C000067797

RAMA OF THE AXE

Ranjith Radhakrishnan is a Bengaluru-based entrepreneur. He is an ex-actor, assistant director, script assistant, toll manager ... the list is long. He is father to a brat and husband to a wife who loves dogs, cats, cows, elephants, her husband and other animals, strictly in that order.

He loves grandmothers' tales and stories from the Puranas and Itihaasas. He also drinks a lot of tea as every right-thinking person should.

This is Ranjith's first novel. He is currently writing part two of the story. Visit ranjithradhakrishnan.com for more information on his works. You can also reach out to him on:

Twitter: @ranjithr_r

Instagram: @ranjithrdhkrshn

Facebook: Ranjith Radhakrishnan

RAMA OF

• THE EPIC SAGA OF PARASHURAMA •

THE AXE

RANJITH RADHAKRISHNAN

First published by Westland Books, a division of Nasadiya
Technologies Private Limited, in 2023

No. 269/2B, First Floor, 'Irai Arul', Vimalraj Street, Nethaji Nagar,
Alapakkam Main Road, Maduravoyal, Chennai 600095

Westland and the Westland logo are the trademarks of Nasadiya
Technologies Private Limited, or its affiliates.

Copyright © Ranjith Radhakrishnan, 2023

Ranjith Radhakrishnan asserts the moral right to be identified as the
author of this work.

ISBN: 9789357762861

10 9 8 7 6 5 4 3 2

This is a work of fiction. Names, characters, organisations, places,
events and incidents are either products of the author's imagination
or used fictitiously.

All rights reserved

Typeset by R. Ajith Kumar, Delhi

Printed at Nutech Print Services, Faridabad

No part of this book may be reproduced, or stored in a retrieval
system, or transmitted in any form or by any means, electronic,
mechanical, photocopying, recording, or otherwise, without express
written permission of the publisher.

Dedicated to the Great Goddess
Maha aishwarya pradhe,
Maha Tripurasundari,
Maha veerye, Maheshi,
Sri Bhadrakali namostuthe!

Acchan & Amma
Life and love,
Sanvi & Eshaan
Joy and hope.

Contents

I

Barasingha

Ramabhadra wiped the sweat off his brow. Perspiration clung to him like a second skin, his muscular body glistening with it. Pearls of sweat beaded his thick beard. He was up well before dawn. Thoughts of Ma flooded his mind, making his heart sink with worry. He had grown frustrated at his inability to do anything about it, caught between his father's intractable nature and his mother's quiet acceptance.

He had made his way to this small clearing in the forest, well away from the ashram, stripped to his loincloth and thrown himself into strenuous physical exercise. He was strong, he knew, stronger than any man he had met, and he had baked that strength into muscle and sinew in the fire of discipline and effort. But he didn't know many people, given that he lived in an ashram located in dense woodland far from the cities and the press of people. His brothers ribbed him about it, as brothers are wont to do.

'I could rest an anvil on your shoulders,' Vishwa had said. 'And still have room for a dozen hammers. We should give the plough bull a rest and strap you in.'

Vishwa exaggerated about such things, but I do have

prodigious shoulders, Ramabhadra thought proudly. He found relief in physical action, in the doing of things. As a child, he had badgered an old Kshatriya renunciate called Veera into teaching him to use a sword. The man had fashioned a mock sword out of bamboo and tried to humour the child. That was until he realised, in amazement, how quickly the boy learnt the exercise forms, how fluidly he moved, and how easily he made the mock sword into an extension of his arm.

Veera had approached the boy's father and narrated everything to him. Jamadagni had agreed to his proposition: Veera would instruct Rama in the martial arts and the use of weapons. He had set aside time from Rama's study of the Vedas, mantras, rituals and chants for his martial arts practice. Jamadagni would watch Rama's training, noting his skill and natural talent. Soon, he started teaching Rama the secrets of Dhanurveda and the science of weapons.

Those days held the happiest memories for Rama. He had taken to the training like a duck to water, an eagle to the skies, and soon gloried in his mastery.

'You have the spirit of a warrior and the blood of a Kshatriya, boy,' Veera had bellowed. 'You are no Brahmin.'

'Maybe I'm both,' Rama had retorted.

Days and years passed, and finally the day came when Veera had expressed his desire to move on.

'Kailasa calls,' he had said, gazing wistfully north.

'Grant me permission, Swami,' he had addressed Jamadagni. 'I've taught Rama all I know. He excels his teacher now. He's no ordinary child.'

'That is true,' Jamadagni had said. 'Go with my blessings, Veera. May you find what you seek.'

Rama had been distraught seeing Veera walk away in the distance. Unshed tears had filmed his eyes as he had vowed to honour the old man by practising every day.

He missed Veera. His easy demeanour and bellowing laugh belied his strict discipline when it came to practice. I hope you are well, old man, thought Rama. I wish we meet again someday.

Dawn had broken. His brothers and the renunciates would have finished their sandhyavandana. The lessons and rituals for the day would have started too. Rama bathed in the Narmada, at a gentle ford in the mighty river, banked by armies of lotuses and lilies. Damselflies were already abuzz, flitting back and forth. The light of dawn bathed the river and the forest in exhilarating beauty.

Rama was at home in the forest and privy to its secrets. He knew where to find the Nirgunda trees. The smoke from their burning leaves kept away mosquitoes and soothed cough. He could track animals by their scent and droppings, and knew the small cave where the fruit bats nested. Once, he had spotted a black panther by the river and, fascinated by the powerful beauty of this elusive beast, tracked it across the Vindhyas for days. During those days, he had survived on roots and leaves, filling his hip pouch with jamun fruit when he found them. When thirsty, he drank water from small wedges he cut into Haridrabha trees. When he climbed to the top of the giant Arna trees, he would see the roof of the forest that lay below him like a massive variegated green carpet. Atop his perch, he would watch the langurs scramble from treetop to treetop in search of mangoes, jamuns and dates. One day, he decided, he would navigate the river all the way to Amarkantak and pay homage to Ma Narmada at the source.

Refreshed by his exertions and the cold bath, Rama's mood lifted. His chores awaited, but he decided to first go see Ma. There was a copse of Anjan trees on the way to her dwelling. The dark reddish-brown heartwood made for excellent firewood and charcoal. The wood was heavy and hard, and cutting it would be a toil. He could take some bark and resin for her. He used the resin to make strong ropes, but Ma said it had medicinal properties. Yes, he would cut the wood on the way back to the ashram. If he hurried, he could gather some Arjuna bark and Sallaki too.

Rama wrapped his dhoti around his waist, lifted the heavy axe to his shoulder and hurried into the forest.

It was the insistent, lively chirping of the leaf warbler that caught Rama's attention as he made his way through the dense foliage. They seemed to have arrived early this year. Soon the silent forest would ring with their chirps and tweets. He turned to the sound and his breath caught. The warbler went quiet immediately.

A barasingha stood ten feet away from him. The stag was big, the biggest he had ever seen, a good five feet upto his shoulders and with a magnificent rack of prongs. He had never seen one so deep in the forest. Barasinghas grazed and moved along the grasslands, away from dense foliage that hid predators, and where creepers, vines and low branches could catch and trap them by their antlers. The stag stared at him, unafraid.

Rama slid the axe to the ground, gently inching it down, not wanting to startle the deer. Strange, his coat was bright reddish brown, and he was alone. It wasn't rutting season yet, and summer was over, his coat should have faded.

'Hello, friend,' Rama said, bending his knees a bit and

hunching to show non-aggression. But he was ready to leap aside should the stag charge. The barasingha grunted and ambled forward, which was the last thing Rama expected. This was a herd animal that bolted at the sight or sound of humans, and yet, this stag had moved closer. The antlers could be lethal if the stag lowered his head and butted him. The stag moved to go past him and stopped when he was abreast of Rama and nuzzled the side of his belly against him.

'Mahadeva!' Rama whispered in amazement as he slowly rested his hand on the barasingha and caressed it. His whisper sounded very loud in the deathly silent forest. Rama glanced up, wary of lurking predators, and saw that a fine mist had descended. He could hardly make out the drooping branches of the Dhavala tree a few feet away. It had been a clear day with scattered sunlight dappling the forest floor a few nimishas, just moments, ago.

The stag moved with its hind legs and turned to face him again. It was too close now for Rama to leap away, and the prongs were inches away from his face. The stag lowered his head and presented his antlers to him. Rama gasped. He did not know what to do.

The barasingha waited patiently. Rama, his mind confused, raised his hand to rub the antlers, hoping this was what the animal wanted. He rubbed the length of the prong and the stag grunted again. Rama withdrew his hand and stared at his palm.

Velvet! The stag was offering his antler. This was beyond strange. Rama grabbed a square of cloth from his hip pouch and dusted the flakes into it. The stag still waited. He rubbed the antlers again, using both his hands. Flakes and small pieces came off. He managed to collect an enormous amount of velvet on the cloth. Antler velvet was precious. Vaidyas paid a fortune for even a tenth of this quantity, so rare was it, and here he was being offered this treasure.

The velvet glowed and glimmered, a dull gold sheen covered the square of cloth he had spread on the ground. When he had gathered all he could, he knelt and wrapped the cloth, bringing the four corners together in the middle. In a blink, the barasingha leapt over his kneeling form. Rama sprawled on his back in surprise, startled by the sudden movement. He turned to see where the stag had gone and found ... nothing.

The stag had vanished into thin air, and the mist had disappeared. Rama sat up in a daze as the warbler resumed his song.

2

Eight Pots of Sand

Rama walked up the path along the small creek that led to Renuka's house. The path and the creek continued to wind their way to a settlement a short distance upstream. The colony had grown from a handful of people a few years ago to at least a hundred settlers now. He had come across three more settlements at various points in the forest, all close to the river or a creek. Rama wondered why so many were living a hard life in the forest when they could have ease and security in Mahishmati. A few, he learnt, had come here from Mahishmati and some from as far as Prayag, Saketa and Vaishali. He must remember to ask his eldest brother Vasu about it. Vasu was the talkative one, made friends fast, and knew a few people from the settlements. It was a passing thought. His mind still wondered at the barasingha, and he was eager to ask Ma about it.

At the edge of the small clearing, a small bamboo hut stood below an Ashwattha tree. A raised platform of stone plastered with clay ran across the front of it. The door was ajar, and a small white cloth hung inside a window to the left of the door. A thatched roof overhung the platform and provided shelter from rain and sun. A few feet to the right stood a cottage, twice as big as the hut. It had two doors. One for the room where Ma stored her medicinal herbs, leaves, resins, minerals and bark, and the other for the room where she saw her patients. Seven pots stood on a platform beneath the window. Ma was sitting next to them in padmasana, her knees folded and feet crossed and resting on her upper thighs, her spine as straight as could be, her eyes closed, a heap of river sand in front of her.

Rama knew what she was going to do. He had seen it so many times before, and still his amazement never diminished. He would watch until she finished.

Ma had birthed five sons—all young adults now—yet she looked younger than all of them. She could be mistaken for our sister, Rama thought. Smooth skin, jet black hair and a slim frame—a younger sister—Rama corrected himself. She still had the open, innocent smile of adolescence, and radiated warmth and grace that put everyone at ease. People unburdened their worries and fears to her while she took their pulse, examined their wounds, or attended to their illnesses. The settlers came to her for healing, for birthing of their babies, for advice on customs and familial matters, and even for intervention in case of a dispute in the community. People from across the Narmada, from the foothills of the Satpuras, came calling as her fame spread. Amba, they called her with love and respect. Rama had chuckled many a time when people from across the river came to meet Amba and stood surprised when they saw her. They always expected an old, wizened matron bent over a staff.

Dakini walked up to him, carrying a bundle of neem leaves in the crook of her arm. She had a toothy grin that was forever cheerful and a wiry frame that was always busy with some chore or the other. Her eyes twinkled as she smiled at Rama.

'How does she do it?' she asked.

'I don't know,' Rama replied. 'She doesn't know either, I think. All she tells me is that she empties her mind and trusts her instincts. That's what she always tells me to do too. She says it comes from her tapasya and her core inner self. She even treats people by instinct, and it has been unerring. This is something inherent in her, not the fruit of a particular mantra or something bestowed by the blessing of a Deva.'

'It will be the eighth pot,' said Dakini.

One pot for each week of her banishment, thought Rama.

'There's a leper in the room,' said Dakini. 'We found him fallen by the river when we went to collect lotus stalks. He's been gruesomely mauled by a tiger or a leopard. It seems as if it happened days ago. Gangrene has set in. Devi knows, how he's still alive!'

'How did you get him here?' Rama said with a gasp.

Dakini averted her eyes. 'Amba carried him herself.'

She glanced at Rama and seeing the shock on his face, blurted out, 'She wouldn't let us touch him. Varnini has gone to the village to seek his family, but I don't think anyone will come.'

Rama clenched his hands in frustration. 'Oh, Ma,' he said, shaking his head in dismay. 'May Mahadeva protect her!'

Renuka twirled the sand in front of her, eyes still closed. She didn't touch the sand, but it arranged itself in a flat, round shape. She dug her hands into the sand and started moulding. Her hands moved with practised ease, like a potter at the wheel. But she had no wheel, and this wasn't wet clay; it was dry sand. Rama and Dakini watched—Dakini wide-eyed and slack-jawed—as Ma fashioned the sand into a perfect round pot. She bevelled the edges of the mouth, caught it by the neck and flattened the base of the pot slightly. The pot was ready.

Rama knew that even if she filled the pot with water, it wouldn't disintegrate or be soaked through. He had seen this almost every day, whenever he accompanied her to the riverside at the crack of dawn to fetch water.

There was another thing she could do. Rama had begged her so many times when he was a child, pestering her till she relented with a smile. He would call his brothers and other disciples to come see 'Ma's Magic'. Renuka would pick a stone, any stone, and enclose it in her palms—rubbing, turning and massaging the stone. She would be quiet and keep her eyes closed, till she smiled and opened her palms to show Rama a drop or two of water she had 'squeezed out' from the stone. Rama would taste the water and exclaim, 'Pure as a raindrop!' Renuka would reply, 'Everyday practical magic.'

Renuka rose and placed the pot alongside the others. 'Rama,' she said, turning and catching sight of him. 'When did you come?'

'When you started with the pot,' said Rama as he walked to her. He held out his open palms to her. Flecks of dull gold velvet shimmered in the morning light.

'Something strange happened today.' He told her about the barasingha as he gave her the wrap of velvet. 'What does it mean? Is it an omen?'

'Perhaps,' Renuka thought aloud. 'A barasingha stag lowers his head only on two occasions. To graze or to butt antlers with another stag during a rut. Otherwise, he faces even his hunters with his head held high. It means that you must face whatever comes your way head on and not turn away from it.'

'I've never heard of a stag behaving this way or seen antler velvet of this colour.'

She handed the wrap back to Rama. 'It is for you. Not me.'

She smiled and put her palm against his cheek. 'My youngest. So quick to temper yet so kind to animals.'

Rama smiled in mock embarrassment.

'Has my husband asked about me?'

Rama knew this query would come and, as always, kept mum. It was 'my husband' now, never 'your father'. Earlier, it had been 'your father' every time she spoke of him, till eight weeks back, when Jamadagni ordered her to leave the ashram. Rama had built this dwelling for her and the two girls had come with her, eager to learn and serve as attendants.

It was an unspoken rule in the ashram that no one should have any contact with Ma, but Rama didn't care. He came here whenever he could, and if his father knew, he hadn't uttered a word to him till now.

'I've asked so many times, Ma ... Why?'

Renuka looked at the earnest bewilderment in Rama's eyes. Eyes the colour of sweet forest honey. She had stalled him before. It wasn't something you could talk to your son about. But Rama wouldn't give up. He never gave up once he pursued anything. He understood far more than he let on, and Renuka sensed that he had good instincts. They led him straight to the nub of the matter when he heeded their call. She would have to reply today and not couch her answers in evasions. That was morally abhorrent to her, and Rama would catch the lie immediately. He had the mien of a raptor at hunt sometimes, this youngest son of hers.

Renuka glanced at Dakini and she slipped away, leaving mother and son alone.

'You have to be a grihasta, a householder, to understand,' Renuka started, casting about for the correct words.

'A rishi and his patni are heart and soul. And Jamadagni is no mere rishi. He is one of the saptarishis, the seven ancient ones, the seven seers of the soul. He is the high adept of Atharva and the Bhargava Guru, the head of the Brighu clan. The same Brighu who brought humanity its first fire and learnt to invoke Agni. Jamadagni has codified the rituals, yagnas and homas revealed to him in tapasya. He has taught the world how to respect their gods. He is the keeper of Rta, that which is true and pure, that which imparts to men civilisation, morals, righteous behaviour and action.

'For one such and for his patni, especially personally, the rules are much stricter. The discipline is harder and transgressions bring harsher punishments.

'A Rishi and his patni are like Agni and Svaha, invocation and oblation, yagna and ghee. Rishi is the vital energy and patni, the pot that holds it.'

Renuka paused and sighed. 'My pot broke.'

Rama stared at her in silence. Ma had danced all around the issue. He sensed the waves of guilt emanating from her. This wasn't an ordinary spat between a husband and wife. It went much deeper. Mahadeva, forgive me, he thought. It sounded close to betrayal. He shouldn't have asked. He wouldn't ask again. He would leave it to the rishi and his patni to resolve it, and try his best not to entangle himself in this mess.

He thought of a way to break the awkward silence and, finding none, stood quiet.

Renuka stared off into the distance.

'Amba,' Varnini cried, startling them both. She came running up to them, heaving her heavy bones and stern countenance with as much dignity as she could muster.

'No one in the village knows who the leper is. At least that's what they claim.'

'It doesn't matter,' said Renuka. 'I will tend to him anyway.'

She wagged her finger at Rama as he was about to speak. 'I don't want you to say a single word against this. It is my calling, my Dharma.'

Rama shut his open mouth.

'More news,' said Varnini, besides herself.

'The hunters have been finding the remains of cook-fires across the deep forest during their forays. Tens of them, in all directions. Yet, they can't find anyone around at all. They say the forest goes unnaturally quiet at night. Been so for the past two, three days. Nobody goes deep into the forest anymore, and never at night. Someone found a skull ... a human skull.'

Renuka and Rama looked at each other in bafflement. The stag, the leper and now, a human skull. Things were getting very strange.

3

Four Mounds of Ash

Renuka remained lost in thought, frowning, worry fraying her composure. Varnini rushed to confer with Dakini.

'What is it, Ma?' asked Rama.

'Prophecy,' Renuka replied. 'Something I had long forgotten, a reading by a saint in my childhood. I remembered now because of the skull ...

... mounds of ash four,
Streams of blood three,
Head of one,
The price to pay,
A test by fire invoked,
Fork in the path of Dharma,
Rests on the edge of a blade.'

Rama felt a chill run down his spine. A prophecy was not child's play. The seers were extremely cautious with prophecy. It gave one only a glimpse of the flow and play of time, and one understood very little of what one saw. It was best to stay clear of it.

'Something about me losing my head,' Renuka continued. She looked at the pots and whispered, 'That seems to be true.'

Rama caught her look and wondered what it meant.

'What about the ash and blood?' he asked.

'I don't know,' said Renuka. 'Even the saint was at a loss to explain.'

Rama looked at her, wondering if she was hiding something from him, dancing around the issue again.

All at once, Renuka clapped her hands, breaking the tension in the air.

'Don't you have chores to do?' she asked.

Rama laughed. Mothers were always after you to do things. His was no different. He humoured her and rattled off a long list of chores involving leaves, fodder, ploughs, wagon wheels and a lot of wood.

Renuka laughed, bidding him stop.

'If you are going to carry that much wood on your shoulders, Vishwa is going to call you the ox with an axe!'

Rama grinned. It was always good to see Ma happy.

Renuka watched as Rama hurried away. She had always felt a strong sense of destiny about her youngest. He was polite to a fault and kind, always mindful of his big frame and strength. Yet, this was not a man whose wrong side you would want to see. Man, she mused, a boy still in his early twenties but with a maturity far beyond his age. He carried an air of easy-going calm very well. But she had seen his eyes spark with anger a few times and then his temper had risen quickly, like a flash flood in the Narmada. The force of that current was incredible.

She knew her answers dissatisfied him, but he wouldn't probe anymore. He had a good head on those huge shoulders.

She hadn't revealed all that the saint had told her. It was a prophecy of her death.

'Your unbecoming, death and becoming' was what he had said but nothing more. The vision had closed for him. The words had been long forgotten but had been dredged up whole and complete today.

Death, she did not fear. As a vaidya, she had seen disease and death at close quarters.

Unbecoming ... her unbecoming had occurred on that fateful day by the riverside. It had ripped her apart inside, torn asunder her heart and mind.

She had been at the riverside, her pot of river sand ready by her side. She tarried by the lotuses that day, basking in the beauty of the place, in the languid light of early dawn, a smile on her lips. A song sprung to her heart, and she hummed her happiness to the wind. It took her a few nimishas to realise that something had heightened her senses. The beauty was somehow extraordinary, somehow supranatural. She had enough merit of tapasya to realise that she was in the presence of a divine being. She had looked around, her curiosity piqued.

Was it one of the gods, or was it a nymph or maybe a celestial musician, a gandharva?

She had heard muted sounds from behind the thicket around the Saptaparna tree. The powerful aroma of its flowers had made her heady. The entire tree had been abloom with whorls of small green-white blossoms.

Giddy with song, joy and fragrance, she had parted the shrubs to see a gandharva. She had been right.

It was a gandharva. And his mate. Completely naked and in coitus, unabashedly given to passion. The female atop the male, oblivious to the world. Lost in the frenzy of their coupling, moving to the oldest rhythm in the world. The beautiful bodies and their eroticism intoxicated her eyes and mind. She gasped as she drank in the voluptuous sight. The restraint of her tapasya flew away with the wind. She lost herself in her own wild, primal imaginations.

By the time she anchored her inner self and found her moorings, she couldn't undo the damage. She had fled in embarrassment from the writhing couple.

———

Jamadagni had received a vision of a sacred ritual in his tapasya. He strived to bring this vision to fruition. He couldn't do this alone. The yoking of the minds of a rishi and his patni was the first and most important step towards the revelation of the rites and rituals, of the needs of the yagna and crucially the mantra, which was the divine vibration, Vak, transmuted to sound. To distil the cosmic vibrations seen, not heard, into thought, then into comprehension, and then into the spoken word, was a rigorous and arduous spiritual task. Seekers of the truth were many, seers of the truth were but a handful. Jamadagni was a seer, steadfast in his pursuit of truth. To get such a vision was the grace of the gods, reserved for the most deserving. But, he couldn't bring the spiritual into the earthly realm without his patni.

The rishi and his patni had yoked their minds, their subtle energies. They had dissolved the partition of individual minds to create a vessel to receive the flow of knowledge. The vessel had to be pure and immaculate, hence requiring cleansing and discipline in thought, word and deed. Because of this, he had immediately realised the disintegration of the yoke and the reason behind it.

It went beyond marital infidelity. It had broken the chain of descent of divine knowledge to man. The vak would not find completion in speech.

The pot had broken. Renuka had wrought her own unbecoming. Banishment, she suspected, was only the beginning of her ordeal.

May Devi have mercy, she prayed, give me a chance at redemption. This was her tapasya now. May She at least let me save the leper, so advanced in disease and so close to death.

She bid Dakini to fetch the short sword for her. There were herbs she had to get herself, after imbuing them with mantra and prayer and cut only at the correct muhurta, the appropriate time. This she alone could do, as she knew the secrets of muhurtas, mantras and medicine.

———

Rama sensed the disquiet in the forest, and he wasn't even deep inside it. He berated himself for being so preoccupied with his thoughts earlier in the morning. The forest seemed pensive, as if waiting for a storm to break. He had found and cut the wood he wanted, also the leaves and the bark. He didn't find a single woodpecker hammering away at the wood, nor a squirrel chittering away at him for trespassing into its territory. Even the trees seemed to hold their breath. The deathly quiet disturbed him.

Muhurtas later, Rama reached the periphery of the ashram, hefting the heavy load of wood on his left shoulder. He heard no sound of rituals, of mantras being recited or the hustle and bustle of the disciples. He saw no gambolling calves. Even Surabhi, in the goshala, refused to moo a welcome. He glanced at the long cottage alongside it. He saw the terrified face of a student disappear behind a window. Rama took a long look around him—the huts of the many renunciates were shut; there wasn't a single person up and about. No sign of the acharyas, shishyas or even his brothers. The silence of the ashram screamed at him. A sense of dread enveloped him, and his throat ran dry. He heaved the wood to the ground and tightened his grip on the axe. He walked towards his father's cottage, reached the small open space in front of it and stopped like he had hit a stone wall.

Ma was on her knees, her short sword hanging by her side, held by a loop across her left shoulder. She was holding one of her sand pots. The other seven formed a haphazard circle around her. Dakini and Varnini stood on either side of her, outside the circle of pots, frozen with terror. Jamadagni sat cross-legged before his doorstep, livid with rage. His wrath seemed to emanate from his body like heat waves from a raging forest fire. Rama felt sweat break out all over him.

Between Jamadagni and Renuka were four steaming mounds of ash. The tops of four skulls shone in the ashes.

4

Three Streams of Blood

'RAMABHADRA!'

Jamadagni's voice was thunder. It seemed to reverberate around the ashram. Rama stood as still as a statue, unable to utter a word. This was the implacable wrath of a saptarishi. Even the devas fled from it. It could cast your soul into damnation and the souls of seven generations of your descendants with it.

'Destiny has decided. Renuka's punishment is proclaimed. Today she will be liberated from her fall. She will be beheaded!'

Rama gasped.

'You will be the executioner!'

Rama fell to his knees, holding on to his axe to keep from collapsing to the ground. He felt bile rise and fought the urge to retch.

'I bade your brothers to bring her here. I ordered them to execute her. All of them disobeyed.'

Jamadagni turned to look Rama straight in the eye. Rama stared back in terror. He found only fury behind those eyes. His father was nowhere to be found.

'Father,' he said, his voice barely a gasp.

'Disobedience is death!' roared Jamadagni and pointed to the mounds of ash.

It took Rama a long moment to wrap his head around the gesture, and then realisation dawned.

His four brothers were the four mounds of ash!

Jamadagni had incinerated them with the power of his tapas, his yogic power.

Rama stared at the mounds, numb with shock. He felt himself drowning in a whirlpool, unable to swim his way up for air.

No! No! He couldn't do this. I can't kill my mother, Rama thought. He turned to Jamadagni to implore mercy.

There were no eyes behind Jamadagni's eyelids anymore. Liquid raging fire filled the sockets. Filaments of flame poured out, streaming down his face and towards his ears and beard. They were like twin volcanoes of fire waiting to erupt. The thick white hair knotted on top of his head and his heavy beard glowed with the heat. His hard, hairy body was absolutely still, like it was carved out of granite.

The High Adept of Atharva had invoked Agni into his eyes.

Rama's mind reeled. He knew he had only a few fleeting nimishas left. He would die, but he wouldn't kill his mother. Rama turned to look at her one last time.

Renuka looked at him, calm, quiet and accepting; her face immobile. Her eyes filled with a sea of compassion. Compassion for him.

Rama's gaze held on to Renuka's eyes. A thought sparked in him. He grasped for it but it disappeared. He struggled to clear his mind. Ma's words sprung from his memory, unbidden. *Trust your instincts.*

Unconsciously, he did what his father had taught him to do to control his mind. He imagined a yagnakund, a fire altar, and fed his fear and desperation into it. Rama gave himself over to pure instinct, and did something he had never done before. He invoked Agni into the fire of the yagnakund in his mind. The fire blazed, and he found calm in the heart of it. He emptied his mind.

The faint thought came rushing back. Wait! The words his father had spoken: 'Destiny has decided'.

Destiny. Not the Gods. Odd word to use. 'Liberated from her fall.' Father had not used the word death at all.

He remembered the prophecy. The four mounds of ash were his burnt brothers. The head of one was his mother's head, and the blade was his axe. He was sure of it. He couldn't figure out the rest of it. Why didn't Jamadagni burn Ma instead? And he could behead as easily as incinerate her. It was not adding up. Something else was at play here.

The barasingha. The omen. What had Ma said? Face whatever comes your way head on.

Rama's mind raced. He had no time to think further. He had to decide now! Rama decided to trust his instincts. He stood up and said in a voice as quiet as murder, 'I accept.'

Renuka put the pot on the ground and bent to rest her head on it. Her hair, tied up in a tight bun, left the neck bare.

Rama stared at the slender neck. 'I beg forgiveness, Ma,' he said. He grasped the wooden staff of his axe with sweaty palms and hefted the axe high above his head. Mahadeva, I put my trust in you, he prayed.

He screamed his anger to the world from the depths of his being.

OM NAMAH SHI—

He swung the axe and beheaded his mother before he could complete the chant.

———

Rama stood quietly with his eyes shut. He could hear the blood pulsing in his ears. He slowly opened his eyes and looked at the lifeless body of his mother. Rama noticed the cut was not clean. The head was on the ground but still attached to the stump of her neck by a ribbon of sinew. And then he gasped.

Mahadeva! Where was the blood?

Not a drop of blood stained the ground. Rama could see the sliced endings of muscle, bone, blood vessels and skin on either side of the cut, but not a drop of blood.

Rama stared in amazement. Dakini had fallen in a swoon and Varnini was on her knees, crying her grief to the earth.

An eerie, piercing sound wafted in from the forest at the edge of the ashram behind him. Tens of similar sounds all around answered it. A strange ululation, strident as a war cry, erupted. All at once, a mass of humanity broke through the jungle, circling the ashram.

Rama stared, slack-jawed in wonder. Was there no end to the strangeness of the day? He glanced at Jamadagni. The fire had gone out of his eyes. His eyeballs had rolled up, and the whites of his eyes stared back at Rama through open eyelids. Jamadagni had transcended into a meditative trance.

Rama looked at the teeming multitude. He had heard of them but never knew there were so many of them. Their name was whispered in dread. Dwellers of charnel houses, eaters of the dead, harvesters of the skulls and bones of those buried in the sky. Today he saw them for the first time. They were the ones who had left the skull in the forest.

As one, the Aghoris charged into the ashram.

Rama felt a thrill run through his body. The Aghoris were smeared in ash from head to toe, some naked, some clad in tiger skin and others in deer hide. Their dreadlocks flew in the air as they ran. Their bodies were adorned with skulls and bones, rudrakshas and metal piercings. They carried staffs, swords, hack knives, spears, axes and trishulas. The air rang with their wailing, piercing cries as they came to a halt around the open space.

They banged their staffs, spears and trishulas on the ground. Their feet moved in a weirdly graceful dance, and they shook their bells and damaroos. The sound was deafening. Rama caught snatches of their chant.

Adi Rudraya
Aghora Mantraya
Aghora Rudraya
Aghora Bhadraya

Hail the great one, Rudra,
He, the sacred chant of the Aghora,
He, the great god of the Aghora,
He, the wealth of the Aghora.

An old Aghori, all skin and bones, with dreadlocks piled high on his head, stepped forward. The sparse loincloth was his only attire. Garlands of bones adorned his neck and rings of bones wound around his wrists and ankles. Thick caked ash was smeared on his body, beard and hair. He carried a

staff, as tall as himself, topped with a human skull. He hit
the ground thrice with the staff, the sound magically louder
than the chants and the music of the Aghoris. The noise died
down at once.

In a deep resonant voice that belied his frame, the old
Aghori sang.

> Delve into the void,
> Merge into the night,
> Mahavidya awakens,
> Behold her might.
> You soak in pleasure,
> Chase hollow delight, Swim the sea of passion,
> Be dead to the Light.
>
> She brings the Light,
> She brings the Sun,
> Burn the body,
> Eat the mind.
>
> Mountain of ego,
> Scorpion of Lust,
> Tread her path,
> Turn them to dust.
>
> Free the Atman,
> Be the Brahman.
> Whip of anger,
> Blade of greed,
> Hark to her song,
> Empty your need.

Free the Atman, Be the Brahman,
Mahavidya awakens, Mother comes,
Mahavidya awakens, Mother comes.

The eight pots shattered into dust, that hung in the air, caught between the earth and the sky. A pattern appeared on the earth around Renuka's dead body. A square nested on the four sides like doorways. The dust settled inside the square, forming a circle of eight lotus leaves around Renuka. A triangle, its points touching the inside of the lotus circle, appeared too. It contained three concentric circles and finally a smaller triangle, with its points touching the innermost circle.

Rama gasped. It was a yantra—a diagram of power, the sacred geometry of a mantra, but this one he hadn't seen before. All it lacked was the bindu, the central point. Realisation dawned on Rama. Ma lay at the exact centre of the yantra. She was the bindu. Some force seemed to ripple through the yantra. It lifted into the air and spun vertically. The triangles inverted. A golden light flashed through it. It spun flat and settled on Renuka.

Renuka's lifeless left hand moved to her head, grasping at the hair. Her right hand drew out the short sword from the scabbard. Suddenly, the body jerked upright. Dakini and Varnini lay senseless on the ground. Rama's hair stood on end. The Aghoris watched with rapt attention. There was a deathly silence all around.

Jamadagni, the whites of his eye still showing, whispered from deep in his trance, clearly and slowly.

'*Tat twam asi*. Though art that.'

Renuka's dead mouth moved. A voice emanated from inside her.

'*Sa Ham*. So I am.'

She cut the ribbon of sinew that held the head to her neck with her sword.

The world went red.

A circle of red mist hung in the air for a long moment, obscuring Renuka and her attendants. Suddenly, it twisted into a whirlpool of red haze and disappeared with a roar.

Rama dropped his axe in shock as he stared at the macabre sight. It was his mother, yet it was not her. The Aghoris fell to their knees, their palms joined in prayer.

An eight-petalled lotus of brilliant white stood in the space. On it, a naked couple, woman atop the man, writhed in the climax of love-making and on them stood Renuka. Her body was bright red. The red of the rudrapushpa. A belly chain of bones and garlands of skulls covered her nudity. A hissing green serpent wound around her torso like a sacred thread, a yagnopaveeta. She held her head in her left hand, hair now loose and dishevelled, and her sword in the right. Dakini and Varnini had torn their clothes off and stood naked, their bodies blue-grey, long hair in disarray. They stared at Renuka, rapture dancing in their eyes.

Rama watched in horror as three streams of blood sprouted from Renuka's neck. Maniacal laughter emanated from Dakini and Varnini as they opened their mouths in anticipation. A stream of blood flowed into each mouth. Renuka's mouth opened over her left hand, and the third stream flowed into it. Try as he might, Rama could not tear his eyes away from the sight.

The old Aghori opened his eyes and said reverentially, 'CHINNAMASTA. Mahavidya has awakened.'

The Aghoris pulled out their trumpets made out of

hollowed-out thigh bones. An eerie, piercing sound rent the air as the Aghoris celebrated.

The streams of blood turned voluminous. A corner of Rama's mind wondered at the copious amounts of blood that was going into Renuka's mouth. Where did it go? Not a drop of it fell from the open cut.

The sea of Aghoris parted.

The leper appeared amidst them. His dead eyes stared at Chinnamasta. His body was a gruesome patchwork of leprous skin, gangrene, bandages and medicinal poultices. His rotting flesh hived off with each step he took. Some unseen force propelled him forward, jerking him by the ankle, hip and shoulder. His ear fell off and at the next step, his jaw broke away. His thigh bone fractured and pierced through his gangrenous flesh as he collapsed in a heap in front of the lotus.

Chinnamasta roared.

The sound sent ice coursing through Rama's body. The three streams stopped and a deluge of blood burst from Chinnamasta's mouth. It bathed the leper, and drenched the four mounds of ash. Her head spun like a top. A rain of blood fell on Rama and the Aghoris.

The last thing Rama saw before he fell away in a swoon was Chinnamasta placing her head on her neck and smiling, like a child, pure and innocent, delighted at getting her favourite treat.

It was Renuka's smile.

5

Two Portions of Blessing

Thirst. Acute thirst awoke Rama. He was sitting hunched next to the doorway of Jamadagni's hut. He opened his eyes to see the old Aghori staring into his face.

'Water. Drink,' he said.

Rama drank his fill, gulping down mouthfuls of water before realising that he was drinking out of a skull. Rama blanched as he moved it away.

The old Aghori watched him.

More out of courtesy than curiosity, Rama asked, 'What is your name?'

'Shiva,' the old man replied.

'I'm Shiva too,' said someone next to him. 'Him too,' he continued, pointing at someone else. 'We are all Shiva.'

'I'm Durga,' said someone else, and Rama realised that there were women amongst them too.

'We are all Durga.'

Rama hastily averted his eyes from her nudity.

'He be shy,' she chortled.

'Who wants to know?' asked the old Aghori.

Rama answered, a little confused, 'Me ... Rama.'

'Mara Mara Mara Mara,' said Old Shiva. 'Death!' He laughed uproariously.

'Ramabhadra,' Rama interrupted.

'Bhadra Mara: happy death,' Old Shiva tittered. 'Bha Draha: to shine and awake. The man is a prophet!'

The Aghoris all laughed.

Rama had had enough. 'My mother,' he asked. 'What happened to her? Is she dead?'

'One who dies before dying, does not die after death,' said Old Shiva.

Rama felt his irritation rise. He'd had enough of prophecies and riddles. He moved to rise.

In a flash, Old Shiva had him by the throat.

'Your mother is alive and so are your brothers, but they sleep a long sleep now. Long will Renuka be remembered,' he said.

Rama gasped. 'Mahadeva!' It was a miracle!

Old Shiva pushed Rama against the wall and brought his face close. Rama stared into his eyes. He put his right thumb on Rama's forehead, between the eyebrows.

'Listen well Mara, trust your instinct, listen hard to the Atharvan and ...'

His pupils contracted to pinpoints, and he spoke in a singsong voice.

'The flint has been struck.
The fire lit.
Empty will the thrones sit,
And blood the crowns gorge,
When comes the dread weapon,
From Mahakaal's forge.'

The Aghori's eyes came back to normal. He blinked in confusion and surprise and let go of Rama. He rose and walked away without a word, and his compatriots followed him.

———

Jamadagni sat on the floor next to Renuka as she slept peacefully. The women of the ashram had bathed and dressed her as well as Dakini and Varnini. They, too, were in deep slumber in the women's quarters. The Aghoris had attended to his sons, and they were asleep in their respective huts.

Jamadagni sighed, held Renuka's hand in both of his and pressed her palm against his chest.

Perhaps she could hear his heartbeat, perhaps her mind, so far, far away now, would see the light of the love he had for her. He hoped it would comfort her in her mindless sleep.

She was the bedrock from where he launched his forays into the mysteries of the universe and the vagaries of Dharma. So much of what he had achieved and learnt was because of her intelligence and insight and ... her humanity. The very quality that had caused her to slip. But that was Renuka, and he would not have her any other way. He would abide by her and accept her punishment, if she so desired. It was the least he could do.

He raised her hand to his lips and kissed it. Tears ran down his face as he whispered, 'Life of my breath, beat of my heart....'

Jamadagni stayed that way for a long while. From the entrance of the small bedchamber, Rama slipped away, unable to confront his father.

Rama had gone in to see Ma—he walked past the scores of scrolls and manuscripts neatly arranged on shelves and tables, to the small bedchamber—but had seen his father instead. Anger came flooding back to him. Jamadagni had no right to be sitting there. He had forfeited it the moment he had proclaimed judgement on Renuka. Rama's hand tightened on his axe involuntarily.

He caught a glimpse of Ma's face, and relief washed through him. She was alive and breathing. He could not thank Mahadeva enough. Ma looked nothing like the terrifying sight he had seen a couple of muhurtas earlier. Then he noticed the third person in the room. The leper. Whole and healthy. He lived and breathed. Adbhuta!

Why was he in his parents' bedchamber? The answer came to him instantly. It was Jamadagni's gesture of love for Renuka. That she probably wouldn't even know, made it more poignant. Nobody knew what state of mind Renuka would wake up in, or if she would remember who she was. But if she did, the leper's tidings would be one of the first things she would ask about. By some divine alchemy, Chinnamasta had restored Ma and the leper. Rama was sure now that his brothers and the girls would also be well.

No. Not Chinnamasta, Rama thought. Chinnamasta Devi ... not that too.

'Ma Chinnamasta.'

At that instant, Renuka smiled in her sleep.

Jamadagni sighed and held her hand in both of his and pressed her palm against his chest.

Rama stood still for a few nimishas and then slipped away.

He sat and waited by the doorway as dusk turned to night. He had returned after checking on his brothers and the girls.

Hundreds of cook-fires sprouted in the ashram and the forest as the Aghoris prepared their meals. A sanyasini came to check on Ma and brought food for Rama and his father. Jamadagni declined the food. As the sanyasini was leaving, Rama heard him call out from the bedchamber.

'Take the velvet from Rama. Powder it fine. Divide it into nine portions, the leper will need extra. Once you have powdered it, place a pinch in their mouths, underneath the tongue. Repeat every fourth muhurta. Bring me the portions for Renuka and the leper. I will take care of them myself.'

Rama handed over the cloth to the sanyasini. His father seemed to know a lot more than he had suspected. His instincts had been right; there was much more at play here. Jamadagni knew. How much, Rama intended to find out, but it was an enormous relief that Jamadagni knew something. At last, in what seemed like a long time, Rama felt relaxation course through him. He let out a deep breath and realised he was hungry.

———

Jamadagni watched as Rama sat by the doorway, a small oil lamp and its weak flicker his only company. Somewhat of a lone wolf, he thought, quiet and preferring his own company, but built like an ox. His thick black hair coiled into a knot atop the head, akin to all sanyasis and renunciates. His dense beard had grown to the collarbone. The spartan existence at the ashram, his own dedication to physical exercise, and the practise of swords and archery had given Rama a hard muscular body. There was no trace of looseness or excess about him. His dhoti circled a tight waist and was cinched at the back between thighs that threatened to burst through the thin cotton. He looked ready to leap even when seated. There was an unmistakable sense of caged ferocity about Rama. Jamadagni expected the flood of Rama's anger to be directed at him.

Jamadagni sat opposite Rama. Neither spoke. Silence wrapped around them like a wool blanket on a hot summer night.

After a long while, Jamadagni spoke, 'Renuka is well. She will recover and be herself soon. Ease the worry eating away at you.'

'Is it Ma who is back or ...,' Rama paused. 'Or is it both?'

Jamadagni smiled. His son had started to probe.

'Mahavidya is an elemental force. She cannot be contained in a human form. It was a mere aspect of her that resonated in Renuka.'

'Why Ma?' Rama asked.

Jamadagni sighed. He stood and said, 'Come, walk with me.'

Rama walked beside him, studying his face intently. He wanted to see how his father danced around the issue.

Jamadagni continued. 'Renuka and I were on a spiritual quest. A divine vibration, a spandana, had revealed itself to me during my tapasya. We needed to recognise, understand and forecast the rules before we could finally grasp it as a mantra.

'We yoked our minds, and after a great effort, recognised it as a vibration of spiritual healing and rejuvenation. Then ... then we slipped, we ... I should have been more alert.'

Jamadagni walked a couple of steps before he realised Rama was standing still.

Rama stared at his father. Jamadagni had said 'we' slipped. He did not blame Renuka, he was blaming himself for his lack of alertness. Rama had no idea what that meant, but one thing was as clear as daylight. Jamadagni did not think less of Renuka. Rama felt his heart go out to his father. He understood the enormous love he had for his wife. The Rishi and his patni were, without doubt, a match for each other.

Without a word, he stepped forward and hugged his father. It took only a nimisha for Jamadagni to overcome his surprise. He understood. He was vindicated in Rama's eyes. So much unsaid, and yet, the boy had forgiven him. Mahadeva bless his noble heart, Jamadagni prayed in his mind. He hugged his son back tight.

And just like that, the night was alive again.

'Let me explain as best as I can,' said Jamadagni. 'Men see the base of the mountain of divine knowledge. The rest lies hidden in the mist of Avidya, ignorance. It needs the insight of a seer to pierce that mist, dispel it and reveal the mountain's full glory. Divine revelations and true prophecies pack their meaning deep and tight. What is apparent is not the full story. It is merely the preface.

'The spandana cannot be abandoned once recognised. Mahavidya graced us by taking it upon herself to bring it to fruition. She used the prophecy of Renuka's death and her inherent gift for healing to bring things to a head. Her blessing is now with Renuka; she will have an enhanced capacity to heal physically and mentally. We have already been given a vision of the yantra, so the sacred mantra, too, will be revealed soon.'

'I've heard of Mahavidyas, Father, but who is a Mahavidya exactly?' Rama asked.

'A Mahavidya is a form of the Universal Mother, the Supreme in its feminine aspect, Adi Parashakti. There are ten of them, some gentle and some terrible to behold. Each has a distinctive power and purpose. Each is a facet of the energy that pervades all creation. A facet of Shakti. The energy is too vast and mindboggling for mortals to understand completely. A momentary glimpse of these forms is considered an immense fortune and that requires decades of discipline and tapasya. And here, we've seen Chinnamasta in all her glory. We truly are blessed, Rama, to witness what happened before. As for Chinnamasta manifesting in your mother, what can I say?'

Jamadagni silently pressed his palms together and raised them to his bowed forehead. He whispered prayers beneath his breath, and then continued.

'Mahavidya bade me proclaim judgement and informed me of the antler velvet. Renuka will rise soon. Neither she nor any of the others will remember any of this.

'This much is clear, son, but it is not the full story. For that, we must go years back in time. The time when things were set in motion. That story is about two portions of blessing.

'Your grandparents, Richeeka and Satyavati, desired a child blessed with an urge for learning and the gift of yogic insight. Your great grandparents, I mean, Satyavati Ma's parents, Queen Ratna and King Gaadhi of Kanyakubja, desired a strong and valiant son to rule the kingdom.

'My father, through his yogic powers and the merit of tapasya, imbued the qualities desired into two portions of pudding. A yogi for himself and a yoddha for his in-laws.

'Call it a twist of fate or the play of the Gods, the portions got interchanged. The yogi was born a prince. Though nurture made him a great Kshatriya, nature or the blessing, impelled him to turn into a rishi. A magnificent one. A saptarishi and the revealer of the sacred Gayatri mantra, Vishwamitra.

'My father, realising that a mix-up had happened, delayed the effect of the second portion by one generation. He could not completely annul the blessing as my mother had already eaten the pudding. The yoddha would be his grandson, born to Renuka and me.

'Today we found out who among our five sons is the yoddha. I had long suspected, but we know for sure today.

'The latent warrior in you has always found expression since your childhood. You threw yourself into training—yoga, archery, swordsmanship. And, you found joy in physical action. You mastered the Dhanurveda. You were the only one who found the fortitude to kill today.'

'No!' Rama protested. 'I did not want to kill her. I would have laid down my life instead. It's just that I thought there was something else going on. That, maybe there was a way out. I didn't have enough time to think. It seems so stupid now. I can't believe I took that chance.'

Jamadagni paused. They were coming close to a dangerous situation now. Something that was best done as early as possible, something that could not be avoided. Was it too early to speak of it or would it fester into self-blame if left for later? Would doing it now put too much pressure on Rama? Would it break him? He thought hard and decided to go ahead.

Mahadeva protect him, he prayed silently.

Jamadagni looked Rama in the eye and said, 'Your brothers thought the same, and they laid down their lives. They refused to harm another despite their father's ... guru's ... orders. They refused even when faced with imminent death.

'You did not shy away from severing your own mother's neck,' Jamadagni whispered.

Jamadagni's words were like a spear through Rama's heart. He had murdered his mother on a mere possibility. Rama held his head in his hands, as he tried to stop his mind from replaying the ordeal again and again. His head throbbed with pain as he went down on his knees. Murderer, his heart screamed. Wracked with guilt, he moaned, and his remorse swept down his face as tears.

Jamadagni's voice was as quiet as death. 'Every yoddha goes through a test of pain. They either crumble or overcome it, but it is a physical test of strength and skill. You, Rama, have undergone an extraordinary test of moral and emotional pain. I've never heard of such a thing before. For upholders of Dharma, there is none harder.'

Jamadagni hardened his tone; his voice grew harsher. Every word rang out in Rama's mind. They were like arrowheads in his skull, piercing his brain, torturing his soul.

'Your first kill, Rama. An unarmed woman. Your mother. You showed no mercy. You swung the axe. You cut her down.'

Rama wailed and dropped his head to the ground. Pain wracked him as his body shook like a leaf in the raging wind.

Jamadagni noticed, with dismay, that Rama was bent over at the very spot where Renuka had been executed.

6

Five Fires

Rama ... son.

Jamadagni's voice sounded like it was coming from a far off place. Rama's mind turned to stone as he plunged into the depths of his sorrow. He had no desire to fight it ... he would not fight it. He was a murderer, never mind that the Mahavidya had revived Ma. He deserved a lifetime of punishment. No ... many lifetimes of it.

Jamadagni watched helplessly. This was a battle within Rama's mind. It was the pain of a noble soul. It was a battle Rama had to fight alone. He raised Rama by his shoulders. Rama's eyes stared blankly back at him.

The Aghoris had all gone silent. From their midst, a lone Durga sang,

Life is a dream,
All must awake.
Who is an Aghori?
One who dreams awake.

Who is the Waker?
The One and True,
Lightning in his eye,
Moon in his hair,
Smiter of sin.
Solace for the soul.

Who is the Waker?
Holder of Ganga,
Heart of Uma,
The fire of creation,
The damaru of destruction.

Who is the Waker?
Lord of Nandin,
Binder of bhootas,
He of Trinetra,
He of Trishula.

Life is a dream,
All must awake.
Death is the awakening.
Seek Him, find Him,
Surrender to the Waker.

Shambho Shiva Shambho,
Shambho Shiva Shambho....

She continued to sing, lost in the ecstasy of her prayer.

Old Shiva walked up to Rama and placed his thumb on his forehead like before.

'I can see, but not intervene. That is forbidden,' he said.

Jamadagni nodded.

Old Shiva's pupils became pinpoints again. 'Emptiness,' he said.

Rama sank deeper in his grief. He was a disgrace to the Bhargavas, the clan of Brighu. Why live like this? An image of the yagnakund flashed in his mind. Yes, that was the answer. He would offer himself to the judgement of his dead ancestors and accept their punishment. He started to invoke Agni. And stopped. No, not enough. He must *burn*.

Rama invoked the Sun. He didn't know how he did it. He turned his will from the very depth of his soul to the energy of the Sun and called it to envelope him, his Atma. He offered his spirit, that energy that resided in his physical body, to the searing inferno that surrounded him.

Old Shiva spoke in a low monotone, 'Rama pursues penitence. He invokes Ag—NO! Mahadeva have mercy! He invokes the Sun.

Jamadagni gasped in amazement. 'How does he do that? How does he know how to? He hasn't been initiated. I haven't taught him all the secrets of Agni Vidya, but he invoked Agni earlier. How?

'He is on a pilgrimage of the soul,' said Old Shiva, ignoring Jamadagni's frenzied questions. 'The fire of the Sun.'

Rama threw himself—his soul—into the Sun. He surrendered to the flames.

Jamadagni saw Rama's body burn with the heat. Steam emanated from his pores.

Rama writhed in agony, in the heat of the searing flames. Burn, he thought, and his soul drew in the flames. More and more. Rama felt himself go white hot. Suddenly, he felt as if he had turned hotter than the Sun. He didn't understand how.

In a blink, the nature of the fire changed. It burned cold. Rama felt the breath in his lungs turn to ice, and lightning coursed through his nerves. The pain was excruciating.

Rama's body turned blue and ice-cold as Jamadagni held him. It twitched uncontrollably, almost throwing Jamadagni off. Only his head held still.

'The fire of Parjanya,' said Old Shiva.

Jamadagni blurted in surprise, 'Panchagni? The tapasya of the five fires! I've never seen it done this way. What is he doing?'

'He charts his own course,' said Old Shiva.

Rama screamed in agony as his brain seemed to shatter into a million pieces. Blinding light raced through it and then there was ... nothing. He floated in nothingness. He shouted and heard not a sound. All was empty.

'The fire of Earth,' said Old Shiva.

Rama's head moved this way and that as Jamadagni held on. The cold disappeared from his body.

Nothing, thought Rama. No direction, no light. Emptiness except for himself. He stood on invisible earth. He could feel the ground beneath his feet, the sand beneath his soles, but not see it. Maybe this was his punishment, he thought. He would go insane like this. So be it. Let my last thoughts be of Ma and Father.

In a flash, he was in a yagnakund, in the sacred fire. Jamadagni sat in padmasana before it.

'The fire of the Father,' said Old Shiva.

Rama gazed at Jamadagni as he sat before the yagnakund. A saptarishi. Seer of the soul. Steadfast in Dharma. The man who would sacrifice his patni and sons to uphold it.

A thought sparked in Rama. He did not grasp for it. He did not pursue it. He let it come on its own.

Suddenly, Renuka appeared, seated before another yagnakund. The flames rose high, enveloping something within. Rama ignored it and gazed at Renuka. Rama called out to her, but she paid no heed.

'The fire of the Mother,' said Old Shiva.

Rama followed Renuka's gaze. She looked at Jamadagni. She looked at him with pride, love and compassion.

Compassion.

The thought raced to the front of Rama's mind.

Steadfast in dharma. Sacrificer of patni and sons to uphold dharma and the divine will. Renuka, too, would have sacrificed her husband and sons if the roles had been reversed. Rama gasped at the nobility of their souls. They held no anger, no prejudice against him. Nor did they pity him. They were happy to serve the cause of Dharma in any way they could. They would go to any lengths for it. His brothers had served Dharma as they saw fit. His parents did not blame them for it, either. But he, Rama, had chosen 'right'. They were proud of him.

It was not guilt he should feel, but rather the determination to seek the course of Dharma, to walk its path to the very end, and perform his part in this leela, this play of Dharma.

That thought echoed in his mind. It was as clear as daylight.

He looked at Renuka's yagnakund and saw the flames part to reveal a mortal figure. Rama stared at his own image. He reached out with his arm and the figure in the other yagnakund did the same. He reached out to himself with his heart and mind, and their fingers touched.

Rama's soul slammed back into his body and his chest heaved as he drew in huge lungfuls of air.

Jamadagni laid him on his back, bursting with relief and pride. They waited for Rama's breathing to return to normal.

A spot of light glowed between Rama's eyebrows, from beneath his skin. It pulsed steadily.

Jamadagni reeled in shock as Old Shiva gasped. 'He carries an amsha!'

'What?' Jamadagni gasped. 'How do you know that?'

'I don't know ... The words just fell out of my mouth. Wait, there is an ancient legend amongst Aghoris about a man who will spark an amsha in himself when he accepts his destiny, and this is the mark of that. The light from the forehead.

'But saptarishi, I remembered that just now ... not when I uttered the word. I swear!'

Light poured out from Rama's agya chakra, the subtle vortex of energy synchronous with the space on the forehead between the eyebrows. Jamadagni controlled his breath and calmed himself. He eased into dhyana with his eyes shut. When he opened them, only the whites of his eyes could be seen. Old Shiva stared into them. Jamadagni sought the light from Rama's forehead with his mind's eye. He studied it, chanting ancient mantras in his mind. Shapes formed in the light. A lotus, a conch, a mace, a bow and a sword. He knew what this meant but there should be one more shape. He wondered why he couldn't see it. He dismissed the thought—he had found the answer he sought.

Jamadagni opened his eyes and joined his palms together. 'The amsha is of the protector, Mahavishnu, himself!'

'He accepts his Destiny! The protector has come! ALAKH NIRANJAN!' Old Shiva shouted out to the world.

7

Amsha

Rama gulped water from the skull. This time he didn't blanch or move it away. Tiredness seeped into his bones. His forehead had stopped glowing. He set the skull down and looked at his father and Old Shiva.

Jamadagni said, 'You did something extraordinary today, Rama. I scarcely thought it possible.'

'I need answers. I need to understand,' said Rama.

'You need to rest now. We can talk later,' Jamadagni replied.

'Not enough adventures for the day?' Old Shiva asked. 'Sleep now. Answers can wait till the morning.'

———

Rama awoke early. He was tired still, but he felt like a new person. Like he had wrung out all that was unnecessary and what was left was what he truly was. He refreshed himself with a bath in the cool waters of the Narmada. Then, he finished his sandhyavandana and prayers, and ate a humble meal of rice pancakes and fruit.

Jamadagni awaited him at the doorway of his hut. Dressed in a saffron dhoti and shoulder wrap as usual, he looked regal and dignified. Today he beamed with pride. Rama touched his father's feet. Jamadagni blessed him, 'Ayushman Bhava.'

'They are okay, they are all okay. In deep slumber still, but healing,' said Jamadagni. Rama nodded. Father and son sat quietly, facing each other, both replaying the momentous events of the previous day.

It was Rama who spoke first. 'I feel changed ... somehow cleansed and free.'

Jamadagni nodded. 'So much happened yesterday and we didn't complete our conversation. I hope I can provide you with answers, but you have proved that you can find many answers yourself, Rama. You are a steadfast seeker of the truth. That is a rare thing.'

'Tell me the rest of the story,' Rama said.

'So, we found the yoddha. You,' continued Jamadagni. 'Like I said, what is apparent is not the full story. Renuka and I were only a small part of all that happened. It was all about you.'

'You mean this was all destiny? Fate?' asked Rama.

'No, Rama, it was all about free will,' Jamadagni replied. Rama looked puzzled.

'Remember the prophecy about Renuka. It was about her unbecoming, death and becoming. The beginning is clear now. It is these three lines that need to be explained.

A test by fire invoked,
The fork in the path of Dharma,
Rests on the edge of the blade.

'In my trance, I could see not only the events but also their spiritual meanings. The 'test by fire invoked' was not the agni in my eyes. It was the agni you invoked in the yagnakund of your mind. You did it by instinct. It was something you have seen me do, but which I had not taught you. Your instinct tapped into your subconscious, which had observed me and learnt.

'You burned every emotion, except one, to do what had to be done. Anger. That is your first lesson.

'The "fork in the path of Dharma" is the point where you chose to act. You could have done what your brothers did, yet you did not. Your choice, your free will was the fork. The blade was your axe.'

'What if I had chosen the opposite?' asked Rama.

'That would have been the death of us all. I would have turned Agni on myself after burning you and Renuka. And the amsha would not have found expression,' Jamadagni answered.

'What about Ma Chinnamasta? And the Aghoris?' Rama probed.

'Mahavidya would have worked her will in some other way. Perhaps some other seer would have gained the insight of the vak. The Aghori can sense the potential presence of elemental forces in people. They gathered in such huge numbers, yesterday, in the belief that such a potential would manifest. They wouldn't miss the chance to see it.'

'And if you had chosen wrong,' interjected Old Shiva, as he walked towards them and seated himself. 'I would have gotten seven skulls. Skulls of a saptarishi and his patni. True treasure! I've been robbed,' he said with a laugh.

Rama grinned. The High Adept of Atharva and the

Aghori. So different, yet so alike. There was so much to learn from both. He was glad he had them around.

'What is this amsha you mentioned?' Rama asked.

Jamadagni glanced at Old Shiva as he answered 'The second test was to imprint what killing really means. You are a brahmin. Ahimsa is your duty, your param dharma. But there is a morality to killing. And a morality to mercy. And a thin, vital line in between the two. That had to be fully accepted by you. Your soul needed to reconcile to the fact that dharma requires killing of the unjust, the adharmic.

'You cannot, must not, shy away from violence when adharma raises its head. Ignoring it will only embolden it. Appeasing adharma in the vain hope that it will leave you alone is a fool's wish. Appeasement will weaken your resolve and lead to cowardice. It makes one adharmic if one lets such base ideas take root.

'If dharma is food, adharma is poison. If you compromise between the two, the only result is a dishonourable death.'

Rama sat silently. Every word his father spoke was clear and true. Dharma protected, protects. Dharma neglected, ruins. It was one's duty to protect dharma—duty towards the gods, one's ancestors, and importantly, to oneself. To tolerate that which is intolerant in dharma was treason to one's own soul.

'You did something incredible in your second test, Rama,' Jamadagni continued. 'The Aghori was witness. How did you do it?'

'Instinct,' Rama said

'You burnt fear, desperation and disgust in your first test, and found anger. What did you burn and what did you find the second time?' asked Jamadagni. Suddenly, he was a father no longer but a guru, testing the learning of his shishya.

'I burnt false guilt, wayward emotion and vagueness of thought. I found compassion,' Rama replied.

'That is lesson number two. Compassion. Anger and Compassion. There is a life lesson for you in these realisations. What is the lesson?'

Rama considered this for a few nimishas and then answered, his voice clear and filled with resolve.

'Compassion for the guilty is treason against to the innocent.

Anger for the guilty is fidelity to the innocent.

Compassion for the innocent and anger for the guilty is dharma.

It is justice.'

'You have tested true, my son,' said Jamadagni, beaming with pride. 'Justice is that thin, vital line.

'Every soul is a part of the Brahman and reincarnates again and again in its quest to merge with the Brahman, the All Soul. The soul does this by experiencing the joys and sorrows of this world created by Brahman himself; by learning to dispel avidya—ignorance—with knowledge, and using it to see through maya—illusion. This is the divine play, leela.

'All gods, goddesses, demigods, elemental forces and so on are manifestations of the Brahman and serve a purpose. They teach us, guide us, bless us, enhance us and lead us on the true path.

'But for the first time, since the creation of man, a divine portion has been added to a man's soul. Yours. There have been divine souls in mortal form before, but they were all born with it. You weren't born with it, but a divine portion has been added to your atma. Even the saptarishis have not been so blessed. That portion is the amsha. This has happened for the first time in the Bhargava clan. Blessed be my ancestors for their adherence to Dharma.

'The amsha announced its presence through the agya chakra between your eyes. The chakra is a lotus with two petals. One is the atma and the other, paramatma. You reached into your inner self with your instinct and viveka—ethical discrimination. And the amsha chose to manifest in you.'

Rama was stunned.

'But ... but ...,' he protested. 'I don't have any divine powers.'

'That is to be earned, to be striven for with rigour. But even the seers can do that,' replied Jamadagni. 'The amsha has a purpose. You fulfil that by your free will, by the choices you will have to make.

'Crisis does not create character, it reveals it. Your character has rung true. Your voyage from now on will be to fulfil a purpose.'

'What is that?' asked Rama.

'The amsha belongs to the protector himself. He chose to spark the amsha in you. The sustainer of the world. Hari himself.'

Rama was struck dumb.

Old Shiva whispered, 'Hara Hara Mahadeva, Hari Hara Mahadeva.'

'The purpose is to protect dharma and render justice,' said Jamadagni.

Rama was quiet for a long while.

'How?' he asked.

'By killing a king,' said Jamadagni quietly.

8

Fast of the Eleventh Day

Rama stared at his father. 'A king?' he asked.

'Not a mere king,' said Jamadagni. 'A Chakravarti Samrat.'

Old Shiva gasped. 'There is only one and ...'

The Atharvan and Aghori looked at Rama.

'And what?' Rama asked.

'It is impossible,' said Old Shiva, shaking his head helplessly. 'Are you sure?'

Jamadagni nodded.

Rama let out a long breath. 'First, my mother, now a samrat. You forget I am a brahmin. This is the job of a kshatriya!'

'You are no longer a brahmin,' said Jamadagni.

'What?' Rama exclaimed, standing up in surprise 'Oh! Because I swung the axe. Strange, to put me to the test, praise me for choosing right and then punish me for the same!'

'Is this is my destiny?' he asked, frustration lending an edge to his voice.

'No Rama,' replied Jamadagni. 'Hear me out. For your second test, what you did was the panchagni tapasya known to and practised by the kshatriya elite only. We, saptarishis, know of it because of our spiritual knowledge, but it is not our responsibility to reveal it. It has to be endowed to a brahmin by a kshatriya king, yet you did it in your own way. Something I did not think was possible. Your unique rite of passage through the two tests has made you one of a kind.

'A Brahmakshatriya! Not brahmin. Not kshatriya. Both.

'You atoned for your sin and assumed the duty of a kshatriya when you performed the tapasya. Not to bear arms to defend dharma is unbecoming of a kshatriya. That amounts to dharma brasht—moral corruption.'

Rama sighed. 'Two portions of blessing, the interchange.'

His father nodded. 'Vishwamitra became a brahmarishi and you, a brahmakshatriya.'

'I wish I could undo it,' said Rama. 'Not only the prophecies, it seems that the Gods also pack their blessings deep and tight.'

'To walk backwards into the future is a sure sign of a fool,' said Jamadagni. 'Don't play at being one. The past cannot be undone.'

'Why can't a kshatriya do it?' asked Rama.

'There is no kshatriya who can. Even Indra himself cannot,' replied Jamadagni.

'The saptarishis?' said Rama again. Jamadagni shook his head.

Rama started to say something and stopped. He thought hard. Indra and the saptarishis could not kill this samrat, and Old Shiva had said it was impossible. That meant only one thing. The answer raced to the front of his mind.

'The samrat has enormous spiritual power, by his own efforts or through the blessings of the gods. That is why an amsha sparked in me.'

His father smiled. 'Walking forwards now.'

Rama retorted, 'And there is a story to it, isn't there?'

'Yes, there is a story to it. The story of the fast of the eleventh day. Ekadashi vrat.'

Rama sat down, eager to hear the story.

'What is his name?'

'Arjuna,' said Jamadagni. 'Karthavirya Arjuna.'

Rama stared in surprise. He had heard the name. The king of the Haihaya Empire. Its capital was along the Narmada, a long way further west. Rama hadn't known he was a Chakravarti Samrat. It was just the name of a king, one in many he had heard among the chatter of the settlers and wayfarers. There was something else they'd mentioned. Rama tried hard to remember, but the memory floated, tantalisingly, out of his reach.

'King Kritavirya and Queen Padmini were childless for a long time,' said Jamadagni. 'They desired a brave and mighty son ...

Rama groaned. 'Not again. Why can't they desire daughters? They can rule as well.'

'True,' agreed Jamadagni.

'Not two portions of blessing?' said Rama.

'Not two portions. Two blessings,' replied Jamadagni. 'Listen to the story. When years of penance didn't bear fruit, Anasuya, the maha sati, advised the queen to observe the fast of the eleventh day—the Ekadashi vrat—and to observe it during the adhika masa or extra month that is added to the calendar every three years. This, the queen did for hundreds of years while practising tapasya. So long did she do it that we now observe the day as Padmini Ekadashi in honour of her faith and discipline. The couple were, at last, blessed with a son, Arjuna, who was destined to rule the world. This was the first blessing.

'Arjuna grew up devout and learned, and inspired by his mother, undertook a tapasya of his own. The second blessing he received made him practically immortal. He has now ruled for thousands of years. He's as old as the mountains, but as youthful and vigorous as a lion in his prime. Arjuna inherited the small kingdom of the Haihayas, conquered Mahishmati, and now the world has grown too small for him. The seven dweepas and seven oceans have been the domain of Arjuna since the time of our clan father, Brighu, who was also his preceptor.'

'Our clan father was his guru?' Rama blurted in surprise. Another question came to his mind, but Rama was impatient to hear the story.

'Brighu, the bringer of fire and Arjuna, the enforcer of dharma. They strove to spread the agni of civilisation through all the realms of men. So driven were they by their ambition, so steadfast in their endeavour, that the success they achieved is likened to the seven flames of Agni.

'They brought light to darkness, and dissolved ignorance through the Vedas. They bestowed the learning of arts and craft, stoked the desire for dharma, taught medicine, sparked the imagination of man and established the performance of yagnas.'

Jamadagni went quiet, lost in thought.

Old Shiva asked, 'What happened next?'

'Arjuna was clever with his requests when he received the second blessing. He asked for valour, victory, youthfulness, a long life, and the ability to know another's thoughts, among other things. He didn't, however, ask for one attribute, or perhaps he thought it was insignificant—Humility. What grew in its stead—Ego—drove a wedge between Arjuna and Brighu.

'The desire to spread dharma became a quest to build an empire. Even people who accepted dharma and saw the wisdom in it were subjugated and a tribute was extracted from them. Arjuna became ruthless. Brighu's dissent led to quarrels at first, but soon his protests fell on deaf ears. Brighu withdrew to his ashram to pursue tapasya, and Arjuna was glad to see him go.

'Ego and its handmaidens—vanity, arrogance, obstinacy and greed—ruled Arjuna's heart now.

'I forgot to mention, there is another thing he requested as a blessing. A thousand arms.'

Sahasrabahu! The word erupted in Rama's mind. That was what the settlers had mentioned.

Karthavirya Arjuna. A Chakravarti Samrat with a thousand arms. Sahasrabahu.

'Arjuna's conquests and marriages with princesses of various kingdoms brought in a period of peace and progress. His popularity soared. He won unstinting support across the land. No king had the strength to challenge him physically or militarily. No king dared to disobey his orders for fear of death or for fear that their own subjects may turn against them. None but Brighu had noticed the worm of ego in his heart. That worm has now become a virulent scorpion and its poison has now spread to all our kings.

'Arjuna fancies himself a demigod, but he is the god of the Cult of the Self, the Dogma of the Ego. His blind devotees—our kings, the kshatriyas—think they are at the pinnacle of mankind. They are drunk on power and pelf, and think that others are beneath them. Brahmins are mere priests subsisting on meagre alms. Vaishyas are traders to extract crippling taxes from, and shudras are slaves to be worked to death.

'The truth is that none of the four varnas are superior or inferior to each other. There is no up or down, greater or lesser. All have different duties and rights. The kshatriyas take away the fruits of the duties of others but forget their own duties. They restrict the rights of others and expand their own. This is a malignant disease. It needs shalyachikitsa, a surgery.

'Perhaps, as a result of this cleansing, the kshatriyas will mend their ways. And instead of another Chakravarti, we will have a true Maryada Purushottam.'

That was why people were moving out of the cities and settling in the forests, thought Rama. To escape their own kings.

'Arjuna destroys society, dharma and the very spirit of the people. No longer are people allowed to choose their own vocation and varna after their education. Arjuna has fused varna with paternity. Your birth determines your varna now. Brahmins who disdain learning and rituals continue to be brahmins. Coward kshatriyas continue to be kshatriyas. A brave and skilful shudra warrior will never get the chance to show his prowess. He will be treated as a servant. Dissenters and rebels are killed. Their corpses aren't allowed a ritual cremation, their families are destroyed. The very kshatriyas who were supposed to protect have turned into tormentors. Who will protect people from the protectors who have gone bad?'

'This is a grave injustice,' said Rama.

'Justice must be served. The kshatriyas are now dharma brasht and the fountainhead of all this is Arjuna. He must be destroyed.'

'Mahadeva or Mahavishnu can finish him in a blink,' said Rama.

'What is wrought by the sins of men, must be unwrought by the virtues of greater men. The gods will help, but the effort must come from men,' said Jamadagni.

Rama thought long and hard, but he couldn't find a way out of this maze. The samrat was physically and spiritually far more powerful. Challenging him would be akin to a lion cub attacking a full-grown tusker in musth. He would be trampled to death in a nimisha.

There had to be a key to unlock the mystery, a secret to his invulnerability, the secret to bring him down, a rahasya.

'Where am I?' said an unfamiliar voice, and the three of them whirled around as one.

Clad in a loincloth and framed by the doorway stood the leper.

9

Thousand Arms, Ten Heads

Chakravarti Samrat Karthavirya Arjuna lounged on his throne, watching his courtiers with barely concealed contempt. Petty little creatures—bent of spine, mouths full of flattery, of a beggarly mien. They vied for his attention and watched his every move from the corners of their deceitful eyes. False humility hung heavy in the air. Did the fools not know he knew the secret longings of their hearts? That he could read their thoughts before they even registered in their minds?

Arjuna glanced at his attendant with half-closed eyes. It was a Naga girl on her knees, holding a golden tray with fruit and mulled wine. She would stay that way as long as Arjuna held court. She was a new one, and Arjuna wondered how long she would last.

The first victory in his campaign that started centuries ago was against the Naga king, Karkotaka. He had conquered Mahishmati then, and the Nagas had fled their land. Of late, he had felt the need to remind himself and his subjects of this. He had sent out search squads to capture them alive. They were a proud people, and it gave him a sly relish to keep them as slaves.

He rested his right hand on her head. His fingers drummed a lazy beat. He felt her stiffen, felt the shame that shot through her heart, and he read her thoughts as he stared ahead.

She thought of morphing into her snake form, with glistening black and red scales and eyes like black pearls, slithering across his chest and burying her fangs in his neck. She knew it was a vain fantasy, but she indulged it anyway. She imagined him writhing in pain as her venom wreaked havoc in his body.

Arjuna smiled. Such delicious thoughts! This one had more spine than his courtiers.

Arjuna kept up the beat as he looked at his minister. 'The tributes?' he asked.

The minister jerked to attention, almost dropping his folio of palm leaves. He rattled off numbers loudly as Arjuna listened absentmindedly, shifting his huge muscular body on his seat and twisting the edge of his slim black moustache. Arjuna looked at the balcony on the left. The queen was in attendance. Surrounded by her daasis, Manorama listened to the minister. She would tell him later in their private chambers if she felt something was wrong with the numbers.

Arjuna looked around the long, magnificent court and the hundred-odd people sitting and standing. He felt supremely bored.

The guard bowed himself in, bringing news that Maharishi Pulastya sought an audience with him. Arjuna signalled to let him in. Interesting! He welcomed the change from routine.

Pulastya walked in, clad in a white dhoti and an angavastra. His face was framed by his flowing white hair, and he clutched his long staff in his right hand. He walked to the centre of the gigantic court as the minister droned on. The minister's voice died before reaching a quarter of the height of the ceiling. The ceiling was held so improbably high by scores of pillars of spotless white marble inlaid with gold. The girth of each pillar was broader than ten full-grown sal trees placed beside each other. Drapes of sheer white hung from the ceiling like thin sheets of ice. The armchairs were hewn from white marble and cushioned in white satin. White, was the marble floor and the carpet that lay like a shroud over a corpse. Arjuna's golden throne blazed like the noon sun, framed by a gold disc with spokes as plentiful as a clutch of water snake hatchlings. The courtiers stood and sat like specks of dirt in the still vastness of the court.

A third arm emerged from Arjuna's back. The court went silent as the hand stretched past the Naga girl's head. The minister continued reading out the numbers, unaware. The arm reached the minister and slapped him. He fell, the palm leaves flying in the air. A moment later the girl dropped the tray in fright. The clang sent a shiver snaking through the court. Arjuna ignored the girl and stared at the maharishi till the tray stopped spinning.

The arm withdrew and disappeared. Arjuna did not stop drumming his fingers.

'Pranaam,' said Pulastya.

Arjuna did not break his stare. The girl bent to retrieve the tray. Arjuna held her by the top of her head and pulled her straight up. His right leg stamped down on the tray. The girl began to shiver. Arjuna resumed his drumming. He probed the rishi's mind. It was blank. Rishis could shield their minds, but this one held his open and empty. He must have known of Arjuna's ability. Perhaps he had left his mind open to show no subterfuge, or he was being too clever.

'I plead a petition of mercy,' said Pulastya.

'Dasagreeva' said Arjuna.

The morning had gotten very interesting.

'It's mercy for him, I plead,' replied Pulastya.

'Your grandson is my prisoner, Pulastya,' said Arjuna. One of Manorama's daasis gasped. The samrat had called the maharishi by his name.

'He lives in his own filth and holds court with the stones and iron bars of his dungeon. I have shown the Lord of Lanka his true place.'

Pulastya stood silent.

'State your case,' ordered Arjuna.

'He will swear never to bear arms against you again,' said Pulastya.

'Useless!' countered Arjuna. 'He is a prisoner now. What can he do? I don't care if by some chance he manages to bear arms against me. I welcome it. I will crush him again ... and rip him apart. He lives in the shade of my mercy. There, I have already granted your petition. Case dismissed.'

'I petition for his freedom,' said Pulastya.

Arjuna roared with laughter. 'I propose a duel. Man to man or, in this case, Man to Asura. He wins his freedom by his own might. Agreed?'

Pulastya gazed at the barrel-chested, bull-necked samrat. A duel would have only one end. Dasagreeva's death.

'Your Majesty, he is but a mere boy. You are sahasrabahu.'

'Yet, the upstart challenged me. He brought the battle to me, Pulastya, and got the beating of his life as his just deserts. I have every right to hold him prisoner till death, or to execute him when I please,' Arjuna retorted.

'That is your right,' Pulastya agreed.

Arjuna waited. Pulastya would not give up so fast. He was bound to know that his entreaties would fall on deaf ears. His real strategy would be something else. His opening gambit had been countered. The real game would start now. Rishis have been past masters at getting kings to dance to their tunes, and deluding them into thinking it was their own idea all along. All their manipulations are couched in the lofty language of the greater good, of morality and dharma.

Arjuna hated them. Schemers, these brahmins were, all of them. They didn't have the courage to arm themselves and fight. That was the honourable way to do things. They used the merit of their tapasya to further their own interests and tried to rule by proxy. All the power, but no accountability. He wondered what the Brighu clan was up to now. No doubt using their tapasya and stature as rishis to spread their sanctimonious prattle. He had snipped all their wings for now. They were free to chant and perform rituals and reveal mantras. But the world bowed to Karthavirya Arjuna, and he could command them on how to use their powers and tapasya. And obey they would, no matter how reluctantly. They knew that he was powerful, far beyond their reach. He enjoyed seeing them chafe at the bit he had firmly put in their mouths.

Priests, he thought with disdain, reminded you of rules and rituals and death every day of your life. Give me a poet any day, at least they taught you how to live well till the day you died. Or even a drunkard, who found solace or happiness in his preferred spirit.

'I plead for a patient ear,' said Pulastya at last. 'The asuras clamour for war again. They seek to overthrow the deva supremacy. Various factions have banded together to attack Indra, as we speak. Others fight amongst themselves, but will join the war if the asuras gain the upper hand. You have brought peace on earth, Samrat. There is a chance that you can win renown as the peace giver in all three worlds.'

Arjuna probed the rishi's mind again. Blank.

'The asuras, rakshasas, daityas and danavas will only accept one amongst themselves as overlord, never a man or a deva. Only one asura has what it takes to unite them. Dasagreeva.'

Arjuna smiled.

'Didn't Kubera unite them? Before Dasagreeva usurped his throne in Lanka?'

'Kubera is a yaksha. He amassed wealth which he freely distributed amongst his subjects, but he was never a leader. The asuras never accepted his writ. They respect only strength,' replied Pulastya. 'You have the strength, but you are not one of them. If you bring your power to bear on them, they will rebel. They will become a nuisance you can do without, and you will also risk disturbing the peace you have created on earth.

'My grandson will swear allegiance to you. He will unite the asura horde, and they will uphold his allegiance. That is the asura code of honour. You can broker peace between the asuras and devas, and win the esteem of Indra and the acclaim of the three worlds.'

Arjuna stared at Pulastya long and hard as he thought.

'Brihadbala, bring the prisoner,' he ordered. His general scurried away.

————

The courtiers covered their noses; some even gagged, as the stench of damp and excrement accompanied Dasagreeva into the court. He wore a dirty, torn dhoti and an insolent smile. A forest of fetters wound around his body. His dishevelled hair hung to his shoulders, his janeu was black with dirt and grime, and he walked barefoot, leaving dirty footprints on the white carpet.

'Grandfather,' he said in surprise. 'Why are you here?'

'To plead your freedom,' said Pulastya. 'I have promised the samrat your allegiance. You will honour my word. Accept his suzerainty and bow to him.'

'Acknowledge the samrat,' ordered Brihadbala.

Dasagreeva looked at Arjuna, smiled and nodded. 'Arjuna,' he said.

Pulastya grimaced.

This time it was Queen Manorama who gasped. It rang around the clump of courtiers, reaching all the corners, corridors, nooks and crannies surrounding them. Then it bounced off the pillars and hung in the air before it faded away leaving a tense, heavy, deathly silence. Dasagreeva grinned at the queen.

The sound of a snap tore through the silence like a sword through silk. With a tiny twist of his wrist, Arjuna had broken the Naga girl's neck. He lifted the dead body by the head and flung it at Dasagreeva. It landed at his feet with a sickening squelch.

Arjuna roared as he stood. His body, bereft of any ornamentation, began to morph and meld smoothly. He grew taller, his legs widened as large as the hind limbs of a bull, ripping his white silk dhoti, now looking more akin to a loincloth. His muscles bulged to a prodigious size, snapping his janeu into two. Arjuna's arms elongated to reach his knees and a gigantic mass of flesh developed on his back. His fists clenched, and the veins stood out against the taut skin. His still handsome face, adorned with a fine moustache, remained completely immobile, but his eyes blazed with fury.

Arms emerged from the mass on his back, huge and muscular. Arjuna grew taller as the arms grew, five hundred arms on each side of him. The whites of his eyes disappeared, turning a deep translucent ochre. Motes of golden light floated in them.

In a single bound, he leapt off the dais and flew across half the length of the court to land before a dumbfounded Dasagreeva. Arjuna held him by the neck, fingers wrapping around the thickness of it, as his other hands ripped the fetters to shreds.

Arjuna roared again, deep and feral. The roar rose to the ceiling, bounced off and boomed across the breadth of the court like a thunderclap. The drapes danced in a frenzy, knotting and snaking together. Even the pillars seemed to shrink, as if in fear of Arjuna's gigantic frame. Dasagreeva trembled in utter horror.

Arjuna lifted him by the neck. His other hands grabbed Dasagreeva's kicking legs and turned him horizontal. A swarm of hands held him tight and rigid in mid-air as a single arm crept up to his ribcage, and started squeezing right over his heart. The fingers pressed into the skin, and the bones began to bend.

'Remember Hiranyakashipu's fate? You will know how it felt,' Arjuna thundered. 'I don't need you, wretch! I will make Kubera king and throw my power behind him. That will be enough. You are worthless!'

'I swear, I swear,' begged Dasagreeva, tears of pain flowing down the sides of his face. The pressure on his chest was unbearable. It felt like his heart would explode any moment now. He fought to get air into his lungs. 'I give you a blood oath,' he gasped. 'I beg forgiveness ... mercy!'

'Mercy, Your Majesty,' said Pulastya. He stood with folded hands, eyes imploring Arjuna.

Arjuna paused and stared insolently at Pulastya. He probed his mind. Not blank this time. Fear and misery ran amok in his mind. Arjuna took his time, soaking in the rishi's desperation.

'Beg!' he ordered.

Pulastya placed his staff at Arjuna's feet. He bent down and raised his folded hands to his head. 'I beg you to spare my grandson's life.'

Arjuna dropped Dasagreeva and planted an enormous foot on his heaving chest.

'Daasa!' he said 'That is what I will call you. Slave!'

He turned and walked back to his throne, arms disappearing and his body shrinking to its usual size. 'You will still bow, Daasa. Not one head. All ten of them. Show me.'

Arjuna sat on his throne and glanced at Manorama. She stood stock-still like her daasis and the courtiers. Fear danced in her eyes ... and something else.

'Your Majesty, my overlord,' Dasagreeva interrupted.

He was on his knees. An array of ten heads had appeared on his thick, wide neck. His main head was the central one, with four heads to its right and five to the left.

All ten heads were displaying varied emotions. So, ten minds too, Arjuna deduced. He probed with his mind, moving from one head to another in an irregular pattern.

The rightmost had its eyes closed, praying to Mahadeva

for mercy and deliverance from this predicament. The head next to it was castigating itself for the insolence that had almost begotten death and had humiliated of the maharishi. Another looked lasciviously at the daasis, imagining carnal pleasures, scrupulously avoiding the queen though. The leftmost thought to gorge on the Naga girl to satiate its gnawing hunger. The central head looked at Arjuna, hoping for mercy. The head to the left of it gazed at Arjuna with open admiration and utter fascination, longing to be him. Another was remembering the verses of the Vedas with deep concentration, while the one next to it sang a raga, soft and melodious, trying to soothe frayed nerves. One more had its eyes roving around the court, observing the courtiers. The last dreamt of ruling the three worlds, of being hailed as an emperor, of being hailed as Ravana.

Arjuna noticed Pulastya watching his grandson, and read the maharishi's mind. He had been honest. He saw the potential and hoped to correctly guide Dasagreeva—to unite the Asuras, to free them from their ceaseless quest for power and glory, and to embrace Dharma. Dasagreeva was of Rakshasa blood but born a Brahmin. Pulastya hoped to mould and fuse his grandson's faculty of learning with his strength of arms to make him a Brahmakshatriya.

Was that even possible? thought Arjuna. He didn't think so. One of his forefathers, Veetahavya had become a brahmin but had lost his kshatra, his warrior spirit. Pulastya's wish was a fool's dream.

The boy had potential and was ambitious too, but he had a streak of cruelty. He wanted to become Ravana, the one who makes the universe scream. Arjuna wondered if Pulastya had detected that streak or had his love for his grandson made him blind to it? Dasagreeva's ambition would remain unachievable as long as I am around, thought Arjuna. I don't want the universe to scream. I will compel it to pay tribute.

Arjuna had sensed a flaw in Dasagreeva. He seemed to overestimate himself, his ambition driving him to overreach. It would prove fatal one day.

Arjuna nodded to his daasa.

Dasagreeva picked up a shard of metal that had broken from the fetters. He cut the palm of his right hand with it, and let the blood ooze and pool in it. He smeared the blood across the forehead of his central head, bent his ten heads to the ground and said, 'I swear a blood oath of allegiance to you. My subjects and I humbly accept the privilege of your overlordship and will forever abide in loyalty to you.

'I bind my words with my blood, my lineage and my honour, with my grandfather Maharishi Pulastya as my witness.'

Arjuna nodded his acceptance.

Pulastya bowed his head. 'Dhanyawaad Chakravarti Samrat Karthavirya Arjuna for your mercy.'

'Be my guests,' Arjuna replied 'Go to your chambers and await my orders. I have further use of both of you. And take your meal with you, Daasa. Sate your rakshasa hunger.'

'Attend to it,' Arjuna ordered Chandragupta, his prime minister.

10

Akritavrana

The leper looked at them in confusion as all three men stared at him. There was not a single disfigurement on his body anymore. His jaw and thigh bone had healed. Leprosy and gangrene had been washed away by the torrent of Ma Chinnamasta's blood. His skin looked spotless and radiant. He was a young lad, maybe sixteen years old. His tuft of hair and janeu indicated he was a brahmin.

'I am Jamadagni. This is my ashram.'

'Saptarishi!' the boy gasped and fell prostrate at Jamadagni's feet. Jamadagni gently lifted him and asked, 'What is your name and where are you from?'

The boy opened his mouth to speak and realised he didn't know what to say. His brow wrinkled in confusion. He looked at each of them, hoping to recognise a face. He gave up in frustration and stood immobile with his mouth agape.

'No need to worry,' said Jamadagni 'You have been through a lot. Sit down awhile.'

One of Jamadagni's shishyas came running, 'Acharya, your sons and the girls have all woken up. They are all fine. I have never seen an Adbhuta like this.'

He glanced at Rama and quickly looked away. The shishya noticed Rama's axe standing beside the doorway and turned ashen with fright. He moved backwards, mumbling, 'I only came to inform ... I'll go back now.'

'Wait,' said Jamadagni. 'I'll come to see them.' He rushed into the hut to check on Renuka and returned soon.

'She is in a deep slumber,' he said to Rama. 'Nothing to worry.'

As Jamadagni and his disciple walked away, Rama saw the leper staring at the axe.

'Parashu ...' he said '... the man with the parashu.'

Rama and Old Shiva exchanged glances.

'What about the axe?' asked Rama.

'Not the axe. The man with the axe ... I was to give it to him. He told me to ...,' the leper replied, grasping at bits and pieces of memory, as he racked his brain.

'Give what? And who told you?' asked Old Shiva.

'Give something ...,' the leper replied, holding his hands out like he was holding a baby. 'I don't know what. The voice in the woods told me.'

'Voice?' said Rama, puzzled.

'It was all around me, everywhere. It was in my head, but I heard it with my ears as well. A kind voice, so beautiful. I wasn't afraid.'

'What were you doing in the jungle?' asked Rama.

The leper thought hard and then stared blankly at Rama. 'I don't know. I can't remember my name or anything else.'

'What did the voice say exactly?' said Old Shiva.

'I would meet a man with an axe ... and he would also have ... have ...,' the leper stopped, staring at the ground as he desperately searched his mind. Suddenly he blurted out, 'Barasingha!'

'What?' said Rama, rising in shock.

'Barasingha velvet. The man would have it and then, I would be reborn and he would name me.'

'The voice meant you,' said Old Shiva to Rama.

The leper stared at Rama in wonder.

'Whose voice was it? Did you recognise it?' asked Rama.

The leper shrugged. 'A kind voice, so calm. I felt so free.

'Free!' he said again, smiling with abandon. 'What is your name?'

'Ramabhadra. Son of Renuka and Jamadagni.'

'What is my name?' the leper asked.

Rama stood flummoxed. 'I don't know,' he stammered.

'You must name me,' said the leper.

'I can't do that. Perhaps, father will. I'll ask him to,' said Rama.

'Your axe?' asked the leper.

'Yes,' said Rama.

'And you have deer velvet?'

Rama looked at him for a long moment and nodded. The leper's smile widened.

'What is my name?' he asked expectantly.

Rama exhaled in exasperation. 'I don't know.... I can't think of anything right now ... I don't know any nice names.'

'The first thing that comes to your mind,' said Old Shiva. 'What is it?'

Rama thought of his first glimpse of the leper. His body had been a macabre jumble of leprosy sores, gangrene, bleeding wounds, and swathes of bandages and poultices. It had been a horrific sight, but now this boy was radiant and whole. Cured of disease and wounds.

'No wounds,' Rama said.

'No wounds?' repeated the leper, looking at himself.

'Akritavrana,' said Rama.

The leper looked mystified for a moment and then leapt with joy, 'I am Akritavrana. Free of wounds. Free. New name, new life.

'Akritavrana,' he repeated, savouring his new name and beaming at Rama with gratitude.

Jamadagni returned a short while later with Dakini and Varnini in tow.

'My sons are all fine,' he said in an aside to Rama. 'I have bid them take rest. They don't remember a thing. I've parried their questions for the time being. These two insisted on coming here.'

'Rama,' said the girls together. 'Amba still sleeps?' asked Dakini.

Rama nodded.

'I'm so happy she is back in the ashram. How did it happen?' asked Varnini as Jamadagni disappeared into the hut.

'Er ... they ... Ma and Father talked it over and ... it's alright now,' said Rama.

'So many Aghoris here. Why have they come?' asked Dakini in awe.

'To meet the rishi and his patni,' said Rama, keeping his answers short.

Old Shiva grinned at Dakini, shook the forest of dreadlocks on his head, and said, 'Hara Hara Mahadeva.'

Dakini moved a couple of paces back, closer to Rama, her eyes never leaving the Aghori.

'Who is he?' asked Varnini as Akritavrana stepped out of the hut wearing a dhoti he had borrowed from Rama. He walked towards the group.

Rama groaned inwardly. Now was not the time for this. The questions would never stop, and he didn't know how to answer them. He would just ask the girls to hush and shoo them away.

'The leper. Akritavrana,' said Old Shiva. Varnini went wide-eyed with shock.

'He's the leper?' she asked in amazement.

'I'm a leper?' asked Akritavrana in surprise as he reached them.

'But he died yesterday, before your brothers came to bring us here. Amba couldn't save him. The gangrene had eaten away too much, and the wounds had bled out too much blood. Don't joke about such things!' said Dakini, her trepidation giving way to indignation at what she thought was a blatant lie.

'I died?' asked Akritavrana. 'Gangrene ... I had wounds?' He looked down his body.

'So that's why you gave me the name.'

Rama looked daggers at Old Shiva. The Aghori grinned back innocently.

The girls looked at Rama. 'Tell us the truth. Who is he?'

Rama could see no way out. 'It is the truth. He is the leper,' he said.

The girls and Akritavrana gasped.

'I really was reborn!' said Akritavrana in wonder. 'How?'

The three of them looked at Rama. Rama stared at Old Shiva, willing him to answer.

'Mahavidya Chinnamasta graced us with her presence and saved him,' said Old Shiva.

'When did that happen? I can't remember anything after coming to the ashram,' Varnini said. She whirled around to face Rama. 'Why can't I remember?'

'Ask him,' said Rama, pointing at Old Shiva. 'He has all the answers.'

'The power of Chinnamasta brought him to life,' said Old Shiva 'Maybe it has affected your memories in some way. Even Rama's brothers don't remember a thing. But some inmates of the ashram have had strange hallucinations, of burning and beheading and blood and what-not. Some swear that they saw a giant seven-hooded snake encircle the ashram and spew thick green fumes of venom. Others saw Indra and Yama astride an elephant and a buffalo killing everyone in the ashram! Mysterious sights that they insist are true, but not a single person has died.'

'It is the maya of the Mahavidya. Who can understand, much less explain it?'

Rama exhaled, letting go of his irritation. Old Shiva was a clever man. He was sowing confusion amongst the residents about what happened. The girls would, without doubt, narrate all this to others, and soon people would start doubting if he really had beheaded his mother. Other, more fantastic stories would sprout, and each person would insist their version was the truth. He looked at Old Shiva in silent gratitude.

Everyone was quiet for a while, staring at each other with a strange mixture of disbelief and wonder.

'How did the Mahavidya come? Who knew how to invoke her?' asked Akritavrana.

'Rama invoked her,' said Old Shiva 'It was all his doing even though he doesn't remember how he did it now. None of us will ever know.'

'Sad,' he said with a deadpan face.

'You are a lucky lad,' Old Shiva said to Akritavrana.

Before he could finish, Akritavrana fell at the feet of a startled Rama. He held Rama's feet with his hands and touched his forehead to them. Rama raised him. 'You don't have to do that Akrita, my friend,' he said.

'Please accept me as your shishya,' said Akrita 'You are my acharya from this moment. My guru.'

Rama stared at him in astonishment.

———

Pulastya and Dasagreeva were ushered into the samrat's private chamber. Scores of lanterns shone from notches cut into marble pillars inlaid with precious gems. Silk curtains swayed ever so gently in the late evening breeze. The balcony commanded a vista of Mahishmati, twinkling with thousands of lamps lit in homes, temples and streets. From so high up, the lamps looked like an army of fireflies stretching all the way to the horizon.

'Pranaam Samrat' they said together; Dasagreeva manifesting his other nine heads in a blink, bowed deeper and longer. His eyes stayed fixed on the velvety moss of the thick carpet woven with intricate designs.

From his balcony, Arjuna continued to gaze at the city— his city and capital. Mahishmati, capital of the world, and the biggest, most magnificent city in all of human history. He turned slowly and walked into his chamber. He probed their minds. Pulastya held his mind blank, but Dasagreeva's was a whirlwind. Thoughts flashed and fled in a fraction of a nimisha, none taking root, all aborted soon after conception. The ten heads fought each other for supremacy unable to agree on a thought, and frantic with anxiety about what Arjuna may demand.

'How goes the war against the devas?' asked Arjuna.

'The devas are hard-pressed to hold their own. It has been aeons since the last deva–asura war, and the devas have grown soft and complacent. They struggle against an army of only a third of the asura clans,' said Pulastya.

'Who leads the Asuras?' asked Arjuna.

'A ragtag group of generals who had fled from battle after Dasagreeva's capture. They seek to burn the chagrin of their defeat at your hands by conquering the weakened devas and regaining their honour. Their success so far has further emboldened them, and they press hard for victory. More and more asuras join them as we speak.'

'If they win, Daasa will no longer be the king,' said Arjuna with a sly smile.

'They will fight amongst themselves and squander the victory,' said Dasagreeva. 'Asuras need a heavy hand over them. None of the generals can match me.' He kept his eyes down and voice meek.

'So, none of them have sworn a blood oath to you?' asked Arjuna.

Dasagreeva stood silent.

'Your authority is as feeble as a crippled kitten,' laughed Arjuna.

'The generals would still obey me ... most of them would. It is the asura code of honour. We value our oaths like none other,' Dasagreeva said in protest. 'I will slay the disobedient ones,' he said with a tinge of anger in his voice.

Good, thought Arjuna. He wanted Dasagreeva insecure, unsure so that he would not throw his strength behind any of the generals. It was important that Dasagreeva obeyed his orders implicitly in the hope of remaining in his good favour.

A great king was not merely a great warrior. His strength could get him the throne, but keeping it and more importantly, ruling well, needed political acumen. Arjuna was a virtuoso in the art of politics. His friends and foes were left splitting hairs, contemplating what he had said and what he had left unsaid. But, sometimes, Arjuna also befuddled them by speaking directly, revealing his aims yet leaving them on unsure footing. He left them with ambiguous possibilities and uncertain outcomes. As a result, they were keen to act exactly as he wanted, lest they fell from his good graces.

'A good time to broker peace,' said Pulastya. 'Dasagreeva will assume leadership and get the Asura army to desist from attacking. Indra will be grateful to you, and Dasagreeva will rise in status. As an equal of Indra.'

Arjuna laughed aloud. The rishi understood little of war and nothing of politics. Typical brahmin advice—ensuring his pound of flesh first. Free his grandson, exalt his status and hide it behind big talk of peace.

'Wrong!' said Arjuna 'Do you take me for some idiot mahatma? To refrain from attacking when in a winning position will only invite contempt. From both, your enemies and your troops. Mercy on a battlefield comes only after you have the enemy's neck beneath your foot and even then, it should not be generous. It should be the barest minimum. If the asuras stop now, the devas will cast off their complacency and reinforce themselves and grow in strength. If they attack the asuras in the future, wouldn't the peace I broker be impotent? Would you have me broker peace again?'

'What do you propose, Samrat?' asked Pulastya.

'Maybe I should remain neutral and let the slaughter happen. Or I should throw him back into prison and watch what happens. Why interfere in the affairs of devas and asuras?' said Arjuna.

'You gave your word, Samrat,' said Dasagreeva, alarmed.

'No. You did,' replied Arjuna.

Pulastya and Dasagreeva glanced at each other, not knowing what to say. Arjuna let the silence grow.

'Go to your people,' he said finally. 'Gather the ones who aren't fighting, get the other factions to join you. Persuade them, compel them, I don't care. Join the siege of Devaloka and lead the attack.'

Pulastya stood stunned. 'You mean to wage war, not bring peace,' he said.

'You will get your peace, Rishi. I will decide how and when,' retorted Arjuna. 'Leave now, Daasa. Do my bidding.'

'I will require some time,' requested Dasagreeva.

'Time is short. Bend them to your will. Show me you deserve to be Ravana. Go!' Arjuna dismissed him. 'Stay Pulastya, you still have one more thing to do.'

Nine heads of Dasagreeva disappeared, and he took leave of his grandfather and Arjuna, walking away and bowing to the queen as she entered the chamber, keeping his eyes on the floor. Manorama was slightly taken aback at the presence of guests in the private chambers. She certainly wasn't dressed to receive them. Her long black tresses were loose and shorn of ornaments, as was her body. A scarlet bustier struggled to contain her full bosom. A diaphanous red skirt stopped just above her knees and danced with the sway of her heavy hips. Her firm flat stomach belied the fact that she was the mother of a hundred sons, and hundreds of years old herself. She didn't bother to adjust the thin white stole that snaked across her upper back and down between her elbows.

'Pranaam,' she whispered when Pulastya greeted her as she glided past him. Arjuna smiled.

'Come, my Queen. The evening's entertainment begins,' said Arjuna 'Use your power Pulastya, open a portal. I wish to speak to Indra.'

'What will you tell him?' asked Pulastya.

'You will find out as soon as he does,' replied Arjuna. Pulastya looked at the samrat with some doubt. He was playing his own game here. Would he sacrifice Dasagreeva to curry favour with Indra? Pulastya watched as Arjuna smiled at him, a knowing look on his face.

Pulastya closed his eyes, focusing his intent and mentally chanting his mantras. The bulbous top end of his staff started glowing with a silvery light. It shot outwards and formed a brilliant circle.

'Pranaam Devendra,' said Pulastya into the light. 'I bring some news of interest to you. We know of the war you fight, and Chakravarti Samrat Karthavirya Arjuna seeks to speak to you about it.'

If there was a reply, Arjuna couldn't hear it. He didn't probe the rishi's mind; he knew it would be blank. The circle of light grew bigger. It hung suspended in air like a huge opaque disc. Suddenly it cleared, and Arjuna saw Indra and Sachi seated in front of him.

'Greetings Arjuna,' said Indra.

'Indra,' replied Arjuna, smiling.

Manorama did not gasp this time; she was lost in the wonder of the spectacle.

Sachi startled in her seat. Her beautiful big eyes glowered at Arjuna's impertinence. Indra stared stonily at Arjuna, as Pulastya tried to hide his discomfiture. First shot across the bows, fair warning given, thought Arjuna.

'Pranaams to Your Majesties,' said Manorama with joined palms.

Indra nodded to her. 'Greetings, daughter of Somadutta,' said Sachi, as she turned to Indra and said, 'Such a lovely girl and such exquisite manners.'

Manorama's eyes shone with happiness. Arjuna understood Sachi's implication and smirked.

'The asura horde has gained the upper hand,' said Arjuna.

'We will deal with them. How does this concern you?' replied Indra.

'I dealt with an asura army five times the size of this horde that troubles you. I won in three days. You struggle.' said Arjuna. Indra's clean-shaven face reddened with anger. 'I slew half the army and captured Dasagreeva,' Arjuna continued. 'How many have you killed and how many captured?'

'They didn't have the power of asuric magic then, at least not to this extent,' said Indra, embarrassed at having to defend himself to a mortal.

'Shukracharya?' asked Arjuna.

Indra brushed off his query in exasperation. 'Why did you seek my audience?'

Arjuna smiled; it was practically an admission of defeat. 'So, the situation is desperate. The devas and Brihaspati have no answer to the horde and their maya. Your weakness is appalling!'

'Careful with your words human, you speak to the King of Devas!' thundered Indra.

'You wish to challenge me to a duel? Are you sure your thunderbolt can surpass my power?' asked Arjuna.

'You sow the seeds of arrogance Arjuna, you will harvest your doom,' replied Indra.

'Your doom has already laid siege around you. It is poor wit and a feeble memory that makes Indra talk of arrogance. Itihasa abounds with your legendary misadventures. Let me see if my memory works. Hmm, weren't you covered with a thousand ... er ... wounds?' Arjuna retorted. He stared at Sachi, willing her to look into his eyes. Sachi's face flushed as she looked away. 'It is only by the grace of Brahma, that you became akritavrana, free of wounds.' Arjuna sneered at Indra.

Sachi had endured enough. 'State the reason for this conversation or I will end this now. I've had enough of your swollen head!'

'The devas cannot defeat the asuras, but I can stop them. The asura king has sworn a blood oath to me today, with Pulastya as witness. I can save you from defeat and dishonour,' replied Arjuna. He stopped and waited.

Finally, Indra asked, 'What do you want? A boon?'

'I have no need for your paltry boons and care less than nothing for your vain curses,' said Arjuna 'I have two conditions. First, you will request my help.'

Indra rose from his throne in anger.

'Second. You will pay tribute to me,' Arjuna finished.

'Arrogant knave!' Indra fumed.

'I will witness your downfall,' said Sachi.

Arjuna laughed at her. 'You will see your husband fall first.'

'Begone!' said Sachi, and waved the portal shut. The brilliant circle winked out in an instant.

Pulastya turned to Arjuna. 'Samrat, it is never a good idea to rile the devas, especially Indra.'

'I've burst the bubble of his empty pride. Once Daasa's forces join the siege, he will have no option but to ask me for help. He is quick to lose his temper. I will rub his nose in the dirt and make him pay through it,' said Arjuna.

Pulastya hung his head in resignation. He had thought Arjuna wise, but the samrat had forsaken wisdom for cunning. Disrespect towards the devas only wrought destruction. Power had blinded the samrat.

'You can leave,' said Arjuna 'Indra will find his own way to reach me. See that your grandson obeys my orders.'

'Pranaam,' said Pulastya, and hastily walked away.

Arjuna felt Manorama's trembling hand clutching at his shoulder. Her face was flushed, and her eyes looked at him with awe and fear and something else. He had seen it in her eyes in the court earlier too.

'Spend the night with me,' she whispered.

A slow smile grew on his lips. He probed.

She imagined him in the court, enormously tall and powerful, his thousand arms outspread. She thought of him as a beast.

'Make love to me as the beast,' she breathed in his ear. Arjuna understood. It was lust that danced in her eyes, stoked by the fire of her fear and fanned by the wind of her awe. Manorama stood. The stole slid off her fair, smooth skin. She loosened the bustier and untied the knot of her skirt. She let his eyes feast on the allure of her nudity and breathe the musk of desire that oozed from her pores. Arjuna's craving rose fast and hard. He grinned.

The night was about to get interesting.

II

Banalinga

Worry gnawed at Rama's mind. Akrita was insistent that he would spend the rest of his life serving Rama, if he didn't wish to be Akrita's guru. He had rushed off to find the thing he had lost and still hadn't returned. Night had fallen, and Rama hoped Akrita wouldn't lose his way in the dark. Old Shiva had sent a couple of his shishyas with Akrita, but Rama was torn between mounting a search for them and staying here to be with Ma when she awoke.

Rama had eaten a sparse dinner with his father and Old Shiva. Then, Jamadagni had retired for the night, while the Aghoris sang and danced in a group around a bonfire in the distance.

Rama lay on his reed mat and thought of the tumultuous events that had occurred in his life. His mind nagged at him that there was something he had missed. Something that had gone unasked and unanswered, something important. His mind couldn't wriggle out that thread from the skein of thought. Abandoning the past, Rama thought of what he should do next, about how to face such a formidable adversary. One man against a samrat, his allies and a vast army. Should he stir up a revolution and a raise his own army? Rama didn't know how he could do that, and who would stand against an army of kshatriyas—all trained warriors?

Rama doubted if any kshatriya would rebel when the status quo served them so well. Rama discarded that train of thought, unable to find a way out of the maze. One step at a time, he told himself. What should he do next? Again, his mind snagged on something, a memory just out of reach. Something unasked but answered. Something that could shine a light on the next step.

Rama felt sleep settle over his eyes and gave up on his rambling thoughts. He would worry about it tomorrow. The faraway song of the Aghoris lulled his senses, his breathing slowed, and Rama drifted into sleep. He felt like a leaf drifting along a gentle bend in the Narmada. Ma Narmada was a cradle, gurgling its lullaby and rocking him to sleep. He felt himself sink deep into the river, into a deep sleep, into the realm of dreams.

He found himself within the dense foliage of the forest. The colours were extraordinarily vivid. They seemed to bleed off the leaves, trees and flowers. Everything seemed strangely liquid, as if a leaf would melt into a pool of brilliant green on his fingers if he touched it. As Rama stood awed by the vista of lambent colour, he realised that the place was familiar. He had been here before.

The place felt like a sanctuary. His mind soaked in the calm, basked in the peace. Softly a voice crooned, mellifluous and clear. The voice in the woods, thought Rama. Akrita was right, it was so calming. He felt so free. The voice was inside him and all around him. Rama felt himself become one with the sanctuary. He could taste the colours, see the crooning tune and hear the shapes of the trees, shrubs and creepers. It was transcendental. And then the song began—

Not one, not many,
Nor any am I,
All or none,
Neti Neti.

Truth so clear,
That it's hard to see,
To seek fire,
With lantern lit.

Neti Neti.
Tree falls in the jungle,
No one to hear,
Mind it has fallen,
Matters not the sound.

Neti Neti.
Could a buffalo be Brahma?
You answer yes,
He answers no,
Both are mistaken.

Neti Neti.
Un-ask the question,
Dive into yourself,
Find the universe.
Dive into the universe,
Lose yourself.

Neti Neti, Neti Neti.
Can Brahma be a buffalo?
You answer no,
He answers yes,
Both are right.

Neti Neti
Question the unasked,
Rope in the light,
Seems snake by night,
Such is Avidya.

Neti Neti
Not one, not many,
Nor any am I
Not you, not we
Not even I,
All or none,
Neti Neti.

The song stopped, and Rama saw the barasingha again. It was at the same place as before, he now realised. Its reddish-brown coat glowed brightly as it galloped towards him. Rama stood rooted to the spot as it raced closer. The 'deer' exploded into a joyous flight of 'pigeons' in mid-stride. Thousands of blue-speckled grey-black bodies swirled around him and flapped away. They turned and dove straight into his chest and disappeared. At the same instant, Rama felt the beat of gossamer wings on his back, and he looked behind to see a giant Luna 'moth' loom over him. Swallow-tailed and shimmery green, it rose to the sky and transformed into the full 'moon'. The moon loomed in the sky; it waned down to a new moon and waxed to full as it spiralled away from him. It became a drop of 'water', clear and teardrop shaped. Suddenly, the entire sky was water. Water flowed above from one end of the horizon to the other. It parted above him and cascaded like twin waterfalls upon him. It rose from his feet to his neck and was all around him. It rose from his feet to his neck and was all around, heaving and ebbing. The 'ocean', Rama realised. There was no shore in sight. A wave, as huge and wide as a mountain, crashed upon him and enveloped him into its indigo depths. A shoal of 'fish' swam by and he swam alongside it. They circled and crisscrossed and swerved and then coalesced into the shape of an 'elephant'. The ocean disappeared as the tusker trumpeted. Its mammoth tusks curved skywards, and oily secretions of its musth ran down its temple. It reached for a creeper around a wide tree trunk, its body fading and its trunk transforming into a 'caterpillar'; its bright green body ran along the creeper and disappeared behind the tree trunk. A 'python' emerged from the other side. It slithered from tree to tree, its yellowish skin with tan blotches stretching yards across. The 'hawk' grabbed it and soared to the air, and Rama flew beside him. The hawk carried the weight as long as it could and dropped it mid-air. The python wriggled and curled as it plunged down and grew smaller into a brown 'snake'. Rama fell rapidly away from it. Suddenly, he was still and saw the snake fall towards him. It reached him and slid into his mouth. Rama couldn't move—he felt the weight of the trees, their roots, within him. Underground creatures crawled inside him; millions of feet trod on him. He was the 'earth'.

The 'wind' blew through the trees, bending them and

shaking leaves loose. It lifted the dust off the ground and Rama rose with it, free of the weight of the earth. It lifted him high in a headlong rush and died down. He hung in mid-air, floated in the 'sky'. He could see no earth below him, only clouds and azure blue skies everywhere. The tuft of hair on his head loosened, and a 'bumblebee' buzzed out. Rama shrank in size and landed on the bumblebee. He rode on its back as it flew from flower to flower. In a blink, there were thousands of bees around. He fell off the bumblebee and found himself on the ground again, back to his usual size. Thousands of hives hung around him as he watched the 'beekeeper' tend to them. The beekeeper walked to a table. As Rama approached him and peered over his shoulder, the beekeeper became an 'arrow-smith'. He laboured over an arrowhead, whetting, and filing, oblivious to the cacophony of festive sounds around him. The sound changed. Hard breathing and soft, sensuous noises caught Rama's attention as the arrow-smith dwindled. Rama looked up into the eyes of a 'courtesan'. A titillating smile playing on her lips as she rode her naked customer in her boudoir. She had a line of them, all naked, tumescent and eager, and went to each to satiate their desire. They disappeared one by one, and she stood alone and forlorn. She sighed and cobwebs formed from her breath, stretching from bedpost to wall. The courtesan blinked, and the 'spider' ran across the web. It broke, and the spider spun a new one. On and on the cycle repeated. The broken webs littered the floor. The boudoir morphed into a kitchen and from the fallen cobwebs rose the 'maiden'. She worked hard, preparing a meal. She blew into the cooking fire to fan the flames and it blazed into an inferno, burning everything in its path. The world was 'fire'. It swept away the maiden as it washed over Rama. It swirled around him, spinning and twisting, carrying him in its wake. The fire set him down before a bundle of clothes and burst into a million specks of flame that slowly winked out.

Rama heard—no, he 'saw'—a soft gurgle from the clothes, walked up to it, and found the 'baby'. It smiled at him and looked curiously at his right hand. Rama felt himself holding something invisible. It had an odd feel to it. The baby laughed and pointed. Rama looked up and saw the 'sun'. It stood shining as the seasons changed around Rama, moving from rain and mist to snow. He turned back to the baby and found it gone. He was back in the sanctuary again.

The whole place seemed to tremble and shift as if it had been uprooted and moved; it, somehow, looked different. He looked about. The foliage was no longer all around him. A few feet away on his right was a desert that stretched to the horizon. The sun beat down on the sand, creating a mirage of shimmering heat. In the far distance, he saw something else shimmer amongst the dunes. It turned and Rama saw a golden hollow disk rotating in mid-air. A chakra. Twenty-one prongs, like arrowheads, projected from the slender ring. It whirred madly all of a sudden, and Rama felt his fingers wrap around the invisible object again. The chakra was a golden blur now. Rama blinked, and it was no longer there. A lone man walked the dunes now. He peered at him and realised that the lone man had sensed his eyes on him. He turned towards Rama.

Rama froze in surprise as two enormous eyes, hanging in air, stared back at him. His fingers wound painfully around the invisible object in his hand. The eyes were a deep translucent ochre with motes of golden lights floating in them. They stared at him in malevolent surprise, and Rama startled out of his dream. He awoke with a gasp and sat up to see Renuka's smiling face beaming at him.

———

Arjuna sat up in a cold sweat and looked around. Manorama slept contentedly beside him, her body loose and sprawled wide, her energy spent from their ardent lovemaking. He reached for the ewer of water. It was an ominous dream that had woken him. He was walking on the dunes of a desert, parched and alone, when he had felt someone's eyes on him. He had turned to find a distant grove where a young man stood staring at him. The grove hadn't been there a moment before. The man was taken aback to see him. The first thought that had sprung to his mind was a single word—ENEMY!

The man had a beam of golden light blazing from his forehead. Who was he?

———

'Ma,' Rama exulted with joy, hugging her as she sat beside him.

'You are alright,' he said with relief and wonder. A child-like smile played on her lips. She looked radiant, brighter than the lamp she had beside her. She was alive and well, and that was all that mattered. He glanced at her neck. It was as before. It was as if the beheading had never happened. Rama's face froze at that thought.

'Thanks to you,' said Renuka.

'You remember?' Rama asked in astonishment.

Renuka shook her head. 'I awoke at midnight. Jamadagni told me about all that happened. It took him a long while to say it all. It's almost dawn now. It was difficult for him to say, difficult for me to hear, but easy to understand what was in each other's hearts.'

Rama clasped her feet. He didn't know what to say. Words would be inadequate and cheap and pathetic.

'You did well, Rama. You did right. So much good has come of one decisive action, which will appear wrong to so many. You did right by the gods, dharma, your manes and your parents. My son has given me a new life,' she said, kissing him on the forehead. Her fingers played over the middle of his brow. 'Amsha!' she crowed with pride.

'Ma Chinnamasta,' said Rama, still clasping her feet.

'Renuka, mother of Bhargava Rama,' she replied. 'Mahavidya's ways are mysterious. I don't know if she will manifest again in me. Maybe it was only a once in a lifetime incident. Time will tell.'

'Father told you of the samrat?'

Renuka nodded 'It is an extraordinary duty you've been given, but nothing less would be expected of an amsha. Strive to fulfil your duty, Rama. Don't be overawed by the sheer difficulty of it. Arjuna wreaks havoc on those he should protect. His valour and strength no longer serve dharma, but rather his vainglory. He squanders his blessings, misuses his strength. A great dharmic king once, a petty emperor of the world now.'

'How do I defeat him?' asked Rama.

'I don't know,' Renuka sighed. 'Trust yourself, trust your instincts. You have done such incredible things already. Answers will come so long as you strive truthfully for them.'

Rama was quiet for a while and then spoke. 'A couple

of important things ... I cannot remember them. I've been wracking my head over it, but....'

'So much has happened, Rama, and so quickly. You will remember in time. Through happenstance or when you are distracted by something else. Or maybe it will come as an omen or as a dream,' said Renuka.

'I had a strange dream,' said Rama 'I don't understand it at all, but I've never had such a vivid one before. It was surreal.'

Renuka nodded. 'I thought you were dreaming while I watched you. I've been sitting here for well over a muhurta. Tell me about it.'

Rama had just finished telling her when Old Shiva walked up and greeted Renuka.

'Pranaam Amba. To be graced with an aspect of Chinnamasta is a blessing.'

'Greetings to you,' said Renuka.

'Don't you ever sleep?' asked Rama. Old Shiva laughed.

'We were waiting for Amba to wake up before we moved on,' he said. 'It has been a blessed journey here, a pilgrimage. The Aghoris will go back happy. We will remember and sing of you and Mahavidya till the day we cast off this mortal coil.'

Renuka bowed her head in thanks.

'Sit and hear about Rama's dream. It will surprise you,' she said.

'The voice in the woods, the one that you and Akrita heard, belongs to one without parallel. A god that wanders the earth as a man or a man who has become a god, both could be said of him. He follows no ritual and has no guru, no human guru. The animals and elements you saw in your dream, transforming from one to another, are his acknowledged gurus. They are twenty-four in number and he attained realisation of the Brahman by observing them. Self-taught and self-realised. The free one, who has cast it all off, clad only in the sky. The unsullied of soul. Avadhuta.'

'Adi Guru,' said Old Shiva in reverence. 'He speaks to you ... you are truly blessed.'

'Dattatreya,' said Renuka. 'Born to Anasuya and Atri, with the essence of the trimurtis.'

'Anasuya,' Rama whispered. 'The Maha sati who guided Arjuna's parents.'

'Not only that. Dattatreya is Arjuna's guru and protector. The one who has bestowed powers on Arjuna,' said Renuka.

Something clicked into place in Rama's mind. That was it. The question that was unasked and unanswered. He had wanted to ask Jamadagni who had blessed Arjuna with such powers.

'Protected by Dattatreya, who is the essence of Brahma, Vishnu and Maheshwara. That's why you said it was impossible to kill Arjuna,' Rama said to Old Shiva. The Aghori nodded.

'Yet, his voice sent Akritavrana to you and came to you in a dream. Why?' asked Renuka.

Rama thought awhile and replied, 'He sends a message and shows the way forward.'

'He shines a light on the path. It is for you to walk it,' said Renuka. 'What was it you held in your hand, in the dream?'

'I don't know ... it was invisible ... but it glowed. It felt like ...' Rama searched for the right word.

'A weapon,' he blurted. 'Mahadeva! What weapon was it?'

'You have to find out. Arjuna misuses his powers, forgets Rta and Dharma. His benefactor urges you forward to set things right.'

'Why doesn't he do anything?' asked Rama.

'What has been wrought by men ...' said Jamadagni as he stepped out.

'... has to be unwrought by men themselves,' Rama completed.

'The eyes are Arjuna's eyes when he assumes his sahasrabahu form. That was him in the desert,' continued Renuka. 'But I do not know the meaning of the chakra and why it had twenty-one projections.

'Arjuna walked the barren desert while you stood in the shade, in this dream wrought by Dattatreya. He shuns the samrat and reposes his faith and goodwill in you.

'I am curious what Akritavrana will bring you. The message is clear. Seek a weapon to challenge Arjuna. A weapon dreadful and divine.'

Dreadful. Divine.

The words blazed through Rama's mind.

'Your prophecy,' he said to Old Shiva. The Aghori looked puzzled.

'The first time you spoke to me ... when you gave me a drink of water in a skull ...,' urged Rama.

'I did?' asked Old Shiva 'I don't remember.'

Rama closed his eyes to concentrate. This was his next step. He hadn't thought to ask his father, but Old Shiva had already answered the unasked. What were the words?

He remembered.

'The flint has been struck, the fire lit,
Empty will the thrones sit,
And blood the crowns gorge,
When comes the dread weapon

From Mahakaal's forge.'

Old Shiva looked at him in surprise.

Renuka looked Rama straight in the eye.

'The brahmakshatriya who carries Mahavishnu's amsha will seek Mahadeva's blessings for a worthy weapon,' she said.

'The flint has truly been struck.'

Rama stayed silent a moment. 'How did he know it was me? How did he find me?'

'A mortal is to carry the amsha of the Sustainer of the Worlds and Guru Dattatreya stays unaware? Especially when the purpose of that amsha is to end the misuse of his own blessings?' asked Renuka. 'He would know. Easy for a man of his spiritual evolution and power.'

The four sat together in the pre-dawn darkness, the weak light of the lamp between them. No one spoke as each thought of the onerous road ahead. An Aghori, a Saptarishi, and a Mahavidya to support an amsha. Surely this would help him prevail over Arjuna, thought Rama. He felt an odd sense of camaraderie with this group. It gave him a sense of adventure. He was being plucked out of a forest ashram and thrown into the world to fight the most powerful man on this planet. No, of the three worlds. He didn't know if he would succeed; the odds were stacked against him. Would he even survive? These moments were precious. His heart wept with joy to see his parents together again. Their love had survived the sternest of ordeals, and they were so courageously stoic in the face of such acute challenges. And the Aghori? So dreadful in appearance, and yet, a poet of life. He had brought so much ease and humour to the most nerve-wracking situations. And he sang such wonderful songs. His heart went out to all of them and he prayed to Mahadeva that he never let them down.

'What lessons did the elements and the animals teach Dattatreya?' he asked in a low voice.

'I don't know, and I wouldn't want to hazard a guess,' said Renuka 'It may seem trivial, even banal, when put in words. Only the lived experience teaches. If we knew, we too would have attained realisation. It is for him to tell you if he so wishes.'

'And when the disciple is ready, the guru will come,' said Jamadagni.

'Acharya!' came a cry. They turned to see Akritavrana running towards them. The two shishyas of Old Shiva were walking some distance behind.

'Your shishya comes,' said Old Shiva, laughing.

'What am I supposed to teach him?' Rama muttered.

'He doesn't remember a thing about himself, but retains his lessons of the Vedas, and knowledge of the Brahman,' said his father. 'Teach him what you've learnt so far and then teach him as you learn more. Perchance, there is something in it for you to learn too.'

Akrita arrived, panting with happiness.

'I found it,' he said, between breaths. He held a bundle of cloth like a baby in his arms. He placed it in their midst and unwrapped it.

It held a stone about a cubit long, smooth and spheroid and black as midnight. Its smoothness made the eyes slide off its surface, and the black seemed to absorb the surrounding light. A little above the midline of the stone were three white almond shapes. Two horizontal ones, with the third vertically centred above the other two. Exactly like the trinetra of Mahadeva. Rama found it hard to look away.

Akrita had brought him a Banalinga.

12

Dhyana

The others gathered around Rama as he held the banalinga in his hands, their sense of wonder rendering them mute. No one could take their eyes off it. Such stones were often found in the Narmada, but most were ordinary lingas for household worship. A genuine banalinga was rare and much sought after. Traders would transport them to Mahishmati and Kashi, where they fetched a handsome price. There were many tests to determine if the stone was a banalinga, but Rama had no doubt about this one. He had never seen one like this—a stone so densely black, so smooth and so uniquely marked. This was of divine provenance. How it came into the hands of Akrita was a mystery. Why would Dattatreya want him to have it?

He looked at the three almond shapes—the eyes of the banalinga. He felt drawn to the small space between them. The utter blackness of it called to him; it tugged at something deep within. He felt himself surrendering to the stone. He stared unblinkingly at the space. His forehead, right above the centre of his brows, throbbed.

Rama blinked as Old Shiva shook him.

'Are you alright?' he asked. 'You've been standing as still as a statue for quite a while now.'

'I know what I have to do,' said Rama. 'This banalinga is for me. It's the means to make my prayers reach Mahadeva, to seek his blessings and protection. I will meditate upon it. I should start today. Now.'

'It is a wonderful thing you've brought me, my friend,' he said to Akrita. The young disciple beamed.

'I take this as gurudakshina ahead of your lessons and accept you as my shishya.'

Akrita bent to touch his feet.

'Arise!' said Rama 'There is a spot in the jungle where I can meditate alone. We must go there.'

'You can use my old cottage,' said Renuka 'I have no use of it anymore, and Akrita can stay with you and assist. I'll tell the girls to spread the word that you aren't to be disturbed.'

Rama nodded his acceptance.

'Dawn breaks. Finish your morning rituals and meet me before you go.'

Rama placed the banalinga back in the bundle of cloth, as Renuka walked away with Old Shiva in tow.

Rama waited at the doorstep with Jamadagni and Akrita. The Aghoris had gathered around the hut to have their last darshan of Renuka and start their journey home. Where was home? Rama wondered. Probably the cremation ghats of Kashi. He marvelled at their way of life. Living among the dead, but so full of life. Worldly accomplishments meant nothing to them. No wealth, no power, no fame could lead them astray. They had their rituals and rites, and didn't seek to impose them on others nor argued the superiority of their ways. They didn't tolerate meddling in their affairs either and were rigorously disciplined in their own peculiar way. They were the true seekers of truth. A hard life, but a free one, and they had such wonderful songs—music for the ears and solace for the soul.

He heard cries of 'Amba' from a distance. The sea of Aghoris parted to let Renuka and Old Shiva through and merged again behind them. The thigh-bone trumpets blew their eerie hymn again, the damarus drummed out their rattling percussion and the bells chimed.

Cries of 'Jai Ambe' and 'Hara Hara Mahadeva' rent the air as the Aghoris spiralled into a rapturous tumult. Finally, Renuka reached them and eased her pot to the ground. Rama turned to Old Shiva and saw the snakes.

There were two of them. Their tails were tucked in Old Shiva's mouth, held between his lips at the corners. He had wound them together creating a small circular cushion on his head, and placed the pot on them. The open hoods of the cobras framed the pot on the right and the left. Their beady eyes stared at Rama, and their forked tongues flicked in and out.

The macabre beauty of the sight struck Rama with wonder. Old Shiva grinned through his thick shaggy beard. Renuka lifted the pot off his head and held it out to Rama, as Old Shiva opened his mouth and let the snakes un-twirl themselves. They moved in and out of his dreadlocks, strangely reluctant to leave their perch. Old Shiva stood nonchalant.

'I made a pot each day for my husband, for his daily worship and rituals. Each would collapse after he finished with it. A new journey awaits you, my son. This is my gift to you. Use it as you deem fit. It will not collapse,' said Renuka.

Rama fell at his parents' feet. They said nothing but their

eyes closed and their lips moved silently in blessing and prayer. Rama rose and accepted the pot. In a jiffy, Old Shiva caught the snakes and conjured them back into a cushion-shape and placed them on Rama's head. Their tails wound around his neck. Rama placed the pot on them and hefted his axe with his right hand.

'Come,' he said, stepping out of the hut and into the now silent sea of Aghoris. Akrita followed with a small cloth bag of supplies.

'Goodbye, Mara, my friend,' Old Shiva said. 'May Mahadeva be pleased with you.'

'Shambho Mahadeva!' the Aghoris roared.

———

Rama sat in padmasana under the Ashwattha tree beside Renuka's hut. He had set the snakes loose at the edge of the jungle when he reached the hut. He had also immediately set the banalinga down before him and bathed it with handfuls of water from the pot. Not a drop of water fell to the earth, the banalinga absorbed it all. He emptied the pot over it.

He prayed to his manes for their blessings and revered them in gratitude. He whispered the Gayatri mantra with folded hands and opened his eyes to gaze at the banalinga. Rama slowed his breathing, gradually increasing the length of each step in his breathing cycle—inhalation, the retention of breath, the exhalation and the absence of breath. He focussed on his intent in his mind—to obtain the divine grace of Mahadeva, to gain his darshan. Rama brought his attention to his breath and focussed on the spot between the almond eyes of the banalinga. He kept his eyes soft and his mind unwavering. His forehead throbbed. He ignored it. Rama withdrew into himself as his sensory organs stopped responding to external stimuli. He kept his eyes shut, and floated into nothingness.

Mentally, he started to chant the Holy Panchakshari.

Om Namah Shivaya,
The Prayer to the Auspicious One.
The greatest Love Song to Oneself.
The Hymn of Bliss.
The Eternal Rapture of the Soul.
The Path from Human to Divine.

His entire being reverberated with the mantra as he chanted on and on. He lost his sense of existence, of his being. His body and mind surrendered to the mantra, and he floated in silence.

Not body, not mind, Neti Neti....

Who had said that? It wasn't his mind; he had cast off his body and mind in his deep dhyana. No, it wasn't a thought. It was the realisation of his consciousness. Rama gloried in the bliss of divine silence and in the thrum of it. To great rishis deep in their tapasya, the vak—the divine vibration—was revealed. They transmuted it to a mantra. The mantra had stripped him of all but his consciousness, and now that, too, transformed into vibration, the nada, the sound of his soul.

'Na ...'

His soul sang, the nada vibrated and the banalinga appeared before him in the nothingness. It wasn't black; it was yellow. The banalinga was an unending pillar of yellow with the almond eyes in front of it. Its girth was enormous, and the surface as smooth as before.

'Mah ...'

The vibration changed, and the pillar turned green.

'Shi ...'

The nada changed again, and the pillar turned red. The red of the rudrapushpa.

'Va ...'

The pillar turned white. Rama could still see the eyes of the banalinga, a shade brighter than the white.

'Ya.'

The pillar turned blue.

Rama's consciousness stood still before the pillar, like an ant before an elephant. The eyes of the banalinga remained closed. It was important that they opened. But Rama didn't know how to do that. All he knew was that his soul craved for it. He desperately wanted the eyes open. That desperation was all he was conscious of. Rama felt an invisible veil between him and the banalinga. He fell away from the pillar and hurtled through the nothingness, careening down and away.

Rama opened his eyes and let his torso slump. He was exhausted to his bones, his legs felt stiff and incapable of bearing his weight. He glanced at the setting sun, a smidgen of light behind the hills. The forest seemed loud after the deep silence he had experienced. Akrita came to him, holding a clay bowl.

'Eat Acharya,' he said. Rama saw it was rice gruel and gulped it down, welcoming the warmth as it settled in his stomach. He felt better.

'Only a day and I'm so tired,' Rama said 'Mahadeva takes a heavy toll on me.'

Akrita looked at him in surprise.

'Acharya, you've been in meditation for twelve days now.'

Rama gaped in astonishment.

'I did not dare disturb you,' Akrita said 'Your body was as still and hard as a statue. It didn't seem like you were breathing at all. I didn't know what to do ... so, I waited.'

Rama was at a loss for words. Twelve days!

Rama tottered to his feet and almost fell before Akrita caught him. He stood supported by Akrita till he felt he could stay upright himself. He walked slowly, getting the blood moving in his legs. He wouldn't stop his pursuit now, he thought. Rama bid Akrita to wait and made his way to the riverside.

———

Arjuna sat in dhyana in the garden adjoining his private chambers. It was his personal garden. Not even Manorama was allowed here. Narrow pathways crisscrossed a well-kept lawn edged with flowering shrubs. They wound around ponds filled with lotuses and lilies, and meandered in the shade of the Ashwattha, Ashoka, Chandana, Bael, Neem and Vetasah trees. He had picked his favourite spot, a marble platform under a gigantic Nyagrodha tree, sat in padmasana, controlled his breath and gone deep into a trance.

A sense of calm and warmth washed over him. He was adrift in the nothingness. A vision came to him; he saw himself sitting in dhyana in the garden. The vision stayed awhile and then dissolved in a burst of colour—vivid and lustrous. The colours were magical. The reds erupted from the ground like a volcano, brilliant blues edged with white streaked across the indigo skies like lightning. Emerald grass overran the burgundy ground, and a turquoise wind blew across the face of a silvery moon.

Visions beset him from all sides. Campaigns of power and orgies of lust held him in thrall. He soaked his senses in them. He roared and gasped, and sported in the hyper-sensory onslaught. Slowly, the visions faded away and Arjuna found himself in nothingness again. In the distance, he saw a sliver of light. It stretched up and down endlessly. He willed himself towards it and stood before a mirror. He saw himself in it.

He was effulgent. His form, powerful and majestic. He marvelled at the beauty the mirror reflected. He glanced up and down the mirror. His image replicated itself a million times, through the length of the mirror, as far as he could see. A feeling of supremacy flooded him. He felt like he could grasp the sun and crush it to atoms. He willed himself to grow. There was nothing to compare this with, but he sensed that he had grown exponentially. He could stride across galaxies. Arjuna gloried in the paroxysms of pleasure coursing through him. He reached out to touch the image. The reflection didn't move.

In a blink, the mirror disappeared. Arjuna froze in confusion. He withdrew his hand, and the mirror blinked back into existence. Arjuna gasped in surprise. The image had turned its back to him.

He stared at the back of his head. He willed himself to go around to the other side of the mirror. Arjuna sensed himself move, but the vista before him didn't change. He quickened his pace. Faster and faster. He thought he was moving blindingly fast, yet his view didn't change. He stopped in frustration. As soon as he stopped, the mirror turned. All the way around. There was a mirror on the other side too. The image had turned its back on this side too.

The image melted like a block of ice in a furnace. Rivulets of liquid flesh ran down his head, shoulders and back. Blood burst from the veins and the arteries, and the bones turned into a white paste. Panic pounded through Arjuna. He couldn't tear his eyes away from the vision in front of him. He willed the image to go back to its original form, but to no avail. The image had collapsed into a steaming, putrid mass. He watched in dread as the mass wriggled. It squelched and contorted itself into a grotesque, misshapen form. Tentacles, horns, fangs and talons formed. Scales and feathers sprouted. Bubbles of red liquid, teeming with worms and larvae, broke out on the surface.

Arjuna gagged and turned away. The mirror burst into a million shards. He felt himself tottering in the nothingness and fought to maintain balance. There was nothing under his feet, yet he felt himself at the edge of a precipice. Unwillingly, Arjuna leaned forward carefully and looked down. He looked into an abyss of oblivion. Somewhere deep down, indescribably far away, he saw three white almond eyes looking back at him.

He screamed and pulled himself away, wrenching himself out of his trance. Under the Nyagrodha tree, Arjuna opened his eyes, bathed in sweat and fear.

———

Rama finished his ritual evening prayers. He sat down on the riverside and gazed out at the expanse of river and forest. The deep silence of his meditation still rang within him. He felt calm and at peace.

The song of his dreams, the song of Dattatreya sprung to his lips as he absent-mindedly played with the river sand.

'Not one, not many...' he sang softly.

Again, and again, he sang, immersed in the beauty of the verse, music and voice.

'Not you, not we,
Not he, not she...'

Rama paused. That line hadn't been in the song. He had added it now. Why?

'Not he, not she.'

He turned over the four words in his head, looking for meaning, lost in thought for a long while. Rama glanced down at the sand beside him. He had unconsciously drawn a beautiful feminine face in it. Rama understood.

Dattatreya sang of the Nirguna Parabrahma, the Absolute without Attribute. Rama had meditated and prayed to the masculine dimension of it—Mahadeva. Why had he forgotten the feminine?

Shakti and Shiva together made the Brahman.

Not just 'he' and not just 'she'.

All Mother and All Father.

An idea came to him, and he gathered all the sand he could. He sat before the heap, closed his eyes, thought of Ma, and beseeched her for help. Then, he let his mind go blank. In his mind's eye, he drew the face again with painstaking detail. His hands moved of their own accord, moulding the sand to what his mind drew. He drew with bhakti, moulded with love, and kept his intent in sharp focus.

At long last, he stopped and opened his eyes. A beautiful, feminine head made of river sand was before him. Rama's heart leapt with joy. The sand held!

Whose face had he created? Rama thought he saw a tinge of Ma in it but he wasn't sure. This wasn't a face he'd seen before. Nevertheless, the head gave off a sense of divine power, of beauty and grace, and it evoked a heady sense of bhakti in him. It urged him towards total surrender. He surrendered himself with abandon and joy. Something awoke and rose inside him. He felt it at the base of his spine. What was that? Whatever it was, it was powerful. He tried to examine it and it died away. Rama didn't care; he gave himself over to the devotion that flooded through him.

This was his goddess, the complement to the banalinga. Wait! He'd thought he saw Ma in it, though the face was different. That was what he felt—love and devotion to a mother. To the All Mother.

Unbidden, the words came to him. Sree Matre Namaha.

I honour the mother of the universe. Rama repeated the words and thought he would burst with joy.

He scooped up the goddess head with care and walked back. He saw Akrita making his way towards him.

'Finish your prayers fast. Come back with Bael leaves,' he said. Akrita hurried away.

Rama reached the Ashwattha tree and set the head down next to the banalinga. He closed his eyes and sought the nothingness again. He whispered a prayer to Ma Gauri, asking for help.

Om
Sarva Mangala Mangalye,
Shive Sarvartha Sadhike,
Sharanye Trayambake Gauri,
Narayani Namostute.

Om
To you, auspiciousness absolute,

To you, fulfiller of wishes,
In you, O three-eyed one, I seek refuge,
To you, O Narayani, I pay salutations.

He whirled the banalinga in his hands. Round and round, faster and faster. In his trance, Rama saw the banalinga float out of his hands. His hands were still, but the banalinga danced. It cavorted with joy and whirled with passion.

Akrita came running back with the leaves. All he could see was Rama's hands moving in a blur, the banalinga an obscure black circle between them.

In the trance, the banalinga stopped dancing and came to rest in his hands again.

Under the Ashwattha tree, Rama opened his eyes, panting with exertion. The banalinga began to sweat. Drops of clear, pure water formed on its hot surface and slowly ran down its body. Rama held it over Renuka's pot, and the water poured in it, filling the pot. Akrita gasped.

As the water filled upto the brim of the pot, the sweating stopped abruptly. The banalinga went cool immediately.

'How did you do that, Acharya?' Akrita asked.

Rama shrugged. 'When Mahadeva dances, entire universes erupt into existence and implode into nothing. He stops when he sweats and then the Narmada flows. That's all I know.'

Rama reverently set the banalinga down. He arranged the Bael leaves around the rim of the pot—half in, half out—the stems of the leaves immersed in the water. Then he placed the goddess head on the pot. His kalasha was ready.

'Akrita, I need flowers for the worship of the devi kalasha,' said Rama. The image of Ma Chinnamasta flashed in his mind.

A red body on a white lotus. 'Red and white flowers. Place them on and around the kalasha. I will go into dhyana now. Replace the flowers everyday till I emerge again.'

Akrita nodded and clasped his hands in prayer.

Rama invoked the blessings and protection of his manes. He controlled his breath and whispered the Gayatri mantra. Shive! He mentally intoned, grant me your blessings, aid me in my quest. He gazed into the eyes of the devi kalasha. After a while, his eyes closed, and he went deep into meditation. Again, he felt himself float in nothingness. This time he chanted the Holy Navakshari.

Om
Aim Hreem Kleem Chamundaye Viche.
Tribute to the Feminine Trinity.
The Lyric of Learning.
The Poem of Good Fortune.
The Shield of Power.

He chanted the mantra thousands of times, his mind unwavering, his intent steadfast. Rama ignored the colours and visions, he let them come and disappear, without entangling his mind and senses in them. He realised he was chanting to a beat, that a small trill rang with each word of the mantra. The trill grew louder and louder. Rama paused his chant and his consciousness filled with joy. It was the nada of the goddess's noopura. The sound of her divine anklet rang through the nothingness.

'Shive...' he whispered in gratitude.

Immediately, the trill was joined by a pulse of percussion. They united in a melody that made his consciousness vibrate. Damaru, he realised. The drum of Shiva. Rama seemed to soar in the nothingness. He flew at blinding speed and abruptly stopped. Before him was the pillar of the blue banalinga. He floated in silence before it. He couldn't sense the invisible veil now.

Namah Shivaya Om, his soul sang.

Rays of light pierced through the edges of the almond eyes. They framed the eyes in a golden light as the music reached a crescendo. Rama watched spellbound.

Golden light burst through the eyes, blazing through Rama. The banalinga transformed into a pillar of light with no beginning or end. The light turned blinding and filled the nothingness. It pulsed once and abruptly blinked out. The pillar of light was now a mirror, a pillar of reflective silver.

Rama gazed into it and saw himself in dhyana under the Ashwattha tree. The black banalinga and the Devi kalasha adorned with white navamallika and crimson rudrapushpa flowers were before him. Two cobras wound around Rama's body. Their tails were at his loins and they criss-crossed across his torso. Their heads with open hoods were above each shoulder, at his eye level. The heads turned to his face, the eyes watching him. A ray of light blazed from his forehead. Rama's consciousness stared at the image in wonder and incomprehension.

Shambho Mahadeva, his soul sang in gratitude.

He looked at the banalinga in the mirror, at the space between the almond eyes, and was pulled forward, thrown against the mirror, and sucked *into* it.

Rama blinked as he awoke from his meditation. He looked down at his body. There were no snakes. No ray of light either, he realised, as he rubbed his forehead.

What had happened? He wondered in confusion.

13

The Battle of Axes

Rama looked around—Akrita was still in prayer; everything was as he had left it when he had entered dhyana. Except it was dawn now. The forest was still, the air quiet.

The eyes of the banalinga had opened in his trance. He had been so desperate to have that happen for the first time. Never had he gone so deep, so far, in dhyana. He had gotten somewhere; he was sure, but what did his experience mean? Why was he shown the mirror in the end? He tried to think it through, but his mind was strangely reluctant. It refused to throw up any theories or ideas. Ma or father would know, but he would have to ask them later. He wouldn't pause now. He meant to go back into dhyana till such time as Mahadeva himself appeared before him.

He stopped forcing his mind and immediately became aware of the sheer bliss inside him. It was more than that—it was *Ananda!* It was like his heart had gathered the music of some divine, joyous rhapsody in it. The damaru was his heartbeat and the noopura his breath. Rama abandoned all thought, and embraced and frolicked in the serenity that washed over him.

Akrita stirred and opened his eyes.

'Acharya! You are back!' he exclaimed.

Before Rama could speak, he continued, 'Nine days you have been in dhyana, or rather nine nights since you started at sunset.'

Rama slowly stretched his legs, rubbing them to get the blood flowing. Akrita lent his shoulder as Rama rose and they walked to the hut. Rama stood in the doorway, reluctant to go inside. The joy in his heart craved the open woodland and gentle light of dawn.

'I'll gather some firewood and cook you some gruel. You must be exhausted and ravenous,' said Akrita, going in.

Rama felt neither hungry nor tired. He felt alive with the energy of his dhyana and the music in his heart. He wanted to savour this sensation without Akrita's chatter. Rama didn't say a word.

Akrita came back puzzled.

'I can't find your axe,' he said. He searched the second cottage and returned empty-handed.

'I'm sure it was in the hut last night.'

'Are you sure?' asked Rama.

'Maybe, I left it near the Jamun tree. I had gone that way yesterday,' Akrita mused. 'I'll find the axe and get you some jamuns too.' He hurried away into the forest.

Rama paced about slowly in the small open space. Thoughts began to form in his mind. He had done something stupendous. What took years, perhaps even decades and sometimes entire lifetimes—even rebirths—of ghor tapasya, he had managed in twelve days and nine nights. Some fruit would come of it, he was sure, since he had managed to open the banalinga's eyes. A spasm of thrill ran down his body as he recalled the dhyana experience. Rama felt as if his heart would burst with pride. He doubted if his clan father, Brighu or even his father, one of the saptarishis, could've managed it. Rama couldn't wait to tell his parents about it, but it would be better still to go back with news of Mahadeva's darshan. He daydreamed about that day. There was a dullness at the front of his head and he unconsciously rubbed at it, lost in reverie.

All at once, the forest came alive. There was some ecstatic, electric vibrancy about it, as if the joy in his heart had spilled over and spread all around. Even the huts seemed to thrum with it. Birdsong wafted in the gentle breeze and the air was fragrant with the scent of abundant myriad blooms. It was as if the forest itself hummed a merry tune and danced light-footed to the beat. The world celebrates with me, Rama thought. He turned to pace towards the Ashwattha tree. He saw an Aghori and stopped in surprise.

They should've all gone by now. Why was this one here, all alone, thought Rama? There was something different about this one. He was a head taller than Rama. The dreadlocks along with the thick shaggy beard and ash-covered body marked him as an Aghori, but he was magnificently muscular. He seemed to radiate extraordinary power. There was no chance that Rama would have failed to notice him amongst the horde of Aghoris that had descended on his father's ashram. This one looked more like a hunter, with tiger skin wrapped around his waist and cinched in place with a wide waistband also made of tiger skin.

The hunter stood like he owned the world. This man would be at home on a throne, squatting on the ground, begging, or keeping a corpse company at midnight at the cremation ghats, thought Rama. Or meditating, his mind added. Or dancing. Or at the van, in the thick of war. Rama looked into his eyes and found he couldn't hold his gaze for more than a nimisha. His gaze slid off the black pupils no matter how hard he tried. He gave up and then noticed the axe in the hunter's right hand. It was his, no doubt about it. He could recognise that axe anywhere. He didn't like the way the hunter held it like it was his own. The hunter gazed at Rama's forehead with the barest hint of a smile. The point on Rama's forehead between his brows throbbed insistently.

'You carry an amsha, yet heed it not,' the hunter chided him.

'Who are you?' Rama asked.

'I am—'

'Shiva,' Rama blurted out and immediately bit his tongue. He hadn't meant to interrupt.

'Aham Brahmasmi!' the hunter said. Rama paused, something puzzled him. The hunter looked around. He saw the banalinga and nodded to himself. He saw the kalasha and smiled. Rama felt his heart leap with joy. He approves, Rama thought. The next nimisha, Rama was angry with himself. Why should the hunter's approval matter?

'Why have you come to my ashram?' asked Rama. 'To return the axe?' he blurted again, half answer and half question.

'Your ashram?' asked the hunter. He raised his left index finger skyward and moved it in a wide circle. 'All this is mine!' The gesture seemed to encompass the forest, the world, the universe itself. Rama snorted his irritation at the gesture. This one thought no end of himself.

'The forest belongs to no one,' he replied, his voice rising.

'The axe is also mine,' said the hunter, raising it and turning it in his right hand.

Irritation gave way to anger. Rama fought to keep it from showing in his voice.

'You are welcome to food and rest in my ashram. I must resume my dhyana soon. Feel free to leave my axe behind when you go your way,' said Rama. The hunter stood quiet.

'Are you a disciple of Old Shiva?' Rama asked. He was sure that he wasn't but he asked anyway. The hunter laughed. It was startling in its innocence.

'Old Shiva?' the hunter asked and raised one eyebrow tauntingly at Rama. 'Dhyana to propitiate Mahadeva,' he said, nodding towards the banalinga. 'Befitting that the one who cut off his mother's head prays to the one that cut off Brahma's.'

Rama exploded in anger. 'I will brook no insult of Mahadeva. No Aghori would ever utter such words that are an affront to Him. Do not speak of things beyond your understanding. Leave my axe here and go. This is my only warning.'

'Take it if you can,' said the hunter as he placed the axe next to the banalinga and moved aside a little. He grinned nonchalantly at Rama, standing at ease with his arms crossed over his chest.

Rama bristled at the insolence. Having the axe was an obvious advantage, but the man had put it down and moved away. It was only a step and leap for Rama to reach the axe. He could do it in the blink of an eye. Did this hunter think himself faster than him, or did he think himself so strong and dextrous that he could, with bare hands, deal with Rama and his axe? Rama decided to ignore the axe.

'Your pride needs to be taught a tough lesson. I will teach it now,' said Rama. He charged at the hunter, his eyes fixed on his target. He reached him in the blink of an eye, his fist already swinging to punch the hunter's jaw. All of a sudden, the hunter seemed to be at three places at once. Standing at ease, then standing with his arms crossed and then adroitly avoiding Rama's blow. The movement was a blur, so incredibly fast did he move, yet each position registered clearly in Rama's vision.

Rama's fist hit empty air. He turned with the blow, pivoted on his left foot, and moved to grip the hunter's neck from behind with his right forearm. Again, he saw the man at three places at the same time. His hands grasped air. The man wasn't there; he had moved a distance away. Rama leapt, aiming a kick to the hunter's chest. Again, he saw the blur of three positions being quickly changed, but, this time, the third was not to avoid the blow. The hunter turned his torso out of the way, grabbed Rama's ankle with one hand, and the back of his neck with the other. Using Rama's momentum and adding a little push to it, he sent Rama sailing in the air. Rama tumbled to the ground, curling as the momentum spun him over and came up on one knee. He exhaled sharply in anger. He raised his eyes to find the axe before him.

'Ramabhadra, harmless as a doe,
Deemed the poor hunter his foe.
His hands with no axe,
And attention so lax,
He sought to catch a tiger by its toe.'

The hunter laughed. There was no mocking in his tone,

rather a gentle chiding. This was no ordinary adversary, thought Rama. His movements looked lethargic, yet he was blindingly fast.

'Acharya,' Akrita called. Rama and the hunter turned towards him. He stood a few feet away at the edge of the open space. He looked at both of them in confusion. In his right hand, he held Rama's axe. Rama stared at it in bewilderment. That was his axe. He recognised the swirls in the wood, the slight indentation in the staff around the clasp of the axe head, and the way the bottom was pitted and scraped. He turned to the axe next to the banalinga. That too was his. The two axes were identical.

'The axe is mine,' said the hunter to Akrita.

'Yes, Acharya,' said Akrita.

Rama whirled towards Akrita. 'Why do you call him acharya?' he asked.

Akrita stared at him and the hunter in turn. 'He is my acharya and so are you. Both of you are identical. I don't know who is real.'

Rama looked at the hunter. He didn't look like Rama at all; he looked like an Aghori. Then why did Akrita see two Ramas?

'Two axes, two acharyas,' said Akrita.

Rama's mind raced. This was a trick. The man was a sorcerer, an asura.

'Asura!' he accused.

'That is a first,' the hunter replied. 'Never been called that before.'

'Give him the axe,' said Rama, grabbing the axe next to the banalinga. The hunter lazily took the axe from Akrita and rested it on his shoulder. He smiled at Rama.

Rama leapt, axe held overhead. He saw a blur of movement and the three positions again. This time he concentrated on the final one. The axe came down swiftly in an arc and slashed through the air. But the hunter had moved two steps beyond the position that Rama had attacked. Rama had not even seen him move. Rama whirled and attacked again, anticipating every move the hunter could make. He slashed and jabbed, he swung backhanded; he feinted left and cut right. His onslaught was unstopping and intense. He brought all his lessons and years of practice to bear, but couldn't land a single blow. After what seemed like a muhurta of untiring, strenuous all-out effort, Rama stood still, his chest heaving, his axe held before him in his right hand. He was covered in sweat and dust.

'Good. You've been taught well,' said the hunter.

Rama roared in outrage and pounced again. A short while later, he stopped, gasping for breath. His opponent had danced all around him, evading and feinting, anticipating his every move with immaculate precision. He hadn't counterattacked even once. He had stood patiently, waiting for Rama to make his move.

Rama thought hard, using the time to regain his breath. The hunter was tiring him out and conserving his own energy. But he would not give up. He had to find a way to defeat this man. Rama raised the blade of the axe to his forehead.

'Mahadeva, help me!' he whispered. He saw the hunter smile. Rama made his move. He didn't focus on any position, instead he focussed on the place where his instinct told him his opponent would move next. As the axe began its downward arc, Rama whispered.

'Namah Shivaya.'

The blur of the hunter's movement paused. Time seemed

to slow down. Rama saw the blade of his axe swing down. It took ages to complete the arc. One axe head crashed into the other with a tremendous clash. He had made contact at last.

'Better,' said the hunter, and he attacked back.

Rama had no time to think. He swerved frantically, the hunter's axe whooshing past within a hair's breadth of his head. The attack was relentless. Somehow, Rama moved out of the way, to retreat and block the axe at the last moment was all he could manage. He moved by pure instinct, but he could only defend. He was losing ground, his brain howled at him. Rama fought on furiously, looking for an opening—a pause in the hunter's assault—to counterattack. His arms, shoulders and torso were covered with nicks, cuts and bruises received from his own axe while trying to stop the extraordinarily powerful blows of the hunter. Rama felt his strength waning. He needed both hands to parry the blows now.

He tried to block a swing to his chest with his axe. It thudded into him, knocking the air out of his lungs. The hunter smiled. He looked as fresh as when he started this fight, as if this was child's play for him. His left hand came up to Rama's sternum, heaved him up and threw him back. Rama flew through the air and landed beside the banalinga. His axe remained with the hunter.

'Acharya,' Akrita called. Rama and the hunter turned to face him. He was again standing at the edge of the open space, holding Rama's axe and staring at them in confusion.

Rama went slack-jawed in astonishment. When had Akrita disappeared and how had he come back with another axe? He wracked his mind for an explanation. Asura maya! Asuras were known to obstruct yagnas and homas of important rishis. This one, clearly, wanted to stop him from continuing his dhyana. He would find out why after he had defeated him, or not—he would just kill him.

'The axe is mine,' Rama roared. 'Throw it to me!'

'But Acharya,' said Akrita.

'Throw it to him,' said the hunter.

'Yes, Acharya,' said Akrita and threw the axe to Rama.

The moment Rama caught it, he launched the axe at the hunter with all his strength. Straight at his head. Rama's aim was unerring, it sped like lightning towards its target. The hunter plucked it out of the air.

Akrita disappeared and reappeared.

'Acharya ...,' he called.

The hunter, neatly, arrayed the three axes in his waistband and said, 'Give them to him.' Akrita obeyed.

Them? Rama saw Akrita throw two axes to him. He caught both, one in each hand. Both were identical, both were his. Rama attacked, fast and furious. The hunter stayed unarmed. Rama roared at the impertinence. He launched a flurry of cuts, slashes and thrusts—none landed. The hunter snatched the axes out of Rama's hands and drove his shoulder into him. Rama reeled back, tumbling over his feet. He fell where Akrita stood. He looked up to see him holding two more axes.

'Acharya ...,' Akrita said.

Akrita still saw two Ramas, but Rama saw the hunter instead. Rama touched Akrita's forearm. Perhaps the touch would help him see what Akrita saw. Rama turned and saw Jamadagni standing before him, exactly where the hunter had stood a nimisha before. Rama let go of Akrita's hand, but, still saw his father before him.

'Who do you see there?' Rama whispered to Akrita.

'You,' Akrita answered in confusion.

Rama felt anger and frustration course through him. This was a formidable sorcerer—a mayavi. Jamadagni looked at him in disapproval. A second figure appeared behind Jamadagni. A rishi again but older than Jamadagni, his long flowing hair and beard completely white. It was his grandfather, Richeeka. He, too, looked with reproach at Rama. Yet another rishi appeared behind Richeeka, and another immediately behind him. Each different from the one ahead. The number of rishis increased every nimisha, till finally, a wizened old rishi appeared. He stared at Rama with piercing eyes.

'I'm Brighu,' he said. Rama realised he was looking at all his manes.

'What do you see? And hear?' Rama whispered again to Akrita.

'I still see you but hear nothing,' Akrita whispered back.

'You forget,' said Brighu, his voice heavy with displeasure.

'Forget,' repeated the images of his ancestors. 'You forget.'

In a blink, along with his manes, Renuka stood before Rama. He didn't bother asking Akrita this time. This trickery was all for him. But why?

'Remember,' Jamadagni whispered, the whites of his eyes showing. Renuka, too, looked at Rama with reproach. 'Have we taught you nothing?'

Rama stared back. This was an illusion. He would not answer. Why was the asura playing these games? He had the upper hand in the fight, while Rama was fighting to stay alive. He could think of nothing the asura would gain by these illusions. Rama stared back, biding time, regaining his breath and planning his next attack. His ancestors, Jamadagni and Renuka had vanished, and the hunter was back. He gazed expressionlessly at Rama, waiting.

'Your illusions do not delude me. The fight isn't finished yet,' said Rama.

Rama rose, eyeing the axes warily. He slowly took the axe from Akrita's left hand. Another axe immediately appeared there.

'Mahadeva, hear me, help me,' Rama whispered. The hunter cupped his right hand to his ear and mimed listening hard.

'I don't hear a reply, Rama. You should worship me to save yourself from this predicament,' said the hunter. Rama snatched the axe out of Akrita's right hand and hurled both axes at the hunter. He kept grabbing the axes appearing in Akrita's hands, and throwing them blindly at the hunter, whispering Namah Shivaya all the while. Rama didn't know how many times he did that. He only stopped when no more axes appeared, and Akrita himself faded away.

Rama looked at the hunter. His aim had been perfect, but the axes hung in mid-air, inches from the hunter's face and body. The hunter hadn't moved one bit; he stayed still even now, looking at Rama. Rama counted sixteen axes. With a sudden arcing movement, the hunter swept up all the axes and tucked them under his right arm. A despairing Rama threw himself at the hunter, who sidestepped and pushed Rama away. Momentum carried Rama forward till he stopped clumsily before the banalinga and the kalasha.

Rama turned and gasped at the sight. The hunter had grown more arms, ten on each side. Each hand held an axe. One more was held by the two hands in front of him. He grew taller as Rama watched, towering over the trees. The hunter had his eyes closed and face tilted skywards. When he stomped his right foot, the ground shook. In the distance,

Rama saw a giant wall of water, as high as the hills, rise and curve along the course of the Narmada.

Rama's mind reeled. Was this Arjuna? How had he got to know of Rama?

'Mahadeva, how do I defeat him?' Rama prayed in desperation. The hunter swirled the axes, making them dance between his arms, up and down, back and forth, building up to a fast rhythm. He whirled them around himself so fast that they seemed to form a circle. A circle of blur with only the axe heads visible. The chakra with twenty-one prongs, Rama's mind screamed. The hunter let out a piercing cry, a roar of exultation. From some unknown source, came the throbbing, bone-rattling, chest-thumping beat of dundhubis, and an eerie trill of bone trumpets rang across the ashram. The day darkened as if the sun was in eclipse. The wall of water fell with a thump that knocked Rama off his feet, and rose higher again. Arcs of blue lightning streaked past Rama and lanced into the earth at the hunter's feet. The thunderclap was ear-splitting. The wind howled through the trees, bending the tops almost to the point of breaking. An iridescent hood of a cobra formed in the sky, its head as high as the clouds. Blue fumes spewed from its nostrils, and swirled around the hunter and across the ashram. The hunter opened his eyes; death was staring at Rama. He brought all the axes together in front of him. Then, holding them perfectly aligned to each other, he twirled them like he was churning buttermilk. The axes blazed in his hands, hot and white. The burning axes liquefied and the hot lava ran and pooled in the hunter's palms like quicksilver.

One brilliant white ray of sunlight fell on the liquid, a needle-sharp jet of water from the wall pierced it, the fumes of the serpent spiralled into it. Lightning arced into it as thunder roared, and the wind spun into a typhoon in the hunter's palms. A column of earth rose and buried itself in the lava. The hunter held it close and breathed over it. His hands came away from the front of his face and Rama saw him hold a single axe in his right hand. An axe with two arcing, vicious blades on either side of the staff, facing away from each other.

Rama looked away. There was something supernatural about this man. It was impossible to beat him. Rama had thrown everything he had at him and come up short. He would still fight to the death, if need be, but he needed help. He turned to the kalasha and banalinga.

'Shive ...,' he whispered and stopped short. He didn't know if it was a trick of light and shadow, or if it was his imagination running amok. But he thought he saw a smile flit across the face of the goddess. He had the strange feeling that the face was teasing him for not seeing what was right before him. Rama emptied his mind and gazed into the eyes of the goddess. He floated into nothingness as soon as he shut his eyes. Rama had no time to marvel at the speed with which he entered dhyana. He saw himself approaching the mirror again.

Rama looked in the mirror and froze in utter shock. His reflection was without a head.

The voice in the woods—the soft, mellifluous voice of Dattatreya, whispered in the nothingness.

Mirror, mirror
What do you see?
My spirits aground,
My dreams aloft,
Tell me, between,
What do you see?

Mirror, mirror
Whither my head?
Whither my axe?
Pray, speak the truth,
What do you see?

The voice sang for him and replied for the mirror as well.

Rama, Rama
What do I see?
Saint, you show me,
Sinner, I see.
Feet that run awry
And head in the sky,
Between,
A sea of pride, high.
When head is lost to ego,
What needs the axe, it must go.

Rama, Rama
I could lie,
Lost head is no woe,
I can give you a halo,
Or three.
For what was,
But never for what could be.
The price for the halo will be,
The morrow's insanity.

Rama, Rama
What do I see?
If truth you wish to behold,
See...

The mirror showed him a lone man walking the dunes in the desert. From the vision in his strange dream, Rama realised, the man was Samrat Arjuna. The mirror drew close to Arjuna, and Rama saw Arjuna fully reflected in the mirror. He saw Arjuna's face for the first time. He was effulgent and powerful and aware of his power. Rama's consciousness told him this was a man suffused with power and pride. Rama remembered Jamadagni's words—Demigod of the Cult of the Self and the Dogma of Ego.

Pride.

Rama understood. His experiences in dhyana had been a blessing from the Almighty. It had been the fruit of the punya of his manes and the prayers of his parents with very little effort from him, but he had taken it to be his own achievement. He had forgotten his pitrus, their sacrifices, their steadfastness in dharma, the trials they had faced and the knowledge they had endeavoured to gain for the benefit of mankind. The worm of pride had burrowed into his own heart. He had been walking on the same path trodden by Arjuna earlier. Rama cringed with shame as this realisation struck home. How could he have been so petty? So blinded by pride? The hunter's prey had been Rama's pride. A tough lesson had been taught to him. His prowess with the axe was tackled with ease by the hunter. So, who was he?

Filled with penitence, Rama prostrated himself in the nothingness. 'Shive, I beg your forgiveness,' his soul cried. The mirror disappeared.

Rama sensed something tugging at him, and he seemed to hurtle through space, only to stop abruptly as if he had hit a stone wall. He felt trapped and immobile, like he was made of stone. Three almond-shaped eyes, akin to the trinetra, appeared and rushed at him. The horizontal eyes settled over his own and opened. Rama gazed out at his ashram, but the perspective seemed strange. It took him a moment to realise what was happening.

He was in the banalinga.

He sensed the presence of the hunter beside him in his banalinga form. But he also saw himself pacing in the open space, walking away from the Ashwattha tree. He saw himself turn and stop in surprise. Rama realised he had travelled back in time.

Suddenly, he saw two pictures at once. Two views. The first view was from inside the banalinga and the second one from inside the Rama, who paced near the Ashwattha tree and stared in surprise at the hunter and his axe. Rama saw and registered each view independently and clearly at the same time. It was not humanly possible he realised. This was divine intervention.

'Who are you?' he heard and saw himself ask in both the views.

'I am,' the hunter replied.

Both the views froze to a standstill.

In the first view, from inside the banalinga, Rama saw the second version of himself appear beside the first. It gazed at the hunter in worshipful adoration. A beam of golden light shone on his forehead. Rama remembered his parents and Old Shiva gazing at his forehead, touching it. Amsha! The word flashed across Rama's mind. This was the sign of the amsha in him.

In the second view, Rama saw only the hunter. He was completely unaware of the second version of himself outside of the banalinga.

The hunter's reply blazed across Rama's consciousness.

I AM.

That was all the hunter had said. That was his complete answer.

I AM.

The view from inside the banalinga, unfroze. The second version of himself dropped to the ground in a full-length namaskara, palms clasped together in front. He strove to complete the thought left incomplete by the hunter.

'...SHIVA!' He blurted in rapturous adoration.

The first version of himself bit his tongue.

'AHAM BRAHMASMI,' the hunter said.

The words echoed across both the views and seeped through the banalinga as well. Realisation dawned on the Rama inside the Banalinga.

The first version of himself was his ego. It saw only the hunter, oblivious to the truth.

The second version of himself was his soul. It saw only the truth. It saw divinity. His soul saw Shiva. The beam of golden light from the amsha that had activated in him, shone in devotion and gratitude in Mahadeva's presence.

Mahadeva had indeed appeared before him. His pride had blinded him to God. Mahadeva had not only responded to his penance, but he had also tested his prowess and broken his pride. Rama berated himself for being an utter fool. Pride was the prize given by the Gods to petty men, and loss of gratitude was the price they paid for it. Pride was the quicksand that pulled you into the depths of misery. He cringed when he remembered how he had called Mahadeva, an asura. In his infinite mercy, Mahadeva had shown him his manes and waited for realisation to dawn on Rama, for him to hark to the voice of his soul and forsake the boastful reasoning of his ego. Rama was filled with deep shame. But for the grace of Ma Gauri, he would still be fruitlessly obeying the urging of his arrogance.

'Mahadeva, my Guru, I have learnt the lesson you were trying to teach. I beg your forgiveness,' Rama prayed in the banalinga.

Immediately, the second view also unfroze, and the first version of himself—the ego version—fell to the ground in full namaskara.

'Mahadeva, my Guru, I have learnt the lesson you were trying to teach. I beg your forgiveness,' repeated the first version.

The two versions of Rama melded together, as the version of Rama inside the banalinga flew out and entered the body of the melded version. He found himself prostrate in namaskara before the hunter.

'Mahadeva, I beseech your mercy,' he cried.

He looked up and saw a brilliant pillar of light.

'You've proved yourself worthy. Arise, Rama.'

The words rang across the ashram and within Rama's head. The voice was gentle, innocent yet enormously powerful. Relief and joy coursed through Rama.

'The axe is yours.'

In the blink of an eye, the pillar disappeared. The deadly, twin-bladed axe hung in mid-air.

14

Parashu

Arjuna sat in prayer under the Nyagrodha tree. His dreams and dhyana had both been profoundly disturbing. His instincts told him that something of great significance was afoot, and he meant to get to the root of it. He had spoken to High Priest Raikava about it. The high priest would use his yogic powers to delve into the meaning of his dream and of the image that had shaken him to his very core in his dhyana. But what was of prime importance, and what he wanted to remedy first, was his spiritual despair. And so, he prayed long and hard to Guru Dattatreya. It was on his guru's blessing that his prowess rested, and now he sought his aid in his time of distress. Even though it had been a long while since he had reached out to Dattatreya, he had not forgotten what he had learnt.

The guru had been unlike any other brahmin Arjuna had ever known, simple and shorn of orthodox ritual piety. He had no concern for the world or for its grasping ambitions and covetous dreams. His reverence for such an evolved soul, verily a God walking amongst mortals, was deep and intense. Arjuna hoped his guru would hear his pleas in the ether and respond like he always had in the past. As always, he could be found only if he wished to be found.

Arjuna emptied his mind and formed a mental image of the chakra just as Dattatreya had taught him. He stilled his breath and concentrated on the chakra. A blazing disc formed in his mind; its thousand triangular projections lost in the effulgence of the light around it, as it revolved. Arjuna fed his fears and frustrations into it and sat in peace. Ever so slowly, the chakra resolved into its full shape. It was only then that Arjuna realised that what was in front of his mind's eye was something different, something he had never seen before. Arjuna watched it in bewilderment.

What he had thought was a chakra, was actually a ring of twenty-one axes, revolving as one with all the axe heads pointing outwards.

The axes were of a kind he had never seen before. Each was double-bladed, with the twin blades arcing menacingly on either side of the handle. These were no simple woodcutters' axes, these were weapons.

Arjuna startled out of his prayers, but remained deep in thought. This weapon was special, something not wrought by human hands. This was not a figment of his imagination or a delusion of a frantic mind. His was not an undisciplined mind, a mind given to fantasy and wishful thinking. Far from it. He was an ardent and seasoned practitioner of dhyana, and his yogic powers—though not of the same rigour and might as that of rishis—were considerable. These visions had not appeared by mere chance.

The young man, the mirror and the chakra of axes—three visions, three omens perhaps. Arjuna hoped his guru would respond to his prayers soon; he would know exactly what the

visions signified. Meanwhile, he would hear what Raikava
had to say.

———

'Pranaam Samrat. May you be ever victorious,' said High
Priest Raikava.

'Sit,' said Arjuna, gesturing to the chair opposite him in
his private chambers. Raikava spread his deerskin on the seat
of the chair and sat in sukhasana. He ran a hand over his bald
head and weak, clean-shaven chin. Nervous, Arjuna thought.

'Have you gained any insight?'

Raikava stared at Arjuna and nodded.

'What does the Avadhuta, your Guru, blessed be his name,
have to say?' he asked.

Arjuna looked at the priest in surprise. The question
was unexpected. Raikava was a man who rarely spoke and
then, too, only what was necessary, his words shorn of
embellishments and sparse like the man himself. This was
a man who had chosen a spiritual path—the worship of
Mahavishnu and none else—and had followed its course
with blinkers on his eyes. The blinkers, he used, were strict
ritual adherence and orthodoxy. He acknowledged that other
paths existed, but disdained even a debate with any of their
followers. To Raikava, his path was paramount, and the world
and its affairs a paltry sideshow towards which he glanced only
on occasion. For such a man to ask about the Avadhuta—a
man who abjured orthodoxy, who had tread a new path to
moksha—was unprecedented.

So, I was right, thought Arjuna. The visions had serious
implications.

'I await his reply,' said Arjuna.

'I'm very keen to hear his thoughts,' said Raikava. 'The future, Samrat, hangs in the balance. A mother's penance, her tapasya of the Ekadashi Vrat, and her son's vigorous dhyana to gain spiritual power and unparalleled worldly success is known to many. Queen Padmini and Chakravarti Samrat Karthavirya Arjuna—mother and son—have been celebrated in song and story.

'But, my yogic powers now reveal that another pair of mother and son have been the recipients of enormous spiritual power—a Mahavidya has appeared in the mother and an amsha of Mahavishnu in her son.'

Arjuna went still, stunned by what he had heard.

Raikava continued, 'Such a circumstance is unrivalled in the itihasa of mortals. And it gets stranger still. Both mother and son were born mere mortals, with no divine power finding expression in their actions, until ...'

Raikava paused and stared at the samrat. '... until the son executed his mother on the orders of his father. He beheaded her.'

Arjuna gasped.

'The mother lives. Mahavidya Chinnamasta manifested in her. The son, in essence, has made his mother a goddess. Did she die? Was she reborn? I cannot say. I can speak only of the little that was revealed to me.

'The son committed matricide, the gravest of all sins, and yet he carries an amsha within. That should have been impossible, for divinity never sparks in such sinners.

'It needs a great deal of spiritual penance to even receive the darshan of God, even more to beget a blessing, and greater still to bring the blessing to full potency. Undoubtedly, you know this, having achieved it yourself. The son has overcome the sin of matricide, an insurmountable endeavour, through his extreme penitence. How he did it is unknown to me, but because of his free will and spiritual rigour, he has awakened the amsha that was dormant in him.'

Arjuna listened to all this, lost in thought, rubbing and tugging at his left earlobe. Raikava waited.

'There is more?' asked Arjuna, after a long while.

'Yes. The incredible doesn't cease here. The son has also done what no mortal has hitherto accomplished. He has become a brahmakshatriya.'

'Impossible!' Arjuna blurted out in astonishment.

'It was, until now,' replied Raikava.

'Who is he?' asked Arjuna.

'I know neither the mother nor the son. I know only of the father who had ordered the beheading of his wife. He is a saptarishi, the High Adept of Atharva and clan leader of the Brighus—Jamadagni.'

Arjuna sank back in his chair and said, 'I know only of the mother. Renuka, daughter of the Ikshvaku king, Prasenjit, king of Kashi, a city I had once sacked. I know not the son.'

Anger bloomed and spread inside Arjuna. 'Brighu was always a thorn in my heel. I thought I had plucked that thorn and cast it aside. I was wrong. The scion of the Brighu clan pricks me now.'

'You deem him your enemy?' asked a puzzled Raikava.

Arjuna probed Raikava's mind. The high priest stared back at Arjuna unafraid, knowing exactly what the samrat was doing. Arjuna nodded, satisfied that Raikava wasn't holding anything back from him.

'That was my first thought, my only thought when I saw

him in the dream. He was as surprised to see me as was I to see him.'

'Unusual,' said Raikava in a pondering tone. 'Such dreams can only be wrought by great spiritual power. So, who seeded the dream in two minds at once? It can not be a coincidence.'

'Is he a threat? What of the future that hangs in the balance?' asked Arjuna.

'It is impossible to defeat you, Samrat,' replied Raikava. 'The secret to your strength is known only to you and your guru. I am not privy to that rahasya, nor can I discover it through my yogic insight. Jamadagni's son doesn't know your secret either, and even if he does, how will he be able to overcome it? Only Dattatreya, blessed be his name, can answer all these questions.'

Arjuna nodded. He would ask his guru only about the vision in which he had seen the disc of axes. Raikava must not know of it. Everyone had secrets, but the secrets of a samrat, once revealed, could easily be tossed around like the coin thrown by a drunk gambler in the throes of his compulsion. Aloud, he said, 'But he carries an amsha?'

'We know of five avatars of Mahavishnu. There may have been many more, but everyone agrees on these five. The manifestation of the avatara was evident from the very beginning—on his arrival on prithvi or at birth itself. These are the scales of balance,' said Raikava, turning his palms upward and moving them up and down. 'The last two avatars—Narasimha and Trivikrama—slew or defeated asura samrats who had ruled the three worlds. There is no such asura samrat today. There is only you, the Samrat of Prithvi.'

He paused to underscore the significance of his words. 'And you deem him your enemy. Your instincts, your very soul recognised the danger, the threat in your dream.' He moved his left palm higher than the right.

'He cannot defeat you because he knows not the secret of your strength,' said Raikava, moving the left palm down and the right one up. 'But, Jamadagni's son atones for matricide, brings to prithvi an aspect of a Mahavidya, sparks an amsha within himself and becomes a brahmakshatriya. Who knows what else he can accomplish in the future? What is the purpose of the amsha?' He moved his palms, alternately, up and down.

'Therein lies the threat. The seers and the rishis watch with disbelief and delight at the immense yogic churn Jamadagni's son's atma has undertaken. A mere mortal dares to course yogic paths previously unknown, to ignite a tremendous transformation,' Raikava put his hands down. 'The scales of balance of the future are in play.'

Arjuna shook his head. 'The threat will not be allowed to fester for long. It will be found and crushed underfoot. The scales will tilt to my bidding. Before long, I will be the one holding the scales.'

Raikava stared at Arjuna in disbelief. His voice grew menacing as his eyes bore through Raikava's. 'I will show no mercy.'

Raikava gulped nervously and went quiet. Silence hung heavy around the samrat and the priest. Meekly, Raikava cleared his throat and spoke in a low voice, 'I wonder if he also deemed you his enemy when he saw you in the dream. We must assume that the import of the dream is not lost on him either.'

Arjuna nodded agreement.

'Then, the immediate step he would take is to gain knowledge of the divine astras,' said Raikava.

'I already possess this knowledge. I can counter any astra he may acquire,' said Arjuna.

'He will seek out your secret then. You will not reveal it, so ...,' Raikava didn't complete.

'Will my guru reveal it? That's what you wanted to ask, isn't it Raikava? He, or anyone else, wouldn't know how to reach my guru, leave alone obtain his grace. I doubt, if even the saptarishi, Jamadagni can reach my guru. The guru himself must decide to reach them.'

'And has he?' Raikava thought in his mind, but remained mute.

'Impossible!' said Arjuna aloud. But what if he has, asked a small voice in his head. The thought filled him with unease, and yet his mind kept going back to it. It was like giving into the urge to scratch a persistent itch. What if he got to know the rahasya, thought Arjuna. Even so, he could do nothing with the knowledge. Only the guru could take back what he had given, no one else. Knowing Arjuna's secret would only fill him with awe, and make him despair for not being able to do anything about it.

Raikava pondered awhile and said, 'If he seeks a way to defeat you, he will try to acquire something unique. A weapon dreadfully powerful and impossible to counter.'

Raikava's words broke Arjuna's train of thought. The image of the revolving disc of axes flashed in Arjuna's mind. 'Could the weapon be an axe?' he asked.

'I have not heard of any such weapon. Why do you ask?' replied Raikava. Arjuna did not reply. Raikava knew nothing of an axe. He would pursue this enquiry with Dattatreya only.

'The Brighus are no longer warrior priests. They confine themselves to ashrams and to the pursuit of tapasya and knowledge. I suspect someone lights the path for Jamadagni's son. Perhaps Jamadagni himself or some other who has tremendous spiritual power. Else, it could be his inherent talent or the power of the amsha he carries,' said Raikava. 'Or, it could be all three.'

'What of the mirror?' asked Arjuna, changing the subject.

'Samrat ...,' whispered Raikava, lowering his eyes and pressing his palms together in front of him. He was reluctant to answer.

'Speak without fear,' said Arjuna 'I would not have sought your counsel if I only wanted to hear what would please me. I have my courtiers and vassals for that. I enjoy their snivelling, but I would hear only the truth from you.'

Raikava's shoulders slumped like he was trying to make himself as small as possible. He kept his eyes down, refusing to look Arjuna in the eye. Arjuna could almost see the waves of anxiety emanating from him. He probed Raikava's mind. It was filled with fear. Arjuna waited. The priest would have to speak the truth as he saw it. Arjuna would know the moment he lied.

'The mirror in your trance,' Raikava's voice was barely audible, 'showed you the displeasure of the Gods ... displeasure at your arrogance ... at the misuse of your blessings.' Raikava's voice faltered and faded away.

Arjuna roared as he stood up. 'I conduct the yagnas as prescribed, as per the rules of the rites. My donations to the learned and funds for the temples are aplenty. I have enforced peace across the seven dweepas through the might of my arms. Why the displeasure, then?'

He paced the room in fury. Arjuna roared again as his fury exploded like a volcano. He smashed his fist into a pillar as wide as the trunk of an Ashwattha tree. The pillar cracked along its length; one half cleaved off with a sickening screech and toppled to the ground. Arjuna didn't even flinch. He stamped the broken pillar lying on the ground and shattered it to a million pieces.

'It must be that wretch, Indra, carrying tales. He will know my wrath soon,' sneered Arjuna. 'Anything more?'

The high priest shook his head with vigour, furtively looking up at the samrat. Arjuna dismissed him with a wave of his hand. Raikava scampered away, relieved to be dismissed, thanking the gods that Arjuna hadn't vented his fury on him. As with all tyrants, the complaint regarding his arrogance and misuse of power had gone in through one ear and out the other. Those lusting for power only hear what they want to, and always find a justification to play the victim.

———

Rama looked down at himself. The bruises, cuts and nicks had disappeared. The feeling of bliss from his meditation sang in his heart again. He had travelled back in time as if the battle with Mahadeva hadn't taken place. Yet, there the axe was, hanging in mid-air ahead of him. He marvelled at what had happened and an intense emotion of gratitude washed over him. Rama mentally offered his prayers to his pitrus, parents, Dattatreya, Shakti and Mahadeva.

He walked up to the axe. It shone in the sunlight. The cutting edges of the twin blades started a foot above the top end of the handle and arced savagely to a foot below it. The handle itself seemed about two cubits in length. Rama moved closer, reached out and tugged at it with his right hand. It didn't budge. He wrapped both hands around the handle and pulled. The axe held rock steady.

'Impatience and impertinence will get you nowhere,' said a voice in mock anger behind him. Rama turned. He had heard that voice before; it sparked some distant memory.

At the edge of the open space stood a gigantic, magnificent white bull. It snorted in indignation, and the huff of breath almost knocked Rama off his feet. Rama was pushed a couple of paces back and he coughed out the dust in his nostrils, kicked up by the snort.

'Pranaam Nandin,' said Rama, pressing his palms together.

'At least, you haven't forgotten your manners,' said Nandin, a hint of a smile in his voice. The muscles of the bull rippled powerfully as it gazed at the axe. 'So, Mahadeva deems you worthy. I wonder why? You fought like a little girl.'

Rama didn't respond to the taunt; he hardly heard it. Try as he might, he couldn't place the voice, so familiar yet not heard in a long time.

In a flash of light, the bull transformed. Now, a grizzled old man stood before Rama and roared a bellowing laugh.

'Veera!' Rama exclaimed in astonishment.

Nandin laughed again as Rama rushed to embrace him.

'You haven't forgotten my lessons,' said Nandin, hugging Rama tight. He held Rama out at arm's length and looked closely at the boy he had last seen ages ago. His gaze lingered on Rama's forehead for a long moment. 'You are a powerful man now, strong as a bull.'

'It was a bull-headed man who taught me to fight,' Rama laughed. 'But I wouldn't be standing with Nandin now if you hadn't taught me well all those years ago.

'I practised and trained every day,' Rama said. 'It's made me what I am. But I never would have guessed you were Nandin. Did father know?'

Nandin shook his head. 'No, he didn't, and I was only following Mahadeva's orders.'

'Why would Mahadeva wish for me to have your training?' asked Rama in surprise.

'He is omniscient, Rama. Nothing is hidden from him. My lessons have aided you thus far, and have helped you prove your worth. The axe is proof. He knew this day would come.'

'I can't budge it from where it floats in the air,' said Rama. Nandin looked across at the banalinga and kalasha.

'Finish your morning prayer and ritual,' said Nandin as he walked to the Ashwattha tree and sat in padmasana.

Rama sped to the river to do as he was told.

Later, when Rama returned, he saw Akrita standing in the doorway of the hut, looking from Nandin to the floating axe, in amazement. He held Rama's original axe in his right hand.

'Acharya, your axe,' he said, holding it out.

'He has got another for himself,' said Nandin. He reverentially lifted the head of the goddess from the sand pot and placed it beside the banalinga. He pressed his palms together and whispered a prayer. He, then, stood and lifted the pot in his hands and walked up to the axe.

'Come,' he said to Rama. He emptied the pot over Rama's head as he stood before the axe. Rama stretched out and held the axe by the handle.

'Om Namah Shivaya,' he whispered. The axe settled into Rama's hand immediately. A wash of golden light spread across the width of the blades. Rama held the axe as high over his head as he could. He didn't know why he did that, but it felt like the right thing to do. A beam of brilliant gold and blue light soared out from the axe and shot skyward. Thunder boomed and lightning streaked into the axe. The thunder seemed to course through the axe and Rama , before thumping into the earth. Slender ropes of lightning ran down the handle and cobwebbed across Rama's body, disappearing into his skin. Rama felt the handle press hard against his palm, as if the axe was trying to hold him back. A piercing roar emanated from the axe, swept across the ashram and whooshed away over the river and into the mountains.

Mahakaal's dreaded battle-axe had announced its arrival, loud and clear, in the realm of mortals.

Rama brought the axe down to his eye level and stared at it in fascination. The handle looked like it was made of wood, but it wasn't. It felt like it was made of earth, but Rama wasn't too sure of that either. The surface seemed to soften a little as Rama's hands curled around it, filling the creases and grooves of his palm, taking on the palm's imprint of it. And yet, when Rama looked closer, he found the handle was as hard as a diamond. The axe blades were of a metal unknown to Rama. It seemed strangely alive, like it was a sentient being by itself. Strange markings ran up and down the handle, with a flare at the bottom of the axe. On the top, where the axe handle connected the two menacing blades, runes—a circle with a point, a bindu, at its centre—were on both sides of the axe. The axe was perfectly weighted and balanced to Rama's liking. It felt like a part of him already, like a childhood friend or a brother, almost as if he'd been born with it and it had grown and matured into manhood along with him. Rama stood enthralled by the divine alchemy of the axe.

As if reluctant to come closer to the axe, Akrita crept up behind Nandin, open-mouthed in wonder.

'The axe has accepted you,' said Nandin.

'What do you mean?' asked Rama.

'It fits perfectly in your hand and is balanced to your liking, yes?' said Nandin.

Rama nodded.

'The physical bonding is over now. This is Mahakaal's axe. You must make it yours. You need to bond with it mentally. The axe will seek to take your measure. This is a divine weapon, won by spiritual power, like the other divine astras. The more spiritual power the weapon senses in you, the more strength it will draw from you and the more potent it will become. You won the axe by penance and a trial of worth. Now you need to realise its full, dreadful capability. This much I know for sure about the axe.'

'I need to undertake more tapasya?' said Rama.

Nandin shrugged, 'It will still be a formidable weapon, even if you don't. But you will have to learn how to unleash the fearsome fury of the axe by yourself, either by tapasya or some other way. That is your personal endeavour, no one can teach you that. The axe will recognise your intent, measure your power, and do your bidding, as it has with all those who have used it before.'

'Others? Who other than Mahadeva himself has used it?' asked Rama.

'In other worlds, other universes, other yugas, those whom Mahadeva deemed worthy have used the axe, but they are known only to Him. What matters is that the axe retains the memory of their usage, the spirit of their doings. Even the battle you fought with Mahadeva is imbued in it. It can teach you a lot if you can make it truly yours.'

'How do I even start?' Rama asked again.

'It is a weapon. The best way to start is to use it as one,' said Nandin. 'But it has been an incredible journey you have undertaken so far Rama. How did you even know what to do?'

Rama sighed.

'My life twists and turns like a whirlwind. Events storm into it, giving me scarcely any time to catch my breath. I am like a blind man in a dark room, searching for things I know nothing about. I stumble and falter, not knowing the right thing to do.'

He looked deep into Nandin's eyes. 'The stakes keep getting higher and higher, yet I find no guide to tell me what is the right thing to do. I move on the inkling of prophecy, the interpretation of dreams and perception of instinct. Please do not think me ungrateful. I am thankful for the smallest bit of help I can get. Only that ... it doesn't make for solid ground beneath my feet; it makes for a razor's edge. I fear ...,' Rama paused, turning away to look into the distance. 'I fear a wrong decision will have catastrophic consequences.'

'Tell me Rama. All that you've been through, the thoughts that have led to your decisions, the instincts you acted on. Tell me everything. Maybe I can help, and if I cannot, it will ease a little bit of your worry ... talking to someone about it,' said Nandin.

Rama looked into the distance and slowly began narrating the extraordinary events that had taken place recently. He left out no detail, no matter how trivial it seemed. He poured his thoughts and feelings into every twist and turn of the story, ignoring Nandin's sharp intakes of breath and whispered wonder. At long last, he stopped, after describing the battle with Mahadeva and the appearance of the divine axe. He still looked away into the distance. Silence stretched between the guru, who had last seen him as a child, and the formidable warrior the boy had become.

Nandin rested his hand on Rama's shoulder and waited until Rama looked at him.

'Rama, what worries you is that the end of your journey is unknown, that neither is the destination revealed to you, nor the next step. Do not add to that worry and turn it into fear. A soldier goes to war not knowing whether he will come back alive or be maimed in battle, whether he will meet his death by an opponent's sword or by a stray arrow of a compatriot. His duty, his dharma, is to fight, and you are no mere soldier, you are a Warrior of the Soul. Remember the beginning, Rama. You swung your axe on a mere possibility and the intense anticipation that you will find a way out. That is your strength. It is truly invaluable; do not sell it short.

'You chart a fresh course, guided by old prophecies, new dreams and the subtle aid of Guru Dattatreya. They do not tell you explicitly what the next step is, Rama, because the next step is whatever you decide it must be.'

Nandin pointed to the goddess's head.

'Nobody told you to do that. To consecrate the head of the goddess, to worship it, to recognise and venerate its auspiciousness. Nobody has done it before, though all knew of Shiva and Shakti, of Purusha and Prakriti. The urging of your soul, the play of your instincts and the deep confidence you have that you will find a way to your goal, has birthed a new mode of worshiping the Sacred Feminine—invoking Her into a kalasha. A new path has opened up, simply by you deciding what will be your step.'

'But,' Rama protested. 'It was an unconscious decision. Probably because I had beheaded my mother. I cannot think of any other reason for doing what I did.'

Nandin smiled. 'Yet it felt *right* when you thought of it, didn't it?'

Rama nodded. He remembered Mahadeva looking approvingly at the kalasha with the head, and his heart leaping with joy.

'Truth doesn't reveal itself with a thunderclap, Rama. It whispers, like a lover in your arms. Intimacy, the love of the soul, that's what truth desires. It comes to you when your mind focusses consciously on it, away from the noise and turmoil, like when you're in dhyana, waiting for that love. Or, when your mind is unconsciously focussed on something else, truth sneaks past intellect and embraces the soul. Or, when the mind is at rest, in deep sleep truth makes love to the soul. So, heed it, for very few are blessed to hear it.

'To act is our duty, the consequences of our actions are lost in the mists of the future, and subject to too many other influences. Doubt has eroded the will of the best of men, rooted their feet to the ground with the fear of the unknown. To seek, understand and embrace the unknown is the essence of the courage of a man. To know the unknown is to be God, it is to be one with Brahman.

'Your actions have brought you this far, Rama. Do your duty and leave the rest to the gods. Everything has becoming, unbecoming, death and becoming again. That lila is known only to the gods.'

Rama nodded in understanding. It was good to have talked to Nandin about this.

'It was the gods always pack their words, and their actions too, tight with meaning,' said Rama. 'The prophecy of my mother's unbecoming was the start of it all.'

'It was the beginning, Rama. The beginning of your

journey,' said Nandin and stopped speaking. He looked off into the distance as if listening to something and then smiled. 'Battle comes calling. The time and the opportunity for you and the axe to take each other's measure presents itself. Remember my lessons. Remember the battle of the axes and remember my words, Rama.'

'What do you mean battle?' asked Rama, but Nandin looked away, leaving the question unanswered.

A circle of brilliant light formed in the open space a little ahead of where the three of them stood. It was as big as the hut and it touched the ground but left no impression on it. The light faded into a dense orb of darkness and out of it stepped a weary but majestic figure.

Desperate eyes and a bruised body, Rama noticed. A weary man clutching at hope but too proud to show it, Rama thought.

'Pranaam Indradev,' said Nandin.

Akrita's loud gasp shook Rama out of his surprise. 'Pranaam Indradev,' he said and turned to Akrita. 'Akrita, I forgot to introduce you. This is Nandin, the foremost bhakta and mascot of Mahadeva himself.'

In a trice, Akrita was prostrate on the ground, palms joined, mumbling a string of incomprehensible words. Nandin tried hard to hide his amusement. Indra seemed not to have heard or seen Akrita at all.

'That is my shishya, Akritavrana,' said Rama. Indra tore his eyes away from Rama's forehead and glanced strangely at Akrita. A nimisha later his eyes returned to Rama's face.

'You see it too?' said Nandin to Indra.

'Pranaam to all,' said Indra. 'Yes, I see it and it brings hope to my heart.' He turned to Rama. 'I come with Mahadeva's instructions. He bids you to join the war against the asura horde in the realm of the devas.'

Rama was dumbfounded. 'M-me?'

'Mahadeva says you are the one who can save us from ruin.'

'But I don't even know how to use this weapon,' Rama replied, holding the axe up between Indra and him. Indra paled when he saw the axe. He involuntarily moved back a couple of paces.

'You wield Mahakaal's axe,' he whispered.

'Yes, but ....,' Rama didn't know what to say.

'What is it called?' asked Rama to Nandin in exasperation.

'Parashu,' said Nandin.

'Parashu? Axe! That's its name?' Rama said in disbelief.

'Well, it is an axe,' replied Nandin. 'No matter what you call it. You want to give it a name, go right ahead. You have the axe now.'

Rama glanced at the still prone and mumbling Akrita. 'I am not naming anything. Parashu it is and Parashu it will be.'

'You refuse to help us?' said Indra. 'Decide now! Time is of the essence. The devas prepare for the final charge as we speak.'

'That bad?' asked Nandin. Indra stood quiet, trying to hide his chagrin.

'What if I fail?' Rama asked Nandin.

'You die. The story of Ramabhadra ends. The axe returns to Mahadeva,' said Nandin.

'And if I refuse to go?' said Rama.

'The choice is yours. The axe stays with you,' replied Nandin.

Rama paused to think. He had no intention of refusing Mahadeva's bidding. He was only stalling for time to decipher the new sensation he felt inside him. His instincts called for him to join the battle. He wanted to test his skills, to fight his first war, against asuras no less. To face death, to test his mettle against the horde that had pushed the devas' army to the wall. To rain death and destruction on them. But that was not what was new. That was just him, his need for action. The edge to his need was what was new. An imperative impulse that called to him to rush, to be in the thick of the battle when the attack happened. It was the axe, Rama suddenly realised. The Parashu understood his instincts. It recognised the raging call of his blood to face his enemies. It fed into his urge to dominate. The axe was already taking his measure and tugging him on.

Rama wondered if Nandin was aware of the nature of the axe. Rama had a lot knowledge of other divine weapons and astras; he had listened to his father expound the rules for their invocation and learnt them all. He knew all about their deployment and the dire effects of some of the weapons. The axe wasn't akin to them. No—this was a completely different kind of a weapon. It needed no mantra to invoke, and it was gauging his emotions and thoughts, and urging him to deploy it to do what it did best. Cut. Rama felt a surge of power inside him when he thought of that. Rama stared at the axe, his mind ticking away at a furious pace. He turned to Nandin and asked, 'Have you ever handled this weapon?'

Nandin shook his head in denial.

'What does this symbol , the bindu with the circle around it, mean?' asked Rama.

'I don't know,' said Nandin.

Rama held it out to him. 'Hold it,' he said. Nandin froze.

'No. I cannot. Mahadeva ...,' said Nandin.

'—gave it to me. He deemed me worthy. It's mine now. I'm asking you to hold it,' Rama said.

Nandin's face went paler than Indra's had earlier. He didn't want to hold the axe. In fact, he suddenly wanted to be very far away from it. Rama shoved it into his arms. Nandin stared at Rama, unwilling to look at the axe in his hands, afraid to drop it and terrified of holding it. Rama walked away, a dozen steps. When he turned, he saw panic in Nandin's eyes.

'I deem you worthy of the axe,' Rama said and waited. Nothing happened. A thick silence blanketed them. Sheer terror danced in Nandin's eyes. Rama felt the urge of the axe still pound through him. It still recognised Rama as its master and none else. So, thought Rama, it was not simply physical bonding that had happened: Rama suddenly felt like he was wading into deep waters. He would have to figure out a way to stay afloat and swim. Mahadeva had left it to him to figure out the secrets of the axe.

'Throw it to me,' said Rama. The axe practically flew out of Nandin's hands. Nandin stared at it in astonishment. He had intended to gently toss it back, not daring to make any sudden movements.

Rama watched as relief washed over Nandin's face—relief at having the axe out of his hands. He remembered Indra also flinching when he saw the axe.

'What happened to the others who held the axe and didn't truly make it their own?' he asked Nandin as he walked back. Nandin and Indra exchanged glances. Akrita was back on his feet now, watching the axe in dumb fascination.

Nandin felt an overwhelming admiration grow for this boy, nay, this young man. Somehow, he had figured out an important facet of the axe's power. A powerful intelligence was at work here, as sharp and cutting as the axe's edge. He had quickly learnt to please Mahadeva and win the axe, and already he was figuring out how it worked. His disciple had truly outgrown him.

'Some went mad, their minds completely obliterated by the power of the axe. Their bodies wasted away to a miserable death. So, I've heard,' said Nandin.

'Some took their own lives. Ended it with that very axe. Unable to master it, losing their grip on their minds and unwilling to suffer more,' said Indra.

'These are the stories we've heard. No one has ever met anybody who has mastered Mahakaal's axe. It is a weapon no one speaks about aloud. Whispers abound, so do many fantastical theories. No one, except Mahadeva, knows the truth. I didn't want to add this worry, too, to the already formidable tasks ahead of you, Rama. I don't want conjecture and rumour to preoccupy your mind,' said Nandin.

Rama nodded. He understood Nandin's concern. Mahakaal's forge had produced a truly dreadful and lethal weapon.

'Can this axe kill Karthavirya Arjuna?' asked Rama. Out of the corner of his eye, he saw Indra startle.

'It isn't the weapon; it is you who must kill him. If you know what I mean,' said Nandin. Rama nodded again.

'Does he have a weapon such as this?' asked Rama.

'He possesses and knows the usage of all divyastras, and he deploys them to their full potency. He also has a secret to his invincibility. I do not know what that is,' said Indra. Nandin nodded in agreement.

'I will do as Mahadeva wishes. I will join the battle against the asuras,' said Rama to Indra.

'Why do you seek to kill Arjuna?' said Indra.

'It's the purpose of the amsha of Mahavishnu he carries. That much I know,' replied Nandin.

'Then it is time to deliver the first blow. Arjuna uses his influence among the asuras to send reinforcements to the horde and keep the siege going. He demands that I beg his assistance in this battle and pay him tribute for his efforts. He will prevail upon the asuras to retreat if I agree. Insufferable arrogance!' said Indra.

'Let's go,' said Rama. He followed Indra into the orb of darkness.

'Shambho Mahadeva,' said Rama to Nandin.

'Hara Hara Mahadeva,' said Nandin. He disappeared in a blink.

'Akrita,' Rama called. 'Go back to Father's ashram and tell my parents all that has happened. Stay there till I come back.'

'Yes, Acharya,' replied Akrita.

As the circle filled with light and blinked out, Rama said, 'That axe is yours, Akrita, pointing to his old axe in Akrita's hand.'

15

Parashurama

Rama looked around in the cold and darkness. It was unnaturally dark—heavy and inky—like it would stain his body black. The silence was stifling, and pregnant with pain and misery. His breath turned to mist ahead of him. Rama had a feeling he was high up somewhere, and he could sense Indra next to him. The weak light from the lone torch on the wall ahead seemed to die as soon as he walked past it. Shadows seemed to ooze out from the walls. Rama reached out and touched the stone wall: hard, cold and damp. He could smell the rot and decay. His eyes adjusted to the darkness. He saw the stone slabs bulge and sag at places. The rocks seemed to moan with agony. He withdrew his hand, and the surface of the stone came off like glue, holding on to his hand, stretching greasily, before finally letting go and collapsing under its weight. Rama grimaced in disgust and fought the urge to scratch his palm.

'Where are we?' he asked.

'In the watchtower of the outer fort wall around Indrapuri, the city of the devas,' replied Indra.

Rama was taken aback. The stories he'd heard of this city

were all unanimous in their description of its fabulous beauty and riches. Just breathing the air here was supposed to be a heady, intoxicating experience for mortals.

'What happened?'

'Come,' said Indra. He led Rama out of the watchtower and walked along the rampart. He stopped beside a sentinel, who was looking out through an embrasure. The sentinel stood up slowly, but Rama realised it was as fast as he could manage. He was battered and bruised all over, barely keeping body and soul together. His weary, empty eyes stared at Rama, unsurprised at seeing a mortal walk the rampart with the King of Devas. He looked like a man hoping for a quick death.

Indra relieved him of his longbow and picked an arrow from his quiver. Rama doubted if the sentinel would be able to string and draw a single arrow if asked to. Indra nocked an arrow and whispered a mantra. He shot the arrow high and long, the arrowhead glowing as it reached its apogee, and sped downward. There was a flash of light that extinguished in a nimisha and the arrow disappeared.

'That should have exploded,' said Indra. 'It should have created a crater five yojanas wide!' He strung another arrow, and whispered some mantra again and shot it straight up in the sky. It hit an invisible barrier high up in the atmosphere. Streaks of golden light flew out, from the point of impact, spider-webbing in a huge inverted semi-circular pattern. In the brief flash of light, Rama saw a black fog stretching for miles towards the horizon and around the serpentine walls of the fort as far as he could see. Rama realised that the first arrow had died out as soon as it had pierced the top of the fog. The fog seethed and undulated with things unseen. A yojana-long tentacle emerged from the haze, its length splattered with giant, glowing suck holes oozing sulphurous drool dripping acidly into the unseen depths of the thick fog. The tentacle was studded with triangular spikes the size of a horse, black and edged with crimson. It withdrew into the black obscurity with a menacing quiet.

'That astra should have sent blinding light in all ten directions. The horde hides their asura forms in the fog, and that absorbs anything we throw at it,' Indra said.

'Anything!' he emphasised again. 'Even my thunderbolt loses most of its power. Our spells of maya don't hold. The fog sucks them in and absorbs their energy to strengthen itself. We cannot counter asura maya with indrajaal. I have barely managed to hold on to the fort; it is only a matter of time before they breach it. There is no possibility of waiting out the siege; we don't even have the time to rest and recover.

'The dome,' he continued, pointing up, 'covers the entire city, blocking out the light of the sun and the movement of the wind. It infuses all of us with despair and desperation. It taints my city with decay and corruption.'

Rama put his head and shoulders into the embrasure and peered into the darkness. A million red twinkling points appeared suddenly in the obscurity. Eyes! Rama realised and withdrew in a hurry.

'My city lies destroyed by their bombardment. It rots with asura maya. I have moved out the children, the women and the infirm, but I will not leave. I make my stand here. The asuras know we are beaten; they await my final charge with glee. They don't seek conquest alone. The asuras seek to annihilate us and lay waste to my realm. But I will not flee. If Indra has to die today, then Indra will die fighting.'

Indra put his hands on Rama's shoulders. 'My prayers to

Mahadeva have been answered. He bade me to get you here. The fate of Indrapuri and the devas, now, rests with you. I hope you know what to do.'

Rama's mind reeled. Mahadeva, what am I supposed to do? He searched his mind for a solution and came up with nothing. He looked down at the axe. Then he held it up between them. Indra flinched and dropped his hands from Rama's shoulders.

'Tell me about the Parashu,' said Rama.

Indra looked at him in surprise. 'You know nothing?'

'I got this axe barely a muhurta before you arrived in my ashram. Mahadeva gave it to me after I battled him ...,' said Rama.

'You fought Mahadeva?' Indra was incredulous.

'I was a fool. My head had been too swollen with pride to think straight,' said Rama with embarrassment.

Indra looked at Rama with perplexity. This man had no idea about the power of the axe or how to harness it. Yet he had fought with Mahadeva, survived it and had been found worthy of the Parashu, Indra sighed thoughtfully.

'I remember something being written about it. I remember because extraordinarily little is known about this famed weapon, and I was fascinated by it. The one who wrote it scores of yugas ago shuddered at the very thought of it. There is only one verse about it. It seems like they were too scared to even write about it,' said Indra.

Cleaver of Minds,
Flame of Fury,
Binder of Spirits,
Striker of Fear,

Bringer of Mrithyu,
Devourer of Souls,
Drinker of Blood.
Beware the One,
Who holds golden and true,
Mahakaal's Parashu.

Rama repeated the words over and over in his head, searching for the meaning, for any message that could aid him. His forehead throbbed with pain. He gave up in frustration. They seemed ordinary words glorifying the axe and its bearer, but then again, why would they be written if they were insignificant?

'What does the verse intend to convey?'

Indra shook his head, unable to help. Rama exhaled a long breath and changed the subject. He couldn't worry about these words when on the brink of battle. He hoped the answer would come to him when he used the axe.

'Who leads the horde?' he asked.

'There is only one whom I thought capable,' replied Indra. 'But, I'm sure, he isn't here. He would have announced himself by now. No one has come forth as the leader, yet they prevail upon us.'

Indra was quiet for a moment and then reached out and touched Rama's forehead with his thumb, whispering something inaudible. He then touched his thumb to his own forehead and said, 'Call for me in your mind and I will hear, no matter the distance. Come now, let us prepare for attack. You need armour. You can't fight barefoot and in a dhoti with these asuras. This is your first battle, Rama, and only you can tip the scales in our favour. I will not bother you with strategy and planning. You do what you must.'

———

Pulastya and Dasagreeva watched through the portal that had opened by the maharishi's yogic power. They were on prithvi, far away from the fort at Indrapuri. Pulastya had forbidden his grandson from joining the reinforcements he had sent to support the horde. He didn't trust Arjuna at all. Arjuna could join hands with Indra, despite their acrimonious meeting. Then destroy the asuras, before placing his demands on the devas. The samrat was cunning; he would play either side so long as it stood to his advantage.

The image in the portal changed as Pulastya scanned the section of the fort from where the astras were being shot. The image was clear and unaffected by the obscurity of the black fog. The asuras had shed their anthropomorphic forms and assumed their true shapes, as was their wont in battle. He had no dearth of eyes to see through. Millions of eyes were available to him, some giving him the strangest of perspectives, depending on the form a particular asura had assumed. He watched from the mosaic vision of an asura hovering above the horde in the upper reaches of the fog. This asura's vision was focussed on the embrasure from behind which the two arrows had emerged.

Pulastya watched as a head and a pair of shoulders appeared through the embrasure, glanced around and withdrew in haste. A thousand images of the face stretched across the compound vision of the asura. Pulastya went still.

That was a mortal, he was sure of it. He had traversed enough of the three lokas to know this. But who was he and why was there a glow on his forehead?

Beside him, Dasagreeva sat in silence. The final battle was at hand. He could feel it in his bones. He had predicted that Indra wouldn't flee, forsaking his beloved city to the ravages of an unchecked asura horde. Indra's pride wouldn't allow him to do so. Especially to a horde led by a nameless, ragtag coalition of generals who had been defeated by Arjuna. Dasagreeva conceded grudgingly that Indra's valour and pride would impel him to fight to the bitter end. No one became the King of Devas by turning tail in war.

Dasagreeva crossed his legs in padmasana and closed all of his twenty eyes. The lips on all of his ten heads moved as he mentally chanted his personal one-syllable mantra, which had been bestowed on him by Pulastya. He emptied his mind of everything but that one syllable. He controlled and stilled his breath. From the depths of his trance, he reached out to the minds of the generals he had sent at the head of the reinforcements. Pulastya had enabled him to access their minds before he had dispatched them, and he was thankful for it. It made sure the generals never forgot who their king was, and allowed him to direct their strategy and help the horde prevail over the devas. He would step in and claim leadership once the battle was won.

He sensed the tension and excitement in his generals as they waited for the battle to begin—the battle that would give them victory. Dasagreeva waited for Indra to make his move.

Arjuna lay in bed, staring at the ceiling, lost in thought. Manorama sat beside him, leaning against the bedstead.

'My love,' she whispered as she caressed his cheek and turned his face towards her. 'I have a solution to your problem.'

Arjuna sat up, looking at her.

'A temple, my love, a shrine to dissolve the displeasure of the gods and win their goodwill. A magnificent temple such as one that has never been built before, known not only for its size and beauty, but also for the forms of Brahman we will install and invoke there. It will also be an homage to your guru, blessed be his name.'

'Tell me more,' said Arjuna, warming up to the idea.

'A temple to the Trimurti—Brahma, Vishnu and Maheshwara. The essence of all three resides in your guru. This way you can please the gods and pay respect to your preceptor.'

Arjuna mused over it, nodding his head in agreement.

'If you think this is not enough, we can do the pratishta of the guru himself with the Holy Trinity. I had thought of a three-towered trikuta temple, but we can always make it a chatuskuta one.'

A small, pensive smile broke out on Arjuna's face. 'A magnificent edifice. No cost spared. Gurudeva, be blessed! I hope that is the solution.'

'That, indeed, is the solution,' Manorama crowed. Arjuna kissed her full on the lips, long and deep.

'I even have the name ready,' Manorama said, basking in her husband's acceptance and approval. She drew closer, kissed him back and whispered in his ear.

'Arjuneshwara!'

Jamadagni and Renuka sat in prayer inside their hut. Night had fallen and the ashram disciples had retired for the day. It had almost been a week since Akrita had brought Rama's news to them. They offered their prayers for his safety—every day after the sandhyavandana in the morning, at dusk and at night—before the small clay deepa they had lit for him in their room. Renuka had made the deepa herself from river sand, and one of them always kept watch over it, filling it with oil when required. The lamp would stay lit until Rama returned home. Renuka wondered when that would be. Time was different in Devaloka. A day there was a year on prithvi.

They had been awe-struck at the news of the Parashu. Rama had somehow made the dreaded weapon of Mahakaal's forge his own. Their son had an extraordinary yogic capacity. It came from a single-minded, even ruthless, focus on his goal. Rama threw himself, body and soul, into the pursuit of his aims. He had found a way to please Mahadeva and obtain the weapon so quickly. It would have taken others decades of ghor tapasya to do the same. Jamadagni wondered how he did it. Rama, himself, would be at a loss to explain it, he suspected. Rama's thoughts and instincts were inextricably linked to action. The very performance of the task he had set for himself opened up pathways of thought in his mind, and he strode those paths with boldness. His primal instincts showed him possibilities that no one else saw and prospects that would have filled others with trepidation.

Jamadagni prayed that Rama's instincts led him true. A misstep would have disastrous consequences. Jamadagni had decided not to use his yogic powers to see the events of the war. The beheading of Renuka had had a profound spiritual and emotional impact on him. It had tamed his irascibility and set his mind firmly on ahimsa. Rama, the brahmakshatriya, would be the sword arm of himsa; he would protect and restore dharma and rta. Violence and killing would inevitably come his way, but Jamadagni's non-violence would be the counterbalance to it—a sanctum of respite from the blood, death and weeping of widows. Whereas, Renuka with the Aspect of Chinnamasta would be the power of healing. To repair and rejuvenate, to provide solace and sound advice. To cure the wounds of himsa and to cultivate ahimsa.

———

Rama waited alongside Indra amidst the deva army. He was clad in armour, strapped tight over his torso. Thigh guards wrapped around his upper legs over his dhoti and shin guards wound around his calves above hand-tooled leather boots. Rama found the armour heavy and cumbersome. He felt as agile as a pregnant buffalo. He had stubbornly refused the helmet, shoulder plates and arm guards, but had accepted the heavy shield.

He had decided to fight on foot and not astride a horse or in a ratha. Indra had nodded and decided the same, and they had walked together to the waiting army—an army made up of bruised bodies, missing limbs and broken armour, defeated by weariness and desperation, surviving on the last dregs of their spirit and courage. The skin and flesh of many soldiers seemed to have been eaten away by acid. Some of the soldiers had had their skins torched, leaving flesh, sinew and portions of bone visible. Few had bothered to get medical aid. They didn't care, or maybe the vaidyas were hard-pressed to attend to all the injured. Rama looked around, but couldn't see a single uninjured deva.

It was an army filled with grim defeat and mounting despair, and only one hope—Rama. Word of his coming had spread. Hope sparked and gleamed in their eyes and slow, painful smiles tugged at their mouths as they watched Rama walk through their midst. The weight of their expectations and the hope of deliverance rested wordlessly, softly and woodenly on Rama's shoulders. He kept his gaze distant, not daring to look into their eyes, in case some of them caught the confusion in his mind shimmering through his eyes. He was wary of looking down and showing a bent head to the men. The sweat of the men and the acrid scent of the medicines added to the miasma of rot and contamination, which hung like death in the still air. The misty air hung over their heads in a smothering silence. Even the horses didn't whicker or stamp their hooves.

He understood that Indra had deliberately planned this, to give his men as much confidence and resolve as he could. Some reached out to touch him as he walked by and pressed their fingers to their foreheads as if receiving a benediction. Rama was puzzled by this before he realised why they did it. He was Mahadeva's blessing walking amidst them, and the devas were only showing respect. Everyone eyed the Parashu with abundant caution, but no one touched it.

Rama prayed in earnest. 'Mahadeva, show me a way, I'm a mere mortal.'

He had accused Mahadeva of being an asura and using asura maya. In return, Mahadeva had given him an axe and sent him to fight the same asuras, thought Rama wryly.

In the feeble light, the army of rathas, lancers, swordsmen and archers assembled behind the cavalry. The attendants and aides carried the torches; none among the army men did so. They would be useless on the battlefield because the asura maya would eat up all the light. Rama glanced at Indra beside him. His face was grim, and he gazed ahead stonily as he raised his sword arm.

A wave of nervous tension ran through the air and wound around the hearts of the men. It raced through their veins, causing muscles to tense, jaws to clench and fingers to tighten around weapons. Indra's signal was quickly passed on to the gatemen. He turned to Rama and whispered, 'For our faith in the gods, for the dharma we uphold. Death or glory!'

Rama stared at him and nodded. 'For the gods, for our ancestors. Death or glory!'

Indra lowered his arm and an instant later, the gates were thrown open.

There was no fanfare of trumpets, blowing of conches, cries, oaths or ululations of any kind. The deva army charged with the sound of thundering hooves, spinning wheels, rattling weapons, rapid breaths and thousands upon thousands silent prayers.

They were inside the fog almost as soon as they cleared the gates. They sped on, the foetid stench of the fog causing their eyes to water and almost making them gag. Senses hyper-alert with excitement and fright, they moved into the womb of the fog. An eerie light, pale green and sickly, emanated from everywhere in the haze. The commander of the troops next to Rama barked hoarsely, and the men slowed down and spread out, with each soldier out of the striking range of his neighbour's weapon yet close enough to rally together should the asuras charge. In the ghostly silence, they waited with nervous anticipation for the attack to begin.

Rama wiped his eyes clear with the back of his hand.

Darkness held no terrors for him. He had spent many a night alone in the forest, roving through underbrush and thickets and sleeping in caves. But where were the asuras? Rama scanned his surroundings. The bleak light obscured much of what was around him. He did not know the lay of the land; he had assumed that it was a clear, flat land as was usual around forts. This he had heard in Nandin's stories long ago when he told him about the great battles. Off to his right, he saw a small copse of trees. They seemed twisted in agony, sap dripping through the rents and rips in the bark and leaves drooping, sickly yellow, black and leprous.

The ground seemed to pull at his boots, sucking them down with a whisper of a squelch. Rama changed his stance, and he noticed the Deva soldiers do the same. Why was there no attack? No arrows were shot at them, and no explosive astras shrieked and thudded around them. The answer came to him an instant before the attack began. There were no arrows because the asuras were right there, all around them.

They appeared in a blink—coalescing out of the fog itself, snapping and snarling as they threw themselves at the devas with deadly ferocity. As grotesque forms materialised before him, Rama wondered if the deva army had run through the asuras in the fog. The fog suddenly erupted with roars, and the clash of weapons and the screams of the dying rent the air. Rama heard flesh rip and blood gurgle out somewhere near him, but he could not tear his eyes off the apparition before him.

It was as big as a rhino but looked like a rat. A rat that had fused the bodies of thousands of rats into it. The mouths sprouted haphazardly over a body bristling with fur and reptilian scales. Fangs the size of Rama's hands lined the mouths. A dozen legs as thick as tree trunks scurried around. Tentacles tipped with foot-long metal claws, wrapped around the deva soldiers and pulled them into the waiting, salivating maws.

Rama felt fury erupt inside him and the axe responded instantly, fuelling his wrath, urging him to swing, to cut. A tentacle had snaked into a deva soldier's mouth, and something black and oily was running through the translucent retractile tube into the innards of the soldier. As Rama attacked, the axe cut through the nearest tentacle, slicing it without the slightest resistance, dropping the soldier it was holding. Rama dodged and swerved through the swinging maze of tentacles. Fangs ripped at him and he met them with the edge of his axe. It slashed across the mouth of the beast, cutting through bone, sinew and tooth as yellow blood spurted out of its body.

The power of the axe astonished Rama. He hacked at the metal claws and the axe cut through them like a sword slicing through silk. Rama felt a rush of exhilaration course through him. He slashed and hacked around the beast, severing tentacles, tearing out its legs, and gouging out chunks of its flesh. The beast screamed in agony, tottering on its few remaining legs, trying to scurry away. Rama leapt on its back and drove the axe deep, cleaving the spine asunder. The beast collapsed, blood bursting out of all of it orifices. Rama jumped off as it fell, searching for his next adversary. Battle-lust danced in his eyes.

He saw the deva soldier on the ground, thrashing in agony, a scream in his bulging eyes and lips pulled back over his teeth in a rictus grin. His stomach was bloated; his skin mottled grey and black. Rama saw something sharp poke out from under the skin of his stomach, stretching it almost to the point of rupture. A hundred more points of protrusion appeared all over his torso. Rama beheaded him. The body thrashed wildly one last time and went still. The hundred points trying to protrude out froze before they could break through.

The battle came crashing back into Rama's awareness. The roars of victory and death rattles. Shattered rathas and slain deva soldiers littered the ground. Nightmarish misshapen forms emerged and disappeared in the fog. He heard Indra thunder his resistance in the distance and the asuras roar back. He threw himself into the thick of the battle, lusting for the fight, the axe thirsting to cut.

'Come, fight me,' he screamed, roving the battlefield, hacking at anything in his path—Asura blood spurting and staining his armour and limbs. He cleaved a two-headed and four-armed rakshasa from head to loin and leapt through as the two halves fell apart, the Parashu already cutting through an asura with the head of a boar, from shoulder to waist.

Rama's fury drove him on, heedless of his shattered and discarded shield. His armour had been eaten away by the acid ichor of a rakshasa that had spat its heart-blood on it. His axe swirled and cut without pause, as wave upon wave of asuras threw themselves at the outnumbered devas. The tide of the pitched battle was in favour of the Asuras. They knew it was only a matter of time, and they were determined to finish it as quickly and ruthlessly as possible.

Not enough! The thought screamed through Rama's head. The axe certainly cut through everything in its way, but he was still using it just as an axe. This was a divine weapon. Nandin and Indra had flinched from it. It could do more. He had to unlock its power and find out what it could do to save the Devas from certain annihilation. Rama searched his mind in desperation for an answer but found none.

He ceased all thought and emptied his mind. 'For the gods, for our ancestors,' he whispered. 'Mahadeva! My pitrus! Show me the way.' The vision of his pitrus from his battle with Mahadeva flashed in his mind. Jamadagni and Renuka standing at the head of a line of his pitrus. Brighu, his clan leader stood at the other end.

'Remember,' Jamadagni had whispered then, the whites of his eyes showing. Renuka too had looked at Rama with reproach and said, 'Have we taught you nothing?'

'You forget,' Brighu had said, his voice heavy with displeasure.

Rama emptied his mind again as he fought a rakshasa twice as tall as him who was armed with a scimitar that dripped steaming venom.

Rama froze for a nimisha. The rakshasa noticed and threw himself at Rama. Rama lopped off his head in an instant. How did his father manage to see the spiritual and material worlds at the same time? Rama had seen his soul and his ego from inside the banalinga, could he do what Jamadagni had done? This is a divine weapon, won by spiritual power, like the other divine astras, Nandin had said. To use his spiritual power was the answer. Rama had to try; he had to find a way!

Cleaver of Minds.

Rama gasped. Indra was wrong. The ancient verse was not about the axe alone. It was about the wielder of the Parashu. Him!

'You forget', Brighu's words flashed in his mind. What was he forgetting? Mahadeva's words blazed across his mind, searing themselves into his brain.

'You carry an amsha and pay no heed to it. Amsha!'

What he had thought was asura maya was Mahadeva giving him the answers he needed.

Rama ran frantically, searching in the eerie light for what he wanted. There. A group of five devas beset by a swarm of snarling and gnashing warped shapes. He flung himself into the swarm. His fury and the excitement of finding a possible way out adding strength and speed to the arcing strokes of the Parashu. He made quick work of the asuras. He disembowelled the last of them and turned to the devas.

'Hold them off me for a few nimishas, I implore you,' he said.

The devas fanned out into a circle around Rama as he stood and closed his eyes. He tamped down his fury and controlled his breath. He sought his inner quiet and calm. The Parashu responded immediately, aiding him again. Rama went completely still. In a couple of nimishas, Rama again floated in the nothingness. So quick, a corner of his mind wondered. Was it because of the banalinga on prithvi or the Parashu here with him?

He sought the mirror and found it. In it, he saw himself standing in dhyana, with his eyes closed. Rama imagined an exact replica of his image in the mirror. It appeared in the mirror. He willed the second image to have its eyes open. In a blink, they were.

The twin images stood in the mirror—one with eyes open and the other with eyes closed.

As the Rama of the nothingness opened his eyes, he saw the twin images standing before him—one with eyes open and the other with its eyes closed.

Cleaver of Minds.

Rama cleaved his mind, dividing it in two. The very core of himself, his soul, his very consciousness, along with the portion of his mind rapt in dhyana, he locked away in the image with the closed eyes.

Then he imagined the battle taking place in the background of the image with the eyes open. He fed his senses, his awareness and instinct into this image.

In the image with the eyes open, Rama saw the reflection of a gigantic serpent in the mirror, creeping closer in silence, its head high above Rama, its mouth wide open.

On the battlefield, too, Rama opened his eyes. The pupils of his eyes rolled up and only the whites could be seen. He spun as the serpent lunged at him with its jaws stretched wider to swallow him whole. Rama hacked its lower jaw to pieces. He sidestepped and swung again, slicing the serpent's neck. He breathed out and went still. His idea had worked!

In the nothingness, Rama again focussed his attention on the image with the eyes closed, on the space between the eyebrows. His forehead began to throb intensely. Rama called forth the light—the amsha from the depths of his soul. His entire forehead began to burn. The agya chakra pulsated like a thing possessed. Rama felt his entire being vibrate with a vehemence that threatened to shake the life out of him.

Something ethereal, as light as down, as nebulous as a newborn's breath—the amsha—settled on his soul. In the mirror, the closed eyes opened. Rama brought the twin images together and united them into one. Light poured out from his forehead in the version of himself in nothingness and from the image in the mirror.

On the battlefield, Rama lifted his face, the whites of his eyes turned skyward. A brilliant beam of light emerged from the furious blowtorch burning at the centre of his his forehead. It pierced the fog and rose all the way upto the dome.

Rama roared.

It was a feral clap of thunder that rolled across the battlefield, struck the walls of the fort and echoed back. The devas and asuras froze, shocked into immobility.

Far away, Pulastya felt a surge of immense yogic power flow in the battlefield and searched for the nearest pair of eyes to see what was happening. He found a pair of eyes, staring at the beam of light in the fog. The eyes moved down to the source, the blazing forehead of the mortal. Pulastya startled. The mortal carried an amsha. NO. He was the Amsha.

Dasagreeva was struck dumb by that brilliant beam of light. His instincts told him that the fate of the battle was suddenly hanging in the balance. It hung on the source of that light. He screamed into his generals' minds.

'Kill him! Now!'

Rama stared into his own eyes in the mirror, floating in the nothingness. The image rushed out of the mirror and merged within him. Rama invoked the yagnakund in his mind and formed the image of the Parashu. He fed the axe to the fire. It hovered over it, absorbing the heat, burning white-hot.

Flame of Fury.

Rama shone the light from his agya chakra onto the Parashu. It seemed to quiver with excitement and turned golden. The bond was complete. He could feel the axe in his mind now. He could control it with his mind.

He had made the axe his own.

In the fog, Rama's pupils rolled down. The image of the rune on the Parashu—the circle with the bindu—flashed in his mind. Rays seemed to emerge from the bindu, like the pattern of a sunburst. Rama raised the Parashu and touched the axe-head to his forehead reverentially.

'Parashu, be true,' said Rama.

Instantly, he saw masses of asuras appear in the fog all around him. He knew they were coming for him. They thought he was outnumbered, but that was false confidence on their part. He saw the horde being egged on by an enormous wolf-headed beast that seemed to be in charge.

'Fall back,' he told the Devas. Icy calm shone in his eyes. He held himself calm and loose.

Binder of Spirits.

He whispered, 'Come to me. Show me.'

Past memories of the movements of all those beings who had wielded the Parashu before him flooded his mind. The placement of the feet, the bend of the waist, the graceful arc of the swing, the leaps and the feints. Rama let loose his fury. The power of the axe surged through him with a vengeance. He unleashed himself on the horde. He didn't wait for them to come to him. He went to them.

Bringer of Mrithyu.

The blades of the axe whistled through the air, lopping off limbs and flesh. Blood and fragments of bones filled the mist. He moved like a dancer in trance. Rama heard himself scream and urge the asuras to fight him. He saw the grotesque bodies split, heads separate from the bodies and fly away in the air.

Devourer of Souls.

He wove through the gaps between them, skirting around their clubs and maces and swords, limbs and tentacles, claws and fangs. He moved so fast that their weapons could cut only air, while Rama cut them down one by one. He saw a small group of asuras back away rapidly from him. He looked around. The ground was littered with hundreds of asura bodies of all shapes and sizes. He saw the five deva soldiers looking stupefied. They flinched when he looked at them.

Striker of Fear.

The beast in charge howled, and a second wave of asuras appeared. They didn't rush this time. They moved with caution. Dasagreeva watched through the eyes of the beast, who was his general. He saw three rakshasas attack the mortal, one on each side and one from behind him. But the man's movements were blindingly fast. He seemed to be at three places at once. He had seen no one move like that. The three attackers were cut to pieces in the blink of an eye, so were the next three and the five after that. The asuras roared their outrage and attacked as one. They exploded in blood and gore as Rama tore through them. He stopped only when there was no one left standing. Even the wolf beast lay dead. Rama noticed that the blood on the axe blades didn't run off the edge or stain the blades. The Parashu absorbed them.

Drinker of Blood.

The ground had grown soft and slippery with asura blood. Rama roved through the battlefield, wading into scores of asuras, slaughtering them and rallying the devas behind him. Bloodlust coursed unabated in his veins. His temples throbbed with the headiness of it. The horde fell back, now faced with a renewed deva onslaught, led by a man who had performed the dance of death and would clearly stop at nothing. The tired and weakened devas had been slaughtered by the dozen, but one man was changing the course of the battle. The asuras *had* to kill him. On his death rested their victory.

Streaks of black lightning raced towards Rama. He sliced the first one with his axe and it died instantly. He swerved through the searing flashes, evading the ones he could and slicing the ones he couldn't. Explosions rocked the ground. The asuras had changed their strategy. Rama looked for the source of the lightning bolts and saw that they were coming from a hillock ahead of him. The fog was clearing, growing less dense with every lightning strike and explosion. They were diverting the power of asura maya from maintaining the fog to attacking him. He could hear Indra's thunderbolt in the distance. It grew stronger as the fog weakened. Rama decided to fight his way to the top of the hillock.

The asuras, however, had the advantage of numbers, and they threw themselves at Rama and the devas. Rama cut through them, dealing death with every blow, but the lightning bolts and astras of the asuras were taking a toll on the devas. He heard their dying screams behind him. Rama knew his strength was ebbing; he would soon be running on rage and bloodlust alone. He had to find some way to finish this battle fast.

The sunburst pattern on the rune flashed in his mind as he severed the head of an asura. The asura survivors fled into the obscurity of the fog. They would be back with reinforcements soon. Rama looked around. He had made it halfway up the hillock.

He invoked agni in the yagnakund in his mind and fed the axe into the heat. If it could absorb blood, perhaps it could absorb heat as well. He stoked the fire into a blazing inferno and let the axe absorb the energy. On the hillock, the Parashu turned red hot. Rama raised the Parashu high and let the heat shoot into the fog on the battlefield. The lightning and explosions stopped immediately, and the fog thickened as it absorbed the heat. But it had no effect on the asura horde.

Rama was mystified as he turned to meet a fresh wave of attack. He cut them all down, working his way up the hillock. He stumbled as he reached the top and almost fell from exhaustion when he realised he hadn't understood the pattern completely.

What he had thought was a sunburst, were not necessarily rays radiating from the bindu outwards to the circle. They could also be rays converging onto the bindu.

Rama called out to Indra in his mind and realised he had screamed out aloud too.

'Indra! Find me. Now.'

In his mind, Rama used the axe to pull the heat back into the yagnakund. On the hillock, he raised the Parashu. The fog had absorbed everything the devas had thrown at it. Rama would suck all of it back now. The Parashu started to glow and Rama pulled the heat and energy from the fog, faster and harder. He saw the asuras were confused about what was happening. He saw them turn towards the hillock—towards him—as realisation dawned. Rama saw panic rush through them. He saw them stop fighting the devas and rush to the hillock to stop him. Rama pulled in the heat as hard as he could. The Parashu shone like molten lava.

Soon, the fog started to solidify, and the asuras started to slow down and stumble as they found their own maya being turned against them. It had no effect on the devas.

'Indra!' Rama called again, and found Indra hovering above him, aboard Uchchaisravas, his flying horse whom he had summoned to find Rama.

'The thunderbolt. Throw it at me,' said Rama.

'What?' Indra exclaimed in astonishment.

Rama closed his eyes to concentrate. He continued to pull the energy into the Parashu. He felt his legs tremble. He opened his eyes. The asuras were trapped in the almost-solid black ice that was the fog. It was now devoid of heat, the energy of life and motion taken away from it.

'Now!' Rama screamed at Indra.

Indra threw his thunderbolt at Rama, who caught it and absorbed it into the Parashu.

'More,' Rama shouted. 'Don't stop.'

Indra threw thunderbolts for as long and as hard as he could. Rama held on for dear life. He felt his breath catch and nausea build up in him. His vision blurred. But, he held on, the Parashu absorbing the heat and thunderbolts together. His instincts told him he needed more.

'More,' Rama whispered. Indra heard. The flow of the thunderbolts continued. The devas watched from the darkness, gathering at the base of the hillock from all corners of the battlefield. They looked on in utter shock at the arcs of red-hot heat and the blinding white flow of the thunderbolts streaking into the Parashu. The lone figure on the crest of the hillock glowed and pulsed with heat and lightning. The power coursing through the air made their hair stand on end.

Rama called forth the light of the amsha. *His* light. It poured from his forehead. Rama gave over all the strength he had to the light, which started shining like the sun. Indra stopped his thunderbolts, exhausted. Rama felt the yagnakund in his mind begin to waver.

Now! Rama's mind screamed. He touched the Parashu to his forehead, raised it high and let loose the energy, the incredible power of the axe. The energy cracked through the air, blinding in the darkness. The fog moaned and shrieked as the axe's power blew the asuras to smithereens. The ground heaved as the energy ran through it. Trees were uprooted and the distant walls of the fort split and plummeted to the ground.

The dome groaned as the axe's power hit it hard. Gigantic cracks ran like spider webs across the dome. The black ice melted and evaporated and with it went away the eerie light. For a long moment, utter darkness reigned. A huge chunk of the dome broke away and fell towards the ground, burning up like a meteor.

A single, glorious beam of sunlight shone through the crack in the dome which began to slowly dissipate. The beam of light slanted across the air and struck the hillock. Indra blew his conch from up above. A cry of victory, of deliverance, of life snatched from the jaws of death. Of homage to the valour of one man, their saviour.

The devas turned to the sound of the conch. They saw Indra circle the hillock. In the beam of sunshine, they saw the lone man with an upraised axe standing atop the hillock. A brilliant beam of light still flowed from his forehead. The Parashu caught the light and shone like gold.

Indra blew the conch once more. It sent a thrill through the devas. Indra's voice thundered across the battlefield to every soldier gazing at the man on the hillock.

RAMA! PARASHURAMA!

As one, the Devas erupted in joy, tears running down their faces, screaming the name of their hero who had won them an unbelievable victory.

PARASHURAMA!

PARASHURAMA!

PARASHURAMA!

16

Arjuneshwara

Dasagreeva sat in stunned silence, his central head lowered in defeat. The other nine heads had disappeared. He felt powerless and puny, like a crippled kitten in the presence of a full-grown, ferocious tiger on the prowl. He picked up the copper ewer and gulped down the water, much of it splashing down his face. He stared at the empty ewer, wanting to crush it into a misshapen lump. It would be an empty show of frustration. Of futility and impotence. He placed it down beside him without a sound and turned to see Pulastya watching him.

He stared into his grandfather's eyes—the unspoken question hanging between them, waiting for an answer. Pulastya shook his head, lost in his own thoughts. Dasagreeva felt the walls of the small hut closing in on him, suffocating him. He fought the urge to go out into the forest. To lose himself in the darkness, to hunt, to kill. To feel warm blood flow down his throat and hear the rattle of a dying life. To rip something—anything—to shreds. He took a deep breath and calmed himself. He needed answers.

Finally, Pulastya spoke, watching the small, steady flame of the lone lamp between them.

'I do not know who he is. He is a brahmin mortal. No, he is more, an amsha. And also, something I hoped you would someday become—a brahmakshatriya. Only a brahmakshatriya can wield so much yogic power in a battlefield while fighting his enemies. Such incredible power, and we haven't even heard of him. But it won't be long before the whole world knows him, I think.'

Dasagreeva was silent for a nimisha.

'His weapon?'

'Mahakaal's Parashu, a weapon I thought was a myth, the whisper of an over-imaginative bard,' Pulastya replied. 'I know next to nothing about it or of anyone who has wielded it before. But that axe has the capability to destroy entire worlds. It is the most fearsome weapon I've heard of.'

'What is the counter to it?' asked Dasagreeva.

'I know of none. Only Mahadeva knows. It is his blessing to the mortal. There is no other way he could wield it.'

Dasagreeva went quiet, turning over the many strands of thought in his mind. Pulastya sat patiently, curious about what his grandson would do next.

'How does one become a brahmakshatriya? Was it because of Mahadeva's blessing again?'

'The blessings of god are necessary for any endeavour to bear fruit, my child. But this is not a boon given by god. It is an individual accomplishment—a journey of the soul that has so far remained un-tread and uncharted. That mortal is the first to travel that path, one that many have sought before but none have found.

'A Brahmakshatriya isn't a great yogi with prowess in weapons or a great yoddha with yogic powers. Nor is he someone who knows how to invoke, use, and recall divine astras. He is all this and much more.

'Many rishis have been great warriors or have been able to defeat great warriors by the rigour of their tapasya, like Vasishta. Many kshatriyas have become great rishis, like Vishwamitra. But neither is a brahmakshatriya.

'How one becomes a brahmakshatriya is unknown to me or to anyone else, but we have now seen one in battle. I can make a few deductions from that.'

Dasagreeva pushed himself closer to his grandfather, listening with interest.

'The beam of light flowing out from his forehead that reached the skies was the physical manifestation of his atma recognising and acknowledging the light of the amsha within him. I know this because I saw a spot of light on his forehead earlier when he was looking out from the ramparts of the fort. What is astounding is that he did this on a battlefield, not when sitting in tapasya. Only a brahmakshatriya can do that.

'You saw the absolute destruction of the asura army in only a nimisha. The army had their life heat—their very vitality—sucked out of them and then were smashed to death while they were still frozen. This needs immense yogic power, and that is possible only through dhyana and the power of tapas. So, this mortal's mind was engaged in dhyana while he fought the asuras. This, too, only a Brahmakshatriya can do.

'He fought a yogic and physical battle simultaneously. And he destroyed the asura maya and the army at the same time.

'How he became a brahmakshatriya is a mystery, but undoubtedly, it was through the journey of his atma. A spiritual process, not a physical one.

'I suspect, only a brahmakshatriya can unleash the full powers of Mahadeva's Parashu,' said Pulastya.

Dasagreeva sighed and closed his eyes in contemplation.

'You understand what this means?' asked Pulastya.

Dasagreeva nodded. 'The mortal has thwarted Arjuna's plans. Arjuna will thirst for vengeance; he will not let this defiance go unpunished.'

'The two lions will, without a doubt, fight. It is the law of nature. The champion and the challenger, two prime predators, will battle to kill.'

'Who will prevail?' asked Dasagreeva.

'The mortal is no match for the samrat, even if he is a brahmakshatriya and possesses an amsha. I do not think he knows the use of any divyastras, while Arjuna knows them all, and no one knows the secret of Arjuna's strength. But then again, he has the Parashu, and he has mastered it. Who knows what else he can make it do ...

'It's too close to say with certainty, but I think Arjuna will prevail,' said Pulastya.

'Either way, do you understand what it means?' asked Dasagreeva.

Pulastya looked puzzled.

'It means, grandfather, that there is no place for me. Not while these two walk the earth. If they are lions, I must be one too.'

'What will you do?' asked Pulastya

'Tapasya. To please Mahadeva and obtain his blessings,' said Dasagreeva with conviction.

Ramabhadra ...

The voice was a whisper in Rama's head. He saw a great
flight of rock-cut steps, straight as an arrow. They began
from beneath his feet, climbed up the mountainside and
disappeared into the clouds. He couldn't see the top of the
mountain or where the steps led to, but he knew he must
climb. Rama looked around, but he couldn't see the decaying
waste of Indrapuri. He was in a grove, sacred and wild. A river
ran silently some distance behind him. The mountain and
the grove seemed untouched by the decay of the asura maya,
instead they thrummed with life and health.

Come....

The whisper echoed in his head.

Rama woke up with a start and saw Indra sitting beside
him. Rama sat up in his cot.

'Where am I?' he asked.

'You collapsed on the hilltop, Rama. We carried you here.
The vaidyas gave you a potion to sleep. It's been only two
muhurtas. Rest. Go back to sleep,' said Indra. Rama looked
around at the scores of injured Devas in cots alongside and
opposite him.

'I dreamt of a mountain,' said Rama, 'untouched by
decay—its top lost in the clouds and an arrow-straight flight
of stairs going up its side. Somehow, I'm convinced it's here,
not on prithvi.'

'The old Mahadeva temple?' asked Indra. 'It's about three
yojanas away, along the Alakananda. There's a small, ancient
stone shrine atop the mountain.'

'I must go there,' said Rama, scrambling out of his bed.

'Now? Rest awhile,' said Indra. But Rama didn't stop. He
walked away, searching for the exit.

'Wait. I'll arrange a ratha for you. It will be quicker.'

'Thank you. Someone awaits me there. I must not delay. Time is different here, isn't it?'

'It's been close to a day here since you came. Almost a year has passed on prithvi.'

'Almost a year,' said Rama in surprise.

Indra sent word for a ratha to be arranged as he walked up to Rama and embraced him.

'I can't thank you enough. You have the gratitude of all the devas. We will remember and honour your victory.'

'Our victory,' said Rama.

'Go, do what you must. May Mahadeva's blessing always be with you,' said Indra. He instructed a soldier to show Rama the way out.

'I will remain here with my soldiers,' said Indra. Rama nodded and walked away with the soldier.

The ratha was already waiting for him when he came out of the arched doorway of what looked like a mansion requisitioned into a makeshift vaidyalaya for the war. The ratha was a magnificent war chariot, with two white steeds yoked to it and a canopy atop the central pole for shade. Protective cladding ran around the sides and the front of the ratha. It gleamed golden in the sunlight and the trim on the edges shone silver. Other than that it was utterly devoid of ornamentation. Sharp blades protruded from the wheel-hubs on either side of the ratha. There was no doubt about the purpose of the ratha; it wasn't for transport or sport, nor was it ceremonial. It was built for battle. Rama sat down on the hard seat and looked around at the niches and compartments in the ratha created to hold an array of weaponry. He wondered how it had escaped the ravages of the asura horde and how the charioteer looked so fresh and unhurt.

'The old temple of Mahadeva?' asked the charioteer.

Rama nodded and dismissed all thoughts from his mind. He would try to catch up on some sleep on the way. The chariot moved smoothly and swiftly through the decay and rot on the empty street. It flew over the holes and bumps on the street without a single jerk, not even slowing down. Somewhere far off, he heard the muted sounds of revelry and a name being shouted repeatedly: 'Parashurama!'

Rama smiled and wondered what Ma would say. She would laugh at the name but be proud nonetheless. The last thing Rama remembered before he nodded off was that he had left his axe behind.

———

Rama stood at the start of the flight of stairs. The mountain and its surroundings were as in his dream, untouched by the asura maya. Was it because of the asura's devotion to Mahadeva? Or was it that the maya was ineffectual here? Rama didn't know. He began to climb but stopped shortly after. He turned to see the river flowing sedately behind him.

'The holy Alakananda,' said the charioteer. Rama ran past the ratha to the river and immersed himself in it upto his shoulders. The river swirled around him, pulling him under and pushing him up. Rama stood still in surprise; he could feel the wet sand beneath his feet as he stood still. The water pulled him under again and then once more, the swirl of water loosened and dissipated. The river flowed calmly again. Rama clambered up the gentle riverbank. He felt completely cleansed in body and mind and revitalised in his soul. His battle-weariness was gone, and he felt a wonderful sense of calm. He walked back to the stairs and paused again. He gazed at the clouds embracing the mountain top, lost in thought.

'Shambho Mahadeva,' he whispered and instinctively turned left and made his way into the grove. He walked slowly, skirting trees and pushing through the bushes. Luckily, the ground was flat and firm. He glanced up at the mountain top and stopped short. He could now see clearly to the top of the mountain, to the small stone gopura of the shrine with a saffron dhwaja atop it, swaying in the wind. Rama moved forward a step and glanced up again. The mountaintop and shrine had again disappeared behind a mass of cloud. He pondered whether to step back and look at the shrine again, but decided against it.

Instead, he stepped forward again and peered up once more. The entire mountain seemed different now. A trick of light, perhaps. He continued forward, keeping his eyes on the mountain. It changed imperceptibly with every step. Rama moved slowly, looking ahead for anything in his path, to check his distance from the thicket he had seen earlier. It was no longer there. He looked around in confusion and realised he was standing in the middle of it. The trees seemed to have cleared a path for him, bending to their sides. He looked up at the mountain and saw the shrine again, but this time the gopura was different. This time it looked as if a gigantic trishula had been planted at the summit, which was reaching for the sky.

'Om Namah Shivaya,' Rama whispered up again. He, now, understood his earlier hesitation to climb the stairs after his dip in the river and the instinct that had made him walk into the grove instead. There may be a shrine atop the mountain, but that was not all. The entire mountain was a fount of energy. Shakti, his mind whispered.

He stepped forward and glanced up again. The mountain was oddly symmetrical now, akin to a golden pyramid, with tiers of triangular projections arranged in a circle as it tapered to a point. There was no gopura now. Something tiny and black stood atop it, clear from even this far away. Utter joy coursed through Rama. The pyramid radiated benevolence, grace and unending compassion. An energy surged up his spine and his mind hushed into silence. It was a silence immersed in syllables and mantras and chants—sounds he couldn't hear but *see*! He felt a tranquillity that was profound, timeless and absolute. The moment seemed to stretch on for eons, and in a blink, the glimpse was gone again. Rama stood quiet for a long while, trying to grasp the meaning of the incredible sight.

He didn't think the devas knew of this facet of the temple, perhaps this was revelation meant only for him. Rama was absolutely certain that this mountain of energy was present in many planes of existence, in many universes. This mountain linga was a point of centrality, a nexus of the spiritual essence of the other lingas.

Rama shut his eyes and brought his palms together. He chanted the holy Panchakshari mantra and stepped forward. He continued to walk with his eyes closed and a prayer on his lips.

Four muhurtas later, he opened his eyes to find himself at the base of the flight of stairs again. He had finished the circumambulation, his parikrama of the mountain linga. The war chariot and its charioteer had disappeared, not waiting to drive Rama back. Rama felt a mild puzzlement at this, but dismissed it from his mind. He touched his fingers to the first step, raised them to his forehead reverentially and continued his chant as he started his climb.

The day was giving way to dusk when he reached the summit. The sky had turned a glorious, deep saffron, and a cool breeze caressed Rama's body. He had climbed the stairs in another four muhurtas. As he stood facing the shrine, he saw a frail, old man—probably the priest—draw water from a small well situated to the right of the temple. Rama rang the bell hanging from the stone arch at the entrance of the shrine. The priest gave him a welcoming smile. He filled his pot with the water he had drawn, walked to the shrine and disappeared behind a flimsy curtain.

Rama walked the short distance to the shrine and stopped. A thought sprang to his mind. He turned towards Indrapuri, a small smidge on the horizon. He pictured the Parashu in his mind.

———

'What do you mean, you can't find him anywhere in the city?' demanded Indra of his sentries.

'My Lord, I'm telling you again. He went to the old temple in a ratha,' said the sentry who had led Rama out of the mansion.

'But my ratha still stands outside. I found no one here when I arrived. I waited for two muhurtas before I went in and enquired,' said another soldier. 'I haven't taken Rama anywhere.'

'A battle ratha and a charioteer were waiting for him when I led him out. He went in it,' said the sentry.

'There is only one usable chariot left in the city. I drove

it here. Which is this other chariot and driver?' questioned
the soldier.

Indra stood completely perplexed.

Rama held his arm out ahead of him, fingers outstretched.

'Come to me, Parashu,' he mentally commanded.

Indra glanced at the axe. 'Rama will have to come back for
this,' he said. 'Continue the search anyway.'

As Indra said this, the Parashu rose from beside Rama's
cot. It flew through the air, smashed through the decayed
window of the mansion and raced into the sky, leaving Indra
and his sentries stunned.

Rama saw a small dot in the sky in the distance and
laughed. It rapidly grew bigger as the Parashu hurtled towards
him. Rama watched the sunlight glimmer on the blades. It
flew straight to him and spun at the last instant. The handle
of the axe flew into his palm as his fingers wrapped around it
firmly. Rama twirled the axe in his hand and smiled. He sat
in padmasana and laid the Parashu across his lap. He waited
for the priest to draw the curtain aside for him to have his
darshan. He knew now what was behind the curtain with
absolute certainty.

The priest drew the curtain aside. Rama gazed upon the
Banalinga. It was the exact replica of the one Akrita had given
him on prithvi.

Arjuna watched the dancers as they posed for the artist. They were in elaborate dance costumes and held their poses gracefully—knees slightly bent, a curve to their hips and their hands in the Nagabandha mudra. The artist sketched them expertly, glancing up to check the pose now and then. He sat cross-legged behind a low flat table on a rug inside the spacious royal pavilion. He looked up to check the poses once more and then handed his sketch to Manorama for her approval.

'Not so much of a smile on the face, and the curve of the fingertips can be a little more. The hand should look like the hood of a cobra and you have to do the eyes again. The eyes are important,' she said.

'Natya is all about the bhava, meaning emotion; raga means music; and tala means rhythm. Bha-ra-ta-natya. If you lose the bhava in the eyes, you will lose the rasa in the posture and the statue or carving will look lifeless.'

The artist nodded and started making corrections to the sketch.

'Send it to the shilpkar in the parnashala after you're done,' she told the artist and turned to the dancers. 'Do not take this lightly. If you wish to dance in the rangamantapa of this magnificent temple, then pour life into your poses. Remember, where the hand goes, there goes the eye, and the mind follows. Where the mind is, there bhava and rasa will bloom.'

The three dancers nodded in response.

'Later, you can pose for the carvings of the apsaras and shilabalikas.' The dancers blushed coyly.

'No need for shyness. Understand that the beauty of your nudity, the eroticism of your curves and the bhava of your posture, is your obeisance to Nataraja, the one who danced the universe into existence. You use what he gave you to pay homage to Him.'

Saying that, Manorama turned to Arjuna with a smile. 'What do you think of the plans, my Samrat?'

'I was waiting for you to show them to me,' said Arjuna.

Manorama gestured to a dozen tables laden with parchment folios.

'These are the drawings for the temple design and the sculptures that will adorn the outer walls. Those are for the interiors and on that table are the drawings for the sculptures on the gopura. Almost everything is done.'

She opened the folio closest to her.

'The design of the temple itself is different. I stumbled upon a shilpkar who had such new ideas. These are his designs, and they are unlike any other temple in the world. Even Indra would be astonished by the beauty of it.'

Manorama noticed that Arjuna's curiosity was piqued. She instructed her daasi to bring the shilpkar in. He arrived only a moment later, as if he had already been waiting for an audience with the samrat. He bowed low and whispered his salutations, 'Pranaam, Chakravarti Samrat!'

He stayed bent till he heard Arjuna's command, 'Rise.'

'Dasoja, show the samrat what you have in mind for the design of this temple.'

Dasoja retrieved a folio and opened it on the table before the samrat. It was the design of the top view of the temple. The outline was star-shaped, made of overlapping staggered squares, with three gopuras in the middle.

'This is a trikuta temple. The three shrines of the trimurti will be directly beneath each gopura. The entire temple will rest on a raised platform about two-and-a-half cubits high. It will form the parikrama pathway around all three shrines,' said Dasoja.

He turned over the parchment and showed him the design for the sides of the raised platform. Three horizontal bands of carvings ran along the entire circumference of the platform.

'The lowest band depicts elephants, to show the strength of the samrat. The middle one will have lions to represent the courage of the samrat, and the topmost band will depict horses, to show the speed of the samrat. The carvings on none of these three bands will be identical to each other,' said Dasoja with quiet pride.

'So many carvings on the platform! The granite will be hard to carve,' said Arjuna.

'Absolutely right, Your Majesty. I propose to use a unique stone. It is called gorara locally. It is soft when quarried and takes to carving with ease; it hardens over time. I will make the entire temple out of it and there will not be a square foot of space left uncarved.'

Arjuna nodded.

Dasoja turned over the parchment. A picture of Arjuna kneeling at Dattatreya's feet and receiving his blessing was drawn in a square.

'This is the lintel piece. It goes over the main entrance of the temple,' said Dasoja.

Arjuna looked over the sketch of the forest-scape. It was intricate and beautiful. It would be a wonder if all this detail could be carved into the stone. Guru Dattatreya was depicted as the three-headed embodiment of the Trimurti, with six arms. One of his right hands was raised in benediction, a rosary hanging from his upraised thumb. The other five arms held a kamandalu, trishula, damaru, conch and chakra.

Arjuna stared at the image, nebulous and uneasy thoughts forming in his head. The picture seemed to tease at some memory, but his mind was reluctant to dredge it up, unwilling to probe for clarity. The image was making his mind stand still, as if in a black fog. Arjuna tried in vain to dispel it. He tore his eyes away from the picture and turned away, holding his arm up for silence before Manorama or Dasoja could speak.

Arjuna paced the room. For almost a year, his prayers to his guru had gone unheeded. He couldn't be found and hadn't responded to Arjuna's prayers. Arjuna had intensified his efforts to keep his growing apprehension at bay, but this picture was now filling his mind with worry.

He opened the flap of the pavilion's doorway and went out. He looked around the site chosen by Raikava for the temple—a few yojanas west of Mahishmati, deep into the forest along the Narmada. It had taken months of search and selection from various sites, the propitiation of the Gods and the calculations regarding the positions of the grahas, to arrive at this site. It was a patch of forest, a hundred acres in size. The trees would be felled, the ground levelled, and a new roadway built to reach the temple. A settlement for the priests and traders, and a vidyapeetha would also come up. Work camps were already being set up, and the plan to denude the site of its vegetation was scheduled for the following week. Arjuna watched High Priest Raikava, Chief Minister Chandragupta, General Brihadbala and Crown Prince Jayadhwaja, his eldest son and heir, confer at a distance. His vassal, King Suchandra, had also joined them. They directed the priests and workers on the tasks to be done that day.

Arjuna paled as he finally realised the connection his mind was so reluctant to make. It wasn't a memory; it was that damned dream.

He had stood in the desert in the dream. A desert denuded of shade and life, of water and comfort. Denuded of the goodwill of the gods. It was Jamadagni's son who had stood in the shade, while he, himself, had stood in the blazing heat of divine displeasure. No wonder then that his prayers had gone unheard. Was it his guru who had seeded that dream in two minds at once? Was his guru displeased and hence unresponsive to his prayers?

Why? his mind screamed. I have done nothing wrong.

A Chakravarti samrat had to rule with a closed fist, not an open palm. A fist that invoked fear and respect. It was the only way to rule. It brought order to the world and sparked obedience in the subjects. An open palm can only give blessings, however, it is not just the needy, but the greedy too who clamour for it. And any gratitude it evokes is only for what more can be taken, never for what has already been given. The gods can afford to have open palms of benediction, a mortal samrat, no matter how powerful he is, can not. And those rishis and the damned brahmins, they always only show you their open palm while hiding the other grasping, greedy one. They always extract their price, and the price is always more than what you imagined it would be. It doesn't matter if it is a blessing or curse, they always stand to profit. It is a kind of spiritual usury, and they are the vilest loan-sharks in the world. And they hide it so well, behind the humble brag of their poverty and the sanctimony of dharma. They are a pestilence that needs to be wiped off from the face of the earth, but he would tolerate them for now. Solely to see what fruit their pursuit of knowledge brought forth. The day he thought they were no longer productive, he would cut them down. He could not afford to have more of them join the ranks of brahmins, so he had decreed that henceforth, varna would be exclusively based on birth. Let them boast of their lineage; when the time came, that very same ancestry would mark them for extinction. Only brahmins like Raikava, who meekly follow orders and know their place in the world would survive his wrath.

When would his guru, who abhorred the affairs of men, realise this? Perhaps he was incapable of understanding. Perhaps he too had become more of a brahmin, and less of a seeker of the truth with the passage of time. Perhaps he himself had outgrown his guru? Yes, that was it. That's why the guru remained unresponsive.

Arjuna's mind remained steeped in turmoil. The worm of apprehension warped into a demon of worry. It wreaked havoc on his mind, flooding it with confusion and stoking the fires of anger. Arjuna struggled to contain the riotous feelings taking hold of his mind. He had to find a solution, not give vent to anger. He walked back into the pavilion. There was a low thrum inside the tent. A glowing disc had appeared on the table, between Arjuna and the dancers.

'Pranaam Samrat.' It was Pulastya's voice.

'Everyone leave!' Arjuna ordered. The shilpkar, the artist, the dancers, daasis and sentries scrambled to obey. Arjuna waited till he was alone with Manorama.

'Tell me, Pulastya.'

The glow faded, and Pulastya appeared in the disc. 'The devasura war has ended, Samrat. The asura army has been destroyed. None escaped alive.'

Arjuna paused in surprise for a nimisha. 'How did Indra defeat them?'

'Not mere defeat, Samrat. Annihilation! It was not

Indra who turned the tide. It was a mortal—an amsha and brahmakshatriya wielding Mahadeva's Parashu.'

Arjuna stood stunned. Manorama glanced at the maharishi and Arjuna nervously. Pulastya waited for Arjuna to respond, but the samrat was lost in a world of his own.

Pulastya's last words echoed in Arjuna's mind. The axe he had seen in his dhyana was Mahakaal's Parashu! He had got his answer despite his guru's silence. And Jamadagni's son had achieved the incredible.

'I don't know who the mortal is,' said Pulastya finally.

'Jamadagni's son,' Arjuna whispered.

It was Pulastya's turn to be surprised. The samrat knew about the mortal and that he was a Bhargava, scion of Brighu's clan. Given the bad blood between Arjuna and Brighu, it was inevitable, now more than ever, that the samrat and the saptarishi's son would end up in battle.

'I take your leave, Samrat,' said Pulastya.

Arjuna nodded. Pulastya let the disc blink out, relieved that the samrat had forgotten to ask about Dasagreeva. The mortal was the latest thorn in his flesh.

Manorama watched Arjuna standing still, not saying a word. She sensed his struggle to keep his anger from boiling over. She had seen him fly into a rage many times before, but this sense of disquiet and bleak melancholy were ominous. It sent a frisson of fear snaking up her spine. She had never seen Arjuna this way. She slipped her hand in his, held him across his tight waist and leaned into him, breathing slowly, not uttering a word.

Arjuna relaxed into the softness pressing against him. His breathing became less ragged and eased into the rhythm of Manorama's breath. His eyes darted around the pavilion until they rested on the drawing of his guru. He stared at it without blinking.

'Not just the gods, even my guru is displeased with me. He showers his benevolence on my enemy, I think,' said Arjuna.

'Who is the enemy?' Manorama asked softly.

'Jamadagni's son. He wields Mahakaal's axe,' said Arjuna.

Manorama looked up at him. Her husband had never known defeat in any of his earlier military campaigns. She had never seen him worry so much about an adversary. Not even that egoistical Asura king. This wasn't something to be taken lightly. This was not the time for empty platitudes.

'If he is worthy of your worry, then he is a formidable opponent. It will be a tough fight this time, or at least an enormously challenging one, but you will do what you always do. Win!'

Arjuna turned to his wife.

'What is really disturbing you is the spiritual pain you have undergone. It is no coincidence that both the challenge and the pain have appeared together. Set your mind at rest. Allow me to do for you, what your mother once did. I will undertake a vrat for your protection and success. I have enough spiritual merit to aid you, and it is my dharma to do so. Everything will fall into place once the temple is built.'

Arjuna hugged her tight.

'The temple! The solution to all the troubles that beset me. Seems as if all the answers I have long sought are coming to me today. Let's speed things up. It's been more than a year already. It'll take many more weeks to cut the timber and level the ground. It'll be better if I burnt the whole area clean. In less than a muhurta, not a single tree or shrub will remain standing.'

Arjuna hastened to leave the pavilion and turned back.

'Thank you, my love. It's my dharma to heed you when you offer good counsel,' he whispered in her ear and drew her into a kiss.

A little while later, Arjuna stood in firm concentration outside his royal pavilion, his breath slow, controlled and gentle. The chakra formed in his mind, whole and clear. There were no axes now, only a glorious thousand-pronged disc. He invoked the mantra for the Agneyastra and chanted it mentally with full focus, imbuing it with his spiritual merit. He raised the small bunch of green grass shoots in his right hand to his chest. The grass began to glow.

He opened his palm and gazed at the shoots. Each blade of grass had turned a brilliant, red hot. He looked up at the site, at the dense forest where the temple was to be built. Shards of molten fire flew from his palm, multiplying in number as they reached the forest, alighting gently on treetops, branches and leaves. They slipped onto the earth and disappeared within the tree trunks. The forest went deathly still. The courtiers, priests and workers stared in astonishment.

The forest erupted into a raging conflagration. The heatwave pummelled through the air, pushing back everyone, except Arjuna, a dozen paces. Tree trunks cracked open, and the sap inside vapourised before it could even drip. The trees crumbled into ash, not a single twig escaping the fire. The flames leapt dozens of yards resembling maniacal demons lost in an orgy of destruction. Hands formed of fire caught flying birds and burned them to a crisp. Rivers of blaze spewed from the innards of the earth. Smoke belched out of the fire, thick, dark and voluminous, blocking out the sun.

Arjuna grinned with satisfaction as the forest blaze reached the skies. No man on earth could imbue divyastras with as much yogic power as he could. The fire raced forward, away from him, leaving heaps of ash in its wake. It would run through the entire area he had marked in his mind. He would then douse the fire and kill the enormous heat using the Varunastra.

Out of the heaps of ash, smouldering earth and billowing smoke stepped a man. The man, who burnt like a human sun, stared at Arjuna with eyes untouched by the fire. Arjuna was taken aback for a moment. His spies were scouring the countryside and forests for Jamadagni. They would have searched here too, but there was no information of there being an ascetic in these parts.

But was this an ascetic or someone else? He stood unfazed and unmindful of his burning flesh. Arjuna invoked the Varunastra and aimed it at the man.

The man laughed as water poured down on him.

'You want to use Varuna's astra on his own son?' he said.

He mumbled something under his breath, his hands moving smoothly through a series of mudras and gestures. The deluge of water lifted to the skies and spread over the entire forest, soaking the blazing fire and extinguishing it. He continued to stare at the courtiers, priests, dancers and workers, as well as the queen who was standing a distance behind Arjuna, at the entrance of the pavilion. His entire body was still covered in dancing flames except for his clear, unblinking eyes. He snapped his fingers and the flames engulfing his body disappeared.

'My name is Apava, and this is my grove,' he said.

The man made of leaf and twig, bark and vine, grass and

shrub, root and sap, flower and fruit stood before Arjuna and his entourage. Raikava fell to the ground in supplication. Behind Apava, the fire died down and the deluge dissipated into a cool, fine mist that sucked the heat from the earth.

Two tears, one in each eye, dropped from the corners of Apava's eyes. They flowed down his face, down the bark he had for skin, down the crevices and bulges of his extraordinary body, which was swelling with water. They fell away from his body as twin streams, soaking into the ground, forming puddles and pools in the depressions in the earth. Myriad roots snaked away from Apava as the ash scattered in the sudden cool breeze. He rubbed his hands on his torso and his hands came away with seeds of all shapes and sizes. He threw them into the wind, and they floated away in the mist, scattering all over the moist earth. As the seeds hit the ground, shrubs and stems sprouted from them and grew prodigiously. Vines stretched from Apava's hair and wound around the growing trunks. Apava breathed heavily and butterflies and moths, damselflies and bees, will-o-wisps and grasshoppers flew out with his exhalation. Earthworms, centipedes and snakes, squirrels and rodents, ants and other foraging animals emerged from under his feet and scrambled into the emerging shrubbery. Apava cupped his hands to his mouth, and he blew into them. As he raised his hands to the sky, a thousand different birds burst into the open air. Full-grown trees started to peep out from the mist and suddenly, the forest was back again.

Apava pressed his palms and closed his eyes in prayer and the forest once again thrummed with life, with chirps and tweets, snorts and mating calls. From somewhere deep in the grove came the defiant roar of a tiger.

Apava opened his eyes and looked accusingly around him.

'I see Kshatriyas drunk on power, who think might is right, who believe their word, wish and whim is the highest dharma—petty tyrants all of them! Pompous fools who disregard the objections of brahmins and attribute selfishness to them.

'I see Brahmins who forget to both teach and abide by true dharma, who blindly perform ritual priestly duties and refrain from correcting the wrongs of their rulers, who live in comfort themselves but forget about their poor brethren who struggle to live but steadfastly uphold dharma.'

Raikava started to quake where he had fallen. He didn't dare to look up at Apava, who had, by now, turned away from the priest and was glaring at Arjuna.

'The wellspring of the sludge of adharma and oppression. Arjuna!

'A name. A curse. A prophecy. This indeed is your day of answers.

'The name. Ramabhadra. Jamadagni's son. Now called Parashurama.' Apava laughed to the sky. 'You know why.'

Arjuna stood in utter stupefaction.

'The curse. YOUR VAINGLORIOUS TEMPLE SHALL NEVER BE BUILT.'

Apava's words echoed in the clearing. He stamped his foot down, and the earth trembled. Arjuna felt his suppressed rage explode within him. He would teach this insolent rishi a lesson for defying the most powerful man in the world.

'There will be another born, of the name the same as yours. His glory will reach the heavens. He will be the true gold to your tawdry glitter,' continued Apava.

Arjuna's many arms sprouted as he grew larger, and his eyes turned ochre. Apava smiled.

'The prophecy. A prophecy of fire and water. Of fire that is the womb of water and water that is the heart of fire.'

'When Mahakaal's dread weapon,
Descends to earth from heaven,
It's master, he will break the world.
Thirsty for blood will the axe be, once hurled.
Lakes of warrior blood five,
The price, arrogance and folly contrive.
The fork in the path of Dharma,
Lies solely in the Samrat's Karma.
To renounce, to reform, this choice he has,
To turn from the dark of Tamas,
To flow with peace, like water,
And stop perchance the slaughter.
Else, if he walks the path of fire,
To pander untrammelled desire,
Beware the loss of the golden horn,
For that day, vengeance is born.
If he swears a battle oath,
Lives forfeit they would both.
For Sahasrabahu
And the master of Parashu,
This fate to escape from,
Is to unbecome, to die, to become.'

'Choose wisely, Arjuna,' said Apava.

It was now Arjuna's turn to speak.

'I'm a warrior, Rishi. The most powerful one on earth. I fear no man, asura or deva no matter what weapon he wields. And no rishi either. Your curse is just a child's tantrum. The temple will be built. It is a warrior's honour to win in battle and his glory to die in one, bested by someone who is better.

'I will bestow that glory to that boy with the axe. I choose the path of fire.'

Apava glanced at the panic-stricken queen.

'You will need all the prayers you can get, Arjuna,' he whispered.

Arjuna leapt at Apava without warning but Apava vanished without a trace. Arjuna's fists found only empty air.

Arjuna roared in frustration; his mind afire with blinding rage. He burned with the urge to hunt, pillage, destroy, to vent his exploding anger. He ran and leapt again, clearing the treetops and crashing into the earth, far away in the distance. He leapt again, this time farther away to the west.

'Bring us horses,' Suchandra shouted as Jayadhwaja conferred with two men who had just ridden up. Raikava rushed to Manorama, his face red with embarrassment at Apava's castigation. Manorama still stared at the spot from where Apava had vanished.

'The rishi sounded ominous. I sense danger, High Priest. This is no ordinary threat,' she said.

'Not ordinary at all, my Queen. Parashurama is a brahmakshatriya and he carries an amsha. The samrat had marked him as an enemy a long time back. The spies have been seeking his whereabouts.'

'Did you understand the prophecy, Raikava?'

'Not entirely. The samrat has chosen war. I guess we all knew he would do that. I do not know what the golden horn is, and I cannot even guess what the last part of the prophecy means.

'Is there some way by which we can prevail on the samrat to choose the path of water instead?' asked Raikava.

Manorama looked into Raikava's eyes and saw fear dancing in them. The man was rattled. He thought the samrat had chosen wrong and would die.

'Organise prayers and yagnas for the samrat's victory, High Priest. I will start my own puja and vrat for his safety. Make the arrangements.

'I have ruled beside him, Raikava, and I intend to do so for a long time to come. A threat to him will not go unpunished by me. You remember the campaign of Mayong? The fools tried to use Abhichara against Arjuna. I sent Jayadhwaja to wipe out that cult of warlocks and their profane magic. Not one soul escaped my assault. This Parashurama will not either.'

Raikava nodded and glanced surreptitiously at Manorama. She noticed this.

'Speak without fear, Raikava.'

'The samrat flies into a rage at the slightest provocation. It has been so for as long as I've known him. But he is thousands of years old, and I'm a mere mortal. You have known him for hundreds of years, your life extended by your tapasya. Was he always like this?'

Manorama paused for a short while and then said, 'Arjuna has lived for so long, seen and done so much, I think he finds life dull and repetitive. Immortality can be a curse and so can extended life. He's seen wives and children be born and die, kingdoms and civilisations rise and fall. On and on the cycle repeats. I've lived long too, thanks to the blessings given to me, and I've given him a hundred sons. An ordinary father or any other king would be overjoyed by this, but Arjuna hardly felt a flutter of excitement. A life without a cause is useless. But an extended life, when all causes, desires and ambitions have been met, breeds emptiness and frustration. The desolation of his soul haunts him. Arjuna rages because of this.'

Manorama turned to the high priest.

'He is a warrior beyond compare, who has had no serious challengers. Until now. Deep down, I think he welcomes it, even if it means death.'

Raikava startled on hearing this.

'Maybe my husband will find a new life, a new meaning with the death of this Parashurama. Arjuna has already "un-become". His enemy's "death" may be the spark for a new Arjuna to "become".'

Raikava nodded. The queen had explained her understanding of the prophecy and it was an intelligent analysis. He hoped she was right, but prophecies were always dangerous. Subtle meanings and hints of intent are hidden in them which are revealed in their own time. Interpretations of prophecies could be many and they usually defied consensus. Never did a prophecy reveal exactly what would happen, and when it eventually did, it was almost always too late.

They watched as Jayadhwaja, Suchandra, Brihadbala and Chandragupta, along with a clutch of soldiers, mounted their steeds and galloped away in the direction in which the samrat had disappeared.

———

Arjuna plunged into the western sea. He dove after a humpback whale and caught it, encircling its stupendous girth with his thousand arms. The whale thrashed wildly in panic. Arjuna held on tight and wrestled the whale to the surface. Then he loosened his grip, letting it slide down to the whale's tail, holding on to it with a vice-like grip. He struggled to stay afloat as he swung the massive creature around, trying to lift it out of the water. He gathered momentum as he kept swinging. Finally, the gigantic form of the whale broke through the surface of the sea. Arjuna whirled it around rapidly, and heaved the whale away into the air, throwing yojanas away.

Victorious, he roared aloud and dove again, all the way to the seafloor. He pummelled the floor with his thousand fists. The deep-sea fish scattered in panic, and the murk of the seafloor rose and swirled around him. Arjuna pounded on, sending shock waves through the water. The floor seemed to moan under his assault. Arjuna could hear someone whispering in the deep water. Perhaps the lack of air in his lungs was playing tricks with his mind, but he heard one word ceaselessly repeated in a watery, soft sigh.

Parashurama ... Parashurama ...

Rage drove him to strike the floor with all his remaining strength and suddenly, the floor trembled and split. The crack in the floor zigzagged on for miles. The crack widened, as if the floor was trying to flee from Arjuna and his assault. All at once, the floor heaved and lifted with an ear-splitting screech.

On the ground above, Jayadhwaja and the others rode past the smashed carcass of the whale in astonishment. They were still many yojanas away from the sea. He was sure this was his father's doing. He wondered how much more destruction his rage had wrought.

'Halt!' Suchandra screamed.

Jayadhwaja's steed neighed loudly as he reined him in. The horse tried to gallop back the way they had come. The others too struggled to control their strangely frantic mounts. The horses quietened after a great deal of coaxing, and Jayadhwaja noticed the eerie stillness in the air. He looked around, nothing moved; even the trees seemed as still as statues. He heard a strangled cry from Brihadbala, turned in puzzlement and froze.

A gigantic wave loomed up in the sky, stretching across the the horizon as far as the eye could see. The wave held still for a moment as if frozen and then collapsed on earth with a deafening crash. The deluge of water rolled towards the group of petrified men, destroying everything in its path. It slowly lost speed, and ebbed away. The wave had died down a few feet ahead of them and had withdrawn along the same path it had come. It left behind thousands of squirming fish, masses of seaweed, uprooted mangroves, rocks and sand in its wake. A sudden gust of wind almost threw the men off their horses.

'Look!' Chandragupta croaked.

A second wave was rising in the sky.

Arjuna floated on the mountainous crest of water and looked down at the tumultuous mass of water dropping away from under his feet to form a trough hundreds of feet deep. He soaked in the colossal, primal force of nature he had unleashed. He plunged into the wave and was driven back into the depths of the sea. Arjuna fought his way up to the surface again and swam onto the next wave that was forming. This one, too, rose high and Arjuna stood atop it, roaring with the ecstasy of power.

———

Rama finished his worship of the linga and sat in padmasana before the sanctum sanctorum. The old priest approached him and held out it.

'For you. For giving us victory, for saving us,' he said.

'Mahadeva saved us all,' said Rama.

'May he always do so. Shambho Mahadeva!' said the priest.

A small necklace of rudrakshas dangled from it.

'I have nothing to give you, I beg forgiveness,' said Rama.

The priest waved the apology away and put the necklace around Rama's neck. A small gomati chakra twinkled beneath the sumeru. He dipped his fingers in the sacred bhasma and traced the tripundra across Rama's forehead and then dabbed on a circle of vermilion in the middle of it, right above the agya chakra. Rama whispered his thanks, and the priest walked away to the inner sanctum.

Rama closed his eyes and imagined the yagnakund in his mind. He emptied himself of all emotion and controlled his breath. Immediately, he felt the Parashu tug at his mind. This was new, perhaps because he had been able to cleave his mind during the battle with the asuras. The Parashu replayed his movements in the battle. Rama saw the flow of his actions once he had given himself over to instinct. His feints and assaults, his defensive, offensive and evasive moves. He studied them and committed them to memory. He thought about them and deduced alternative actions and stratagems. The visions faded away and Rama focussed his mind on the banalinga again. He instantly went back into dhyana, but was completely different this time.

The voice was back, the familiar voice in the woods that had beckoned him to this shrine.

The yuddharatha and sarathi are yours, Rama ... Call them with a focussed mind and they will appear ... Yours also is this ...

A magnificent bow appeared in his mind, as tall as him. It was revolving—the bow string winding around the lower end of it. He saw himself in the vision, reaching out, hefting up the bow, marvelling at its enormous weight. A twin of the bow continued to revolve in front of him. It disappeared with a blaze of light. Two identical bows, Rama mused, just like the two identical banalingas.

In his mind, he unwound the bowstring, gossamer soft and as fragile as a spun spider web. He tied one end of the string to the notch at the top end of the bow, gently, fearing it might break.

As soon as he was finished, the bow twanged alound, and Rama's heart leapt with joy.

Rama raised it to his forehead, prayed to his pitrus and thanked Mahadeva. He drew the bowstring back, stretching it to the maximum easily. He marvelled at his own strength.

In the shrine, Rama's hands moved on their own accord, mimicking what ever he was doing in his dhyana.

The bow disappeared.

'Call and it will come ...'

The nothingness became suffused with sound, something indecipherable being repeated over and over.

Listen ...

Learn ...

Rama felt his forehead throb. This was Mahadeva's blessing, he realised. A reward for the completion of the extraordinary task he had set before himself. He had proved himself worthy by defeating the asuras and understanding the mysteries of the Parashu.

Agneyastra ...

The sound resolved into the clear syllables of the mantra. It rang in the nothingness and in Rama's mind. He saw himself chant the mantra and perform the mudras to invoke the astra, nocking it on a bow, to imbue an object with it, using his yogic power to unleash the full potential of the astra and then recalling it. He learnt of the safeguards he would need to limit the range of the weapon and to counter it. He remembered the lessons his father had taught him; how awestruck he had been when Jamadagni had told him about the divyastras. Now he would have them. 'Shambho Mahadeva!' he intoned and focussed his mind on the voice in his head.

Varunastra ...

The mantra changed and Rama listened with rapt attention, eager for the knowledge of the divyastras and aspiring for more.

Aindrastra ...

It was a long night of learning for Rama.

———

The priest climbed the last of the stairs and rang the bell at the entrance of the shrine. He had left Rama there last night, still engrossed in dhyana when he had closed up. He had climbed back up to the temple in the pre-dawn darkness; dawn was breaking now, suffusing the air with a gentle golden light. Rama was nowhere to be seen. He walked forward, looking around, and made his way to the knee-high outer wall encircling the shrine. Then, he glanced down.

'Mahadeva!' he exclaimed in surprise. He moved along the wall, all the while looking down at the base of the mountain till he reached right where he had started from. He could now see a clear pathway that wound its way all around the mountain and through the trees and shrubs of the grove at its base. A path that was well worn and traced a parikrama of the mountain. A path that had not been there yesterday.

———

Rama opened his eyes and blinked. Mahadeva had blessed him with the knowledge of so many divyastras. He thanked Mahadeva again and looked around in surprise. He was in a completely different temple than the one he had been in earlier, where the priest had given him a rudraksha mala.

———

Arjuna sat on the beach with the sea debris, wrecks of boats, smashed trees and carcasses of thousands of marine life forms strewn around him. A group of men waited at a distance, unsure and afraid, as the sea still heaved turgidly. Arjuna leaned back on his hands as he stared at the grey expanse of water. Jayadhwaja approached him with caution, wary of the sound of the wet earth beneath his footsteps. This was not where the beach was supposed to be. Yojanas of land had plummeted into the ocean in a blink. Millions of lives had ended with no comprehension of what was happening. He wondered how far along the coast the destruction had spread.

He stopped more than an arm's length away from Arjuna.

'Father,' he whispered. 'Two of our spies returned today. They've found Jamadagni's ashram.'

17

Tripura

Rama looked around at the dense vegetation around him. Giant trees reached for the sky. Creepers wound around them in swarms and their roots snaked into the moist ground. A deep hush enveloped the place. The huge Ashwattha tree a little ahead of him had a raised altar running around it. Hundreds of small figurines of Nagas smeared with turmeric lined the altar. Hundreds more were across and around the clearing, straining to keep the jungle from overrunning them. Two shrines were ahead, bathed in the silky soft light of dawn. A sinewy old man stood before the smaller shrine, which had only a peetha in it. He moved to the bigger shrine with a basket of interwoven leaves that held flowers in it.

Rama rose and the old man turned at the sound of the Parashu scraping against the hard granite slabs that led to the steps of the shrines. His right hand swiftly moved to his left hip, and he almost dropped the basket. He appraised Rama for a nimisha, his eyes darting around the shrine and the jungle before finally coming to rest on the axe.

'Pranaam purohita. What place is this? And which temple is this?' said Rama.

'Who are you? How did you come here?' replied the purohita, tearing his eyes away from the Parashu with effort.

'I am Ramabhadra, son of Jamadagni. I ... err ... somehow woke up here. I was elsewhere before.'

The purohita had an odd look on his face as he looked at Rama. It seemed like he was turning something over in his mind. 'This is the shrine of Bhadrakali, the smaller one is of our pitru, Yogeeshwara and the sacred grove is of the Nagas. This is my clan temple, and I am Anantha,' he said.

From a shrine dedicated to Shiva to a shrine dedicated to the Devi in her warrior form, wondered Rama. 'A warrior who worships the Nagas but isn't a kshatriya. A purohita who is not a brahmin. Must be an interesting story,' he said aloud.

'How did you know?' asked the priest.

'Callused hands, scars on the upper arms and shoulders. Your right hand instinctively reached for your sword, which you hang at the left hip. You have a litheness to your body and a warrior mien to the way you carry yourself. So, not a smith or a farmer, rather a swordsman. Your sword probably lies at the feet of the Devi, in her shrine. You seek her blessings for some venture. No yagnopaveeta, so not a kshatriya and not a brahmin.'

Anantha nodded his acceptance of Rama's observations.

'Which land is this?'

'Tripura. That is what they call it now. North and east of Mahishmati, closer to the eastern coast.'

I am back on prithvi, and further east of the ashram, thought Rama.

'Who rules here?'

'Karthavirya Arjuna. Through his vassals.'

'Vassals? More than one of them rule here?'

'This place is a federation of three kingdoms, hence it is called Tripura. Though the kingdoms aren't ruled by kings in the true sense, but by three creeds. The leader of each creed rules akin to a king.'

'What do you mean, it's called Tripura now? What was it called earlier?' asked Rama.

Anantha shrugged. 'We've only been here a few years. They have erased the old name. It is forbidden to know it or speak of it.'

Rama stared at Anantha, puzzled. An odd kingdom with strange people who were migrants here. This must be at the heart of the reason why he had arrived here.

'You weren't surprised when I said I woke up here,' he said.

'You are the second person to say so. The first person we found at this shrine said the same thing and that he awaits your coming.'

'Who?'

'Here he comes,' Anantha gestured down the narrow serpentine pathway leading away from the shrines. A group of men stepped into view. Amidst them was Akrita.

'Acharya!' Akrita exclaimed as he ran to Rama and fell at his feet.

'Blessings of Mahadeva on you,' said Rama. 'How did you get here?'

'I've been meditating on the banalinga near your cottage, as a part of my daily routine. At first, nothing extraordinary happened. Then, one day, it showed me visions, Acharya—visions of your glorious victory over the asuras. I saw that beam of light streaming out from your forehead. I told your parents about the visions and their joy knew no bounds. A couple of days back, I fell into a deep sleep during my dhyana.

It was as if the banalinga was drawing me into it. I woke up to find myself here and the "voice in the woods" telling me you would come.'

Rama drew Akrita away from the purohita and the four men who were conferring with each other.

'I wonder why we are here, Akrita. What is the purpose behind our arrival in this strange land?' asked Rama.

'And why now, Acharya?' said Akrita.

'What do you mean?'

'The three kingdoms of Tripura hold a congregation and fair tomorrow. On the great plains to the north. A day's trek away. It happens once in twelve years. I've been trying to find out as much as possible about this land.' Akrita lowered his voice as he said, 'These people here are rebels of some sort. They plan to attack the fair and kill the three kings.'

'Who exactly are they?'

'From what I've been able to gather, they are shudras who have taken up arms against Samrat Arjuna. They rebel against his iron tyranny and the social order he has imposed. These people have sworn revenge for the ouster of the Nagas from Mahishmati and the sacking of Ahichchatra, their homeland. They wander in the forests in search of something, raiding the vassals of Arjuna, killing when they can and retreating to their secret forest strongholds.

'They've moved south over the years and have now reached here. They wait here for the answer to their search. They intend to worship at this shrine before they battle against the three kings of Tripura, whom they've fought for years now. Their women and children are safe somewhere deep in the forest. They call themselves the "Malaya Kshatriyas".'

Rama glanced at the small group of men. Mere mortals, but they had found the spine to stand against the might of Arjuna in their own small way. And they had possessed the fortitude to endure hardships all these years. He walked to the group and addressed Anantha.

'Akrita tells me you search for something. Perhaps it has something to do with why I am here, allow me to be of help. I stand against Arjuna and it is my dharma to aid any who do the same.'

'It is not my place to accept or reject your offer.'

'What do you search for?'

'Not what. It's who. We seek our Uddhatr.'

'Redeemer?' asked Akrita.

Anantha nodded. 'He that will upraise the land and settle us down.'

'What does that mean?' said Rama.

'Await the High Priestess, the matriarch of our clan and our leader. She will decide on your offer.' The group sat down before the shrine of Bhadrakali and pressed their palms together in silent prayer. Rama and Akrita moved a distance away and waited.

After a short while, they saw what looked like a glimmer of light winding its way through the trees behind the shrines. Soon a middle-aged lady, austerely dressed in an ivory coloured dhoti and an angavastra draped across her chest cinched below her right armpit, stepped into view. She held a lamp in her hands and murmured a prayer as she meticulously put one foot ahead of the other in such a way that the heel of one foot would touch the toes of the other and so on. She kept her eyes on the ground as she made her way to the shrine and placed the lamp before the murthi of

Bhadrakali. The lady reminded Rama of his Ma. The light at the end of the lamp's wick flickered. Playful, just like Ma's smile, Rama thought. She prayed awhile, retrieved the swords from inside the shrine and handed one to each of the now standing men. Then she applied a blood-red tilak to their foreheads, and the men raised their swords to their foreheads. She murmured her blessings to all of them while they strapped their swords at their hips.

The purohita whispered in her ear and she turned towards Rama and froze. She kept staring at him. The group of men tensed at her reaction. Their hands darted to their sword hilts, and their eyes flicked between Rama and his axe. Rama stood still and at ease.

'Does the phrase "Mahakaal's dread weapon" mean anything to you?' she asked.

Rama held out the Parashu to show her. The men also drew out their weapons.

'With the beam of light on his forehead and Mahakaal's Parashu, comes the Uddhatr to you. Devi Bhadrakali be praised, our prayers have been answered, our quest has ended. The Uddhatr has arrived,' the priestess said.

The men looked at her in confusion and a little disbelief. 'Do you not see it?' the priestess demanded of the men. She whirled towards the shrine and lifted a small metal tray containing powdered turmeric. She whispered something and flung the fine yellow dust at Rama's head. Rama looked at her without flinching. The dust floated in the air at the level of Rama's head. The beam of light coming from his forehead shone a glorious golden yellow through it. The men gasped and fell to their knees and touched their heads to the ground. Akrita watched this with his mouth agape.

'The Redeemer lives! The Redeemer has come!' The priestess exulted as she, too, fell to her knees. Rama moved to the peetha of Yogeeshwara and bowed his head in prayer. The yellow dust was caught within the beam of light emanating from his forehead, and as he moved his head it moved, too, with it. He approached the shrine of Bhadrakali and sat before it in prayer. Mahadeva had given him the divyastras and had readied him for battle. He prayed to the goddess for protection and her aid to help defend himself against attacks he may not know how to counter. A vision of himself smeared with turmeric flashed in his mind. The beam of light bathed the black murthi with a glow that made it look golden. The yellow dust floated towards the murthi and settled on it, covering it from head to toe. Rama lost himself in prayer.

> *'Bhagawati rakshaam dehi!*
> *Rakshaam bhagawati dehi!'*

After a while, he opened his eyes. The turmeric had slid off the murthi, collecting in a conical heap at the goddess's feet. The priestess tore off a square of cloth from her angavastra and swept the dust into it. She wrapped it up and handed it to Rama.

'The goddess protects you. This is her blessing.' Rama tucked it away in his waistband.

'I am Bhargavi, the Matriarch of the Malaya Kshatriyas. I never thought I'd live to see the day the Redeemer would stand before us. What does the Uddhatr command? Your people live to obey,' said the priestess.

My people, Rama mused.

'What does it mean, priestess, to upraise the land and settle us down?'

'Ancient lore handed down over generations. The man who predicted your coming, with the light and the axe, was a great mantravadin, a speaker of spells. It is him we pray to, the peetha is his symbol, and the sankalpa is of Yogeeshwara. The lore states how the Redeemer will save us. What it means is for you to either know or to find out.'

Rama sighed. Another puzzle for him to figure out, but he would not worry about it right now. The answer would come to him when the time was right. But some inner conviction told him he would find some answers, at least, at this shrine.

'The ceremony for their swords?' he asked.

'They are dead men walking from this day on. The quintet has vowed to kill the leaders of the three creeds or die trying. They will return only if they succeed. So, they will leave as dead men unmourned by their wives and mothers. If they return after killing the leaders, they will be legendary heroes. If they don't, they will be duly mourned. But a wife or mother will cast out the man who comes back unsuccessful.'

'We have fought many wars, killed many, but lost many of our own too. We cannot afford an upfront attack right now, so we send these squads to target the heads directly.'

'The squads before this one?'

'The first squads succeeded, ages ago, but then the kings got wiser, nay warier and since then it has become harder and harder. The previous five squads have all failed, but we will keep trying. *Dhairyameva hi vidhi!* Courage is destiny!'

'The creeds are a scourge on the face of the earth,' Bhargavi spat the words out. Rama started to ask what she meant, but thought the better of it. It would be better if he saw and judged for himself. Petty misunderstandings and slights escalated to blood feuds sometimes. Each side invariably painted the other in the worst light possible.

'I will go to this congregation myself. As a guide for our trek, I need him,' Rama said, pointing at Anantha.

'Do as the Redeemer bids,' said Bhargavi as she bade Anantha accompany Rama and Akrita. A short while later, the trio set out from the shrine.

———

They stopped at a small cave on the side of a hill, well covered by foliage. Anantha set about building the fire for cooking with twigs and dried leaves. Rama watched him silently. The man had set a fast pace and led them down trails that twisted and turned and disappeared into the foliage. Rama guessed the trail would twist back on itself at some point. No wonder these people were able to evade capture and hide their locations for such a long time. They'd learnt the secrets of the jungle well. Rama felt a vague but persistent sense of unease, like there was some impending urgency. He couldn't wrap his mind around it.

'The cave will hide the light of the fire, but what about the smoke?' said Rama to distract himself.

'The air moves out of a vent high in the roof that opens out on the other side of the hill. The smoke will be lost in the evening mist, anyway. Down this hill is the Valley of the Dead; across it is a small thicket. Beyond that are the plains where the congregation gathers. Better to camp here, Swami. The valley is not a good place to be in after dark,' said Anantha.

'You still won't call me by name. At least you've stopped calling me Uddhatr. Thank you for that small mercy.'

Anantha grinned sheepishly.

'What is this Valley of the Dead?'

'A place of evil, the execution site for captives who refuse to forsake dharma. It is the true visage of the adharma of the three creeds. You will see it with your own eyes in the morning.'

Anantha offered to stand watch for the night, which Rama flatly refused. The three of them would take turns. Anantha immediately claimed the second watch, which was gracious of him since he would have to split his sleep. Rama said he would take the first one. They finished their supper of gruel and fruit. Anantha and Akrita cleared small stones and gravel from a small section of the floor inside the cave, to settle down for the night. Rama stood watch at the mouth of the cave. He noticed a faraway glow coming from the Valley of the Dead. It had to be a huge conflagration to be seen across the forest at this distance.

'What is that?' he asked Anantha.

'Flesh is burning, souls are screaming! I hope they find salvation,' Anantha whispered, staring at the distant blaze. He muttered a prayer under his breath.

'They burn people?' Akrita spluttered.

'They will burn the world,' Anantha replied as he turned back into the cave.

Rama waited for a muhurta before creeping in to the cave, gently waking Akrita, his hand over Akrita's mouth to keep him silent. He led him to the mouth of the cave and silently signalled him to stand watch. Rama hefted his axe and slipped into the dark of the forest. He roved around in the dark to find the trail to the valley, stopping and scanning the bent leaves and shoots, the tell-tale turns in the grass. Where the foliage was dense enough to cut out the moonlight, he skirted around the trees and rocks, always returning to the direction of the blaze. He hacked through a thicket, impatience replacing the uneasiness in his mind. An owl hooted loudly in the distance, and the forest turned unnaturally quiet again. Rama paused, going completely still, listening for the small quiet sounds of the forest at night. Impatience grew; he sensed he was near. He started to hack his way through.

He was still some distance away when he heard the screams. The screams of children. He sprinted, jumping over rocks and crashing through the underbrush and cutting through the branches in his way, till he burst into a clearing and froze. Hundreds of dead and dismembered bodies littered the clearing. Heads and limbs had been hewn from torsos, bodies cleaved in half, eyes gouged out and genitals sawn away. The stench of stinking human flesh hammered into his panting lungs, and he fought the urge to retch. Crows and vultures tore at the bodies and scavenging teeth, small and large, ripped at the flesh. The screams were never-ending from the huge bonfires still a distance away, but there were smaller fires close by.

Rama ran, clumsily picking his way through the bodies and feasting animals, and stumbled into another nightmare. A field of dead bodies strung up high, all on similar wooden devices. A long vertical shaft of wood planted in the ground, with a horizontal beam running across the top of it. The bodies had been bound and nailed to them. Some were on fire, the smell of burning flesh adding to the miasma. There were heaps of ashes where the flesh and wood had finished burning. Some of the structures were covered with swarms of ravens covering the entire bodies; some had only skeletons hanging, the bones picked clean of flesh. Rama ran on—nobody to save here—but unable to tear his eyes away from the horrific sight till the heat of the fire nearby forced him to turn away.

Three gigantic pyres blazed in the night, dispelling the darkness and bathing the gruesome scene in stark yellow light. A pyre each for men, women and children. Clumps of soldiers mutilating and torturing the men, whipping and assaulting the ones that dared to get off their knees. Women stripped and mauled and defiled by laughing, taunting soldiers. Some stood numb to the ordeal while others kicked and screamed and clawed at the soldiers. They were dragged by their hair into the waiting, salivating circles of soldiers. The children turned their eyes away, screaming aloud their terror into the night. The uniforms worn by the soldiers and the design of their armour varied, but there were three dominant colours— white, black and blue. Men of three armies, Rama realised as rage exploded within him. The Parashu thrummed in his hand as it responded. Rama leapt into the midst of a group of soldiers engrossed in their lustful, depraved violations. He cut through the group before they could even realise what was happening, some cut down in the throes of lust. He pulled the woman out of the heap of corpses, while simultaneously running up to the second group and cut them down to the last man. The naked woman who had scrambled to her feet, snatched up a sword.

'Get the other women and follow me to the children,' Rama screamed.

He ran towards the children and saw the soldiers realizing the incoming danger, drawing their weapons and preparing to meet his attack. Rama cut through swords and maces, armour and flesh, spouts of blood arcing around him. The soldiers didn't stand a chance. Rama moved extraordinarily fast, and the soldiers seemed at a standstill, unable to even see the swing of the axe as it raced to end their lives.

'Cut out their uniforms to cover yourselves. Stay with the children,' Rama shouted towards the women and turned to free the men. A semi-circular wall of soldiers stood facing him, weapons at the ready, officers screaming orders. Rama flung his axe at the right edge of the semi-circle. The Parashu swung through the soldiers one by one, lopping off their heads, cleaving through their arms and shoulders. It swiftly returned to Rama's outstretched left hand as the front line of soldiers collapsed en masse. Right where they stood.

It took a couple of nimishas for the other soldiers to realise what had happened. Comprehension sparked, and the impulse to move and attack raced out of their minds. But Rama was already among them, cutting through them before their muscles had even found time respond to the signal from their brains. He was a whirlwind of death amongst the soldiers and no one escaped. He finally stopped, chest heaving, drenched in his own sweat and in the blood of the soldiers, when he couldn't find a single soldier still standing. The night was suddenly silent except for the crackle and pop of burning wood.

He rested the handle of the axe against his thigh and waited to regain his breath. The men Rama had freed scrambled to run to the women and children, ignoring their wounds and the pain of mutilation. Tears welled up in Rama's eyes as he saw the heap of bodies on the three still-burning pyres. He'd been too late to save them. Anantha and Akrita ran up from the distance, streaks of vomit on their bodies and clothes.

'Tell the men to strap their wounds with whatever they can find. Every useful weapon must be retrieved and distributed among the men, the women and the children who are old enough to use them. After that, we will perform what rites we can for the dead captives. They deserve that. Leave the soldiers to the animals. Go!' he instructed Akrita.

Anantha tore his eyes away from the carnage wreaked by Rama. 'More than five hundred soldiers! And you killed them all! Pity the man who stands against the Uddhatr.'

'The sentry alerted you I'd left the cave?'

'How did you know that?' Anantha was surprised.

'His signal, hooting like an owl was just wrong enough to easily distinguish it from genuine hooting. I guess it woke you up from your slumber. I counted five sentries on the trail from the shrine to the cave. The forest holds no secrets from me, Anantha.'

'The sentry saw you too late, else we would have caught up with you earlier.'

'Take all the captives to the sentry and ask him to lead them to the next one. Give them refuge in your forest strongholds. Tell the matriarch that I wish it so.'

Anantha nodded.

'Return soon. I mean to go to this congregation and meet the three kings of Tripura tomorrow.'

———

Rama, Akrita and Anantha watched from within the cover of the thicket as a great tumult of people gathered around the hundreds of tents and makeshift stalls selling farm and forest produce, trinkets, sweetmeats and wine, cloth and dyes and a variety of other items. Taverns and food houses were doing roaring business, as were pushcart vendors. Courtesans stood gaudily dressed before heavily draped and cavernous tents. Street artistes wandered about the crowd, playing their raucous tunes and berating passers-by to loosen their purse strings. Fortune-tellers squatted in the shade of awnings, and they certainly didn't lack customers! A long line of people stood at the lone entry gate, waiting to get in. The whole encampment was enclosed within a giant circular fence. The borders were being patrolled, and the entry was heavily guarded—all by men in black uniforms. Groups of soldiers wearing all three colours walked among the crowds inside the enclosure.

'Security is very heavy today. We have a poor chance to fulfil our oath,' said Anantha.

The night's slaughter had made the soldiers wary. Scouts had been sent to scour the forests and they, no doubt, found the trail of the freed captives. A few scouts had returned to muster reinforcements, but not a single soldier had been able to reach the captives. Rama had killed all those who had tried. The Malaya kshatriya sentries would take care of the captives on the trail.

'Where are the kings?' Rama asked.

'In their respective royal tents at the very centre of the enclosure. Around a giant statue of a man and a woman holding a plough. The emblem of Janamarga. This is their territory; it is their turn to host the congregation. The Janamargis decided to hold this fair here, near the town and the surrounding small hamlets, rather than in the capital, to show how concerned they are for the ordinary folk. It is all pomp and show, not real concern. There is a vast tent inside the enclosure, where the three kings and the administrators of each kingdom meet and confer. And entertain their guests and preach to the faithful and apportion the slaves to each creed. This will continue over the next four days. They make a big show of it, each of them proclaiming their superiority.'

'What are the three creeds?'

'Each creed is different from the other; their core beliefs stand in opposition to one another. Yet, they find common cause in one thing. Denying the Vedas and the Shrutis, denying our dharma and imposing what they call the 'true way'. Theirs is but a temporary alliance against the majority, who are followers of dharma, who are worked to the bone and cruelly exploited. However, members of these creeds are growing in numbers and once they become the majority, they will wipe the followers of dharma off the face of the earth. And then, they will begin a war with each other for supremacy. Whatever may be the lofty ideals they proclaim, there is only one thing they truly believe in. Violence ... against body and soul.

'The first creed is Janamarga, the path of the people. Their philosophy was first propagated by their leader, Vadin—The Teacher. Ages ago. The leader of this creed now assumes the title of Vadin in his honour. They claim all men are equal, but we know that is not so. They preach that those who have the ability, talent or intelligence above that of the average, owe their lives, and the fruits of their endeavours to the masses. From each according to ability, to each according to need, they claim. While it may sound noble, need has given way to greed. All the land, all the property belongs to the kingdom, no one can own anything in their own name. In other words, an elite group runs the kingdom with Vadin as the head. Elite among equals, rotten hypocrites! They live off the work of the masses, who toil like slaves and are all followers of dharma. Any revolt is crushed brutally, by the very ones who once called themselves revolutionaries. They now plan to spawn a class of so-called thinkers, philosophers, poets and dramatists who will take their message out of the confines of their kingdom. They do this to gain influence and prepare grounds for a surreptitious invasion later.

'The elite Janamargis teach that no god exists and all that the rishis do are tricks of legerdemain and illusion. By teaching so, they make themselves into gods that walk the earth, brutal and vindictive gods. Black is their colour. Those guards at the entry, clad in black, are Janamarga soldiers.

'The next is Prakashamarga, the path of light. Their soldiers wear white uniforms. They claim that there is only one God, theirs. He is Alipta, The Anointed, mortal son of the god Vallabha. They deny the Absolute Brahman and any of its forms, be it Mahadeva or Devi. They say all humans are born sinners. A woman is allowed devotion to their god but can hold no position of authority. Her husband is her master; she is his property. Salvation is possible only through Alipta, who died for the sins of all humans. No other way is possible. All of the Alipta's teachings are in a single grantha they call Satyaveda. They claim it contains all the wisdom in the world and every word is true, though I think it is full of stupid notions. Like the claim that the sun revolves around the earth. That anyone who doesn't forsake dharma and join their ranks is doomed to eternal fire, even the Janamargis.'

Rama stared at Anantha incredulously. 'People believe this nonsense?'

'More than you think. The prakashmargis are wolves that wear the masks of sheep, and very few people seek to see what's behind that mask. Most believe what they are shown, the mirage of "selfless service". It all happened because of Arjuna's tyranny that left many in desperate straits. The prakshmargis were there to help. They had only one condition. Deny the Vedas, dharma and our rituals and customs, and bring as many friends and family members into the fold.

'They malign and spit on the teachings of dharma. They brand our rituals as superstition and vile sorcery. That hasn't stopped them from stealing and adopting the same teachings and rituals as ours. They have merely changed the names.'

Akrita laughed out loud at the absurd hypocrisy. 'If they eat up rituals and practices they decry and understand little of, they'll end up getting a terrible bellyache and indigestion!'

'You said they deny Mahadeva and Devi. I've heard sanyasis devoted to Mahavishnu call him Vallabha in the ecstasy of their devotion. They are devotees of the Protector, then?' Rama asked.

'No Swami. They deny him too. Vallabha is the name written in their book, supposedly revealed by one of their earliest prophets. Their god has nothing to do with Hari or Hara,' said Anantha.

'And the third creed?' Rama asked.

'Shantimarga, the third creed, condemns all—Sanatana Dharma, Janamarga and Prakashamarga followers—to eternal fire. Only Shantimargis, it seems, can ascend to heaven. A place of ever-flowing wine, where ever-willing women craving coitus await them. That is their concept of salvation. They condemn Alipta as a mere messenger, one among many. Their head is called the Pratham and their colour is blue.

'There are two things that all three creeds indulge in with passion and glee. The destruction of temples and murthis. Not a single temple stands in these kingdoms, they forbid even the names of the Gods to be uttered.'

Anantha stopped his discourse, and the three were silent for a while.

'Why hasn't Arjuna put them to the sword?' Akrita was the first to speak.

'Tributes continue to reach him. The creeds are not powerful enough to deny him that, and Tripura is too small a kingdom for him to bother about. The three leaders understand that individually they don't stand a chance, and therefore, they must unite to grow and spread. Their bards already rove the surrounding kingdoms, spreading their message of intolerance and hate. The alliance is one of convenience. They seek to grow furtively until the samrat falls or his power weakens,' said Anantha.

'It is Arjuna's tyranny that has spawned them. His new social order, where one's entire life and endeavours are based on the varna of one's birth, has stifled society and has led to perverse creeds like these. It is fear of Arjuna that confines these adharmis here. Once Arjuna's power disappears, their dreams of worldwide dominance will take wings. They will run amok, grow in strength, and there will be no one to rein them in. Very dark times await humanity if that is allowed to happen. All it takes is for good men to do nothing for adharma to spread,' said Rama.

'Acharya, there must be good people among them too,' said Akritavrana.

'Without doubt. But all three creeds are absolutist, they will brook no one leaving their fold or questioning those in power. That would shake the very edifice of these creeds and show up their empty claims. Absolutism needs an unthinking populace and obedient foot soldiers to survive and grow,' said Anantha.

'Bad ideology always trumps good individuals. The great majority will toe the line drawn by their leaders, and will always blame others who don't believe in their claims, for anything that happens to them. But it's our duty to provide a way out to those who want to escape these creeds.'

'Let's go to the fair and see if we can talk to these kings,' Rama added.

'They will not allow you to enter with a weapon,' said Anantha.

'They cannot stop me with my weapon, but I want to see the congregation for myself. I will not unleash violence until then. How did your squads get in?'

'By stealth, in the wee hours of the night. It will be impossible now, with so much security after yesterday's slaughter. They will start also worrying about the missing search squads soon.'

'Go back to your trail sentry and send word to the matriarch to call off the attempt on the lives of the three men by the quintet at this time. I feel there's going to be trouble soon; these men will not take kindly to good counsel. But I must see for myself.'

Anantha nodded with reluctance.

'One more thing,' and Rama whispered something in Anantha's ears, who looked at him in surprise.

'Courage is destiny,' he whispered again and slipped away. Rama plunged his axe into a boulder behind him. The boulder didn't shatter, it accepted the Parashu. The blades disappeared into it till only the handle could be seen sticking out. It looked as if the rock had grown around the axe and imprisoned the axe within itself.

Rama and Akrita joined the long line of people making their way to the site of the fair. The sentries were vigilant, checking every person, sack and cart. Rama made himself as conspicuous as he could, trying to get ahead quickly and loudly, berating the slow movement of the line and creating a ruckus. A sentry pointed at him when they were still quite a distance from the entry. His dirty dhoti and blood-stained body was causing much interest. Six soldiers approached them and asked them to step aside. They were marched between a tight ring of soldiers to the lone tent beside the entry gate. They were presented to an officer seated behind a wooden desk.

'Who are you?' the officer asked.

'That doesn't matter. I created all that noise to get noticed and to get here fast. I come with information about last night,' said Rama. A sudden ripple of tension raced through the tent. The soldiers unsheathed their swords.

'What about last night?' the officer barked.

'You already know what, but I know who, why and how. But that is not for your ears and certainly not for theirs.'

'We will make you talk. There are ways to make anyone talk.'

'There are easier ways to lose rank. Would you like to be digging toilet pits for them? Or cleaning the stables?'

The officer stared back, confused, angry and distrusting. Rama leaned forward slowly and whispered, 'Tell the general that his man among the Shantimargis has come with a report. He will be upset that you know my identity now, but he will be very pleased to hear what I have to say. Possible promotion for you in it.'

'Which general?' asked the officer, not believing Rama.

'If you don't know that, then you must be very low in the pecking order. Find someone who knows or take me inside, I'll find him myself. But I will never tell you what I know;

you do not have that privilege. I hope the general doesn't find out that you threatened to torture me,' Rama said as he moved to the end of the tent opposite the desk, the soldiers reluctantly parting to give way. He squatted on the floor and closed his eyes.

'Be quick,' he said dismissively as Akrita sat beside him.

It was at least three muhurtas before the officer returned. Rama heard the stomp of military boots enter the tent. Four more soldiers, he guessed and opened his eyes. The officer stood red-faced and angry, and behaved obsequiously towards the thickset and heavily muscled man beside him. This man had better armour and more decoration on his uniform. The three soldiers with him looked like his personal guards.

'As I said, you must be pretty low in the pecking order to take so long to get someone,' said Rama. The officer's face turned purple with rage.

'That's him,' he said to the thickset man, pointing to Rama.

'That's not him,' said Rama to the officer, ignoring everyone else. 'This is not the general, I mean.'

The thickset man gestured to the soldiers standing around, and Rama was hoisted up onto his feet. A soldier held his arms tightly behind him and the other placed the edge of his sword on Rama's throat.

'Talk or die,' the thickset man said.

Rama kept his eyes on the man. 'Your search squads haven't returned, have they? They won't. They are all dead. I will tell you where their bodies lie. You can verify my information and then take me to the general.'

Rama told them about the locations. Orders were sent out. The thickset man gestured again, and Rama's feet were kicked out from under him. He crashed to the ground. But he dusted himself off and grinned at the soldiers standing before him.

It was well past noon when a soldier darted into the tent and whispered in the ear of the man behind the desk. The man's face flushed, and a vein started throbbing on his forehead. He turned angrily towards Rama, who looked back at him nonchalantly.

'Let me guess, your soldiers have been beheaded.'

The man startled out of his seat, suspicion dancing in his eyes.

Anantha's first task was complete, thought Rama. 'It's about time we introduced ourselves,' he said.

'I'm Suketu,' the thickset man said at last.

Rama grinned, and Akrita hid his smile behind his hands. 'Ketu, the headless one,' Akrita whispered, loud enough for all to hear.

'Enough!' Suketu roared and punched the desk.

'Apologies for my assistant,' said Rama. 'Sometimes he is a tear looking for a cheek to run down, sometimes a shiver looking for a spine to run up. But always ready with a wisecrack.

'But this matter is serious. We have long watched the Shantimargis; we know they yearn to overthrow us. I think they use this fair to finally move against the Vadin. Please take me to the general quickly. There is no time to waste.

'Look at me,' he added 'The blood on me is of our soldiers. Did your fellow men die in vain? I know exactly who did this. The answer will surprise you. I beg you again. Hurry, who knows what else may happen today.'

'What is your name?' Suketu asked.

Rama's grin was broad. 'I am Shiva.'

Suketu stared at him for a long moment and then, exited the tent with his soldiers. The officer stayed back, still red-faced, eyes darting from Rama to Akrita.

'Are you Rahu then?' Akrita asked. The officer stared stonily as Akrita doubled up with laughter.

The general walked into the tent with his squad of guards and a plainly dressed assistant carrying a bunch of scrolls. Rama observed the general—a full head of grey hair and a beard to match, shining grey armour and a ramrod-straight spine. He turned his attention to his assistant, examining his hands, his eyes, the cut and fabric of his clothes and his shoes.

'I've never seen you in my life,' said the general.

'Neither have I seen you,' Rama retorted, and then turned to speak to the assistant. 'Salutations to the spymaster.'

The assistant and Rama stared at each other. Finally, the assistant nodded, and Rama knew he had deduced correctly and played the game right. Tyrants never allow their army officers to spy for them or to even handle spies for them. It is too risky to hand so much power to a general who already commands armed men. The spymaster is always someone close to the leader. A close relative even, someone over whom the leader had absolute control. Every soldier and officer except Suketu exited the tent.

'I'm Upananda,' said the spymaster as he set the scrolls down on the desk. 'Who are you, Shiva?'

'A man who seeks to give information and hopes to gain a reward.'

'Where are you from?'

'Medi,' said Rama. He had heard Ananta speak of it while lying in wait for the scouting parties.

'The capital of the Shantimargis! What work do you do?'

Rama grinned sheepishly. 'I'm sort of a tax collector.'

Upananda raised an eyebrow.

'Some people carry heavy burdens, especially in their

purses. I ease their burden and collect a small sum for my trouble,' Rama deadpanned.

Upananda glanced at Akrita.

'My apprentice. He spots the overburdened poor souls and helps me collect tax without hindrance. He's learning the trade very nicely.'

'We do such a pious task and yet, people malign us as scofflaws and cut-purses. Imagine that!' said Akrita. 'What has the world come to?'

'Why are you here then?' Upananda asked.

'The fair. People come here to ease their burdens, and we do all we can to relieve them. But now I expect a big reward for all the information I will give you as well as a recompense for the time we've lost.'

'The man claims to be a cut-purse but is built like a warrior. Both of you wear janeus. Never heard of a brahmin cut-purse before.'

'Precisely why! It is the most effective disguise.'

'You could've killed them for all I know. There is blood all over you,' said Upananda.

'If that were true, would I just walk in here, unarmed, and hand myself over to you? I was trying to save lives, Upananda. But...'

'Tell us what you know, or I will torture you myself and you don't want that to happen. You will beg for death, but I will keep you alive just to enjoy your pain. You have already hinted at the Shantimargis, what more information do I need?'

'The Shantimargis didn't do this. That was a ruse to get you here. Only Janamargi soldiers were beheaded; the other corpses were left untouched.'

Upananda nodded.

'It was an attempt to cast suspicion on the Shantimargis. Actually, a Malaya kshatriya called Anantha beheaded them.'

'So, the Malaya kshatriyas killed the soldiers and the scouts?'

'They were all killed by one man. Only one.'

'Impossible!' said Upananda.

'He's in this congregation now, spymaster. I saw the killing with my own eyes. I scoured the Valley of the Dead for a living soldier, but I couldn't find any. He killed them all.'

'If this is your information, then you clearly don't value either your life or your assistant's,' said Upananda.

'I was right about the scouts; I was right about the beheadings. Why would I lie about this? I will tell you one more thing you might have already guessed. Your captives have been taken to the secret Malaya kshatriya strongholds in the forest. Am I right?'

Upananda nodded again. 'So, this man who killed all the soldiers, is he a part of the Malaya kshatriya squad, or has he been hired by them?'

'I'm not sure, Sire. I've told you all I know, and I am ready to identify the man. I'm at your service.'

'Why come to me at all? You know we hate your kind, idolators, and brahmins at that.'

'In the hope of a reward. Money knows no varna and no creed. Artha is the greatest creed. It lies above and below all else. Am I right?' said Rama.

Upananda didn't reply.

'I'm passing through, on my way to meet Samrat Arjuna and pay my respects. Perhaps a little something from you can make the journey easier and faster.'

Upananda considered him carefully.

'What does this man look like?'

Rama described Anantha to Upananda.

'What do you think of this whole thing, Shiva?' asked Upananda.

'Well ... beheading is what the Shantimargis do—so I've been told. Perhaps, he was hired by them.'

'But they lost soldiers too.'

'That's all a part of their plan. A few soldiers lost will strengthen their deniability. And if that man is ever caught, they can always wash their hands off him. If he dies, no one is the wiser and if he succeeds, they win.'

'First, you said the Shantimargis did it, then you said that they didn't. Then, you said a Malaya kshatriya beheaded them, but that they were killed by only one man. Now we are back to the Shantimargis. You inch closer to torture, the more you speak.'

Rama paused for a while and then asked, 'Was the beheading the only thing that was peculiar?'

Upananda gestured at Suketu who ran to convey orders. A soldier rushed back into the silence sooner than anyone expected. 'Pardon me, sire but the bodies ... they are all marked on their thighs. The mark is that of the Prakashamargis.'

Anantha had done his second job well too.

18

No God, Dead God, False God

They stood before the corpses of Janamarga's soldiers. Necks without heads and the Prakashamarga symbol etched on their left thighs with a sharp implement. Suspicion burned in Upananda's eyes as he glared at Rama.

'How did you know?'

'I didn't. I suspected. This is a deep, deep game Upananda. Did the Shantimargis do it to cast blame on the Prakashamargis, or is it the other way around?' said Rama.

'Or is it all the doing of Malaya kshatriyas and are you their agent, seeking to play the three kingdoms against each other?' Upananda glanced at Suketu, and the sword was back at Rama's throat in a blink.

'Would I walk in here with such a fantastic story? You have discovered so much since I came to you, yet you suspect me. The perils of the spy game ... one doubts one's own shadow. I've said all that I know. Don't blame me if that man murders one of your leaders, God forbid, it be the Vadin. One man killed them all. I swear it. Will you be able to stop him if he goes after your leader?

'Torture us or kill us later ... if we cannot find this man for you. But reward us richly if we do. What do you say?'

It was a long moment before Upananda said anything. 'Take them around the fair, guard them well. If he can't find the man by dusk, behead them both at the Ring of Reason and Faith.'

Rama made a big show of peering intently at every passer-by as he trudged along with a dozen soldiers surrounding him. Suketu watched them like a hawk. They circled around the fair twice—Rama glancing at the gigantic circular tent in the midst of the three royal pavilions whenever he could. A great deal of noise was coming from inside it, and it was guarded like a fortress.

'Why the charade? You could've easily fought your way in here?' Akrita whispered.

'Yes. Very easily. But I want to give them every chance. Best to win the minds of people, to change them for good. It will prevent more such creeds from cropping up. And, as you said, there are good people in the creeds. Let's give them a chance to see what's wrong with their beliefs,' Rama muttered.

When they had finished the second round and arrived back where they had started, Rama asked, 'Is that tent the Ring of Reason and Faith?'

Suketu nodded.

'What if the man is already in there?'

'Impossible. The teachers of the creeds, select faithful, and the slaves to be allotted their respective creeds are the only ones inside. No one can carry weapons here except the guards.'

'Your kings are in there, aren't they? That's why you don't want to take me there. A dozen soldiers against two unarmed men and yet you are wary of us.'

Suketu didn't answer.

'What if he is disguised as a slave or as one of the faithful? If he's strong enough, he can snap a neck in an instant. Worse, what if he's disguised as a soldier?'

Suketu sighed and led them to the tent. 'This phantom of yours better be in there, Shiva. The day draws to a close. Death waits to devour you at dusk.'

Akrita opened his eyes big and wide. 'A soldier and a poet. Surprises never cease.'

The din grew as they neared the tent. Sentry guards saluted smartly and allowed the group to pass. The noise came from the full-throated cheers and hurrahs of the faithful. A man clad in white was on the dais at the centre of the stage, whipping up the devotees into a religious frenzy as he called upon Alipta to bless the sinners. Captives were corralled in a ring between the circular dais and the huge number of faithful seated around it. Rama paused, listening to what the man was preaching, his mind thinking ahead.

'Are the kings on the dais?' he asked.

Suketu nodded.

'Too many people, Suketu. They are all seated in circles around the dais, not in straight lines. It's easy to miss the faces. I need to draw him out. I need a distraction.' He walked towards the dais. 'Buy me some time; check if the man is amongst your soldiers. One thing I forgot to mention. The man's weapon, it's an axe. Not an ordinary woodcutter's axe. It's a deadly weapon, you can't mistake it.'

Rama fixed his eyes on the people on the dais as he walked down the aisle leading up to it. A dozen people were on it, some in black, some in blue, and the rest in white. All three creeds—no, not creeds, cults—were putting on a show and revelling in it.

'Sinners we are all, seeking forgiveness,' the man in the white raised his hands skywards.

'Sinners! Sinners!' his flock of faithful cried. Some rolled and twisted on the ground, their faces contorted into weird grimaces.

'Wash your sins in the pure blood of the Alipta. Sit not in judgement, sinners we are all. Let he who has not sinned be the first to cast a stone in judgement.' The Prakashamarga preacher's plea was impassioned.

Akrita seized the chance. He scrambled around, found a small pebble and threw it at the man. It hit him straight on the face. The man reeled in shock and went quiet. It took a few nimishas for his followers to realise that he was standing with his mouth agape in surprise.

'I'm not a sinner, Bhrata,' said Akrita loudly.

'I'm a Pitah,' the man screamed in outrage.

'Not mine.' said Akrita.

'Sinner! How dare you?!' someone in the crowd cried.

Rama paused as Akrita strode up on the dais.

'I'm not given to sloth. I work hard to gain knowledge and I respect my gurus. Nor do I have pride in what I know, I seek to learn more, as a true Sanatani should.'

The flock and Pitah gasped.

'I do not succumb to lust, envy or wrath. I remain centred on my aim, which is to know the truth and gain moksha. I live the life of a renunciate. My food is sparse and satvic, that means I don't indulge in gluttony either. So, tell me, teach me, how am I a sinner?'

'You were born one, fool. To consider oneself pure, is the sin of pride. It is high conceit. Only the Alipta is pure,' retorted the Pitah.

'Look who speaks,' the Pitah turned to the congregation. 'A sanatani, and a brahmin at that. The worst of the lot!'

'Sinner! Sinner!' the flock chanted. Derisive laughter erupted in the crowd.

Rama saw a quick signal pass from Suketu to the black guards. They held back from interfering. The guards of the other creeds noticed this too, as they stood around in confusion. Their officers rushed to confer with Suketu. They dispersed in a bit and Rama saw them inspect their respective guards. Rama watched the dais closely—all this activity would be noted; he waited to see who would signal to find out what was happening. An austere, simply dressed man gestured from the dais and Suketu ran quickly to him and whispered something to him. The man dismissed Suketu with a small wave of his hand. Rama had found the Vadin.

'My sin was born when I was?' asked Akrita.

'It was born when your parents lay together and their parents before them, back all the way to the first man and woman. Anything born of human flesh is sinful,' said the Pitah.

'Hmm ... and the soul?'

'You have only one life, sinner, to cleanse your soul of sin. It is possible only by devotion to the Alipta—only he can save you. Accept him into your heart, forsake these heathen gods, and gain paradise. Else burn in eternal fire. Come, this is the perfect opportunity, join the fold and deny the superstition you call your faith.'

The flock in front of the Pitah chanted, 'Heaven is mine! Heaven is mine!' The Janamargis and Shantimargis booed.

'Else, your fate is to be a slave and serve the faithful.'

'What god condemns everyone to sin? Is such a being a god?' Akrita's voice was loud. The crowd gasped again. Angry mutters erupted. Rama saw Suketu restrain a Prakashamargi officer from moving to evict Akrita. A heated argument erupted between them with fingers being pointed at Akrita and Rama. Rama pretended to be scrutinising the crowd keenly.

'Listen,' Akrita continued. 'Maybe this neck of woods hasn't seen a rishi or a vedantin in a long time and has remained bereft of the light of knowledge and wisdom. I will tell you what little I know.'

'A worshipper of many will teach us about the One?' the Pitah mocked. 'I doubt this creature even has a soul. Who let you on this dais, slave?'

The faithful laughed. A great cheer rung around the tent as a bearded man, clad in a flowing blue robe, stood suddenly.

'Hail the Pratham!' A section of the crowd screamed raucously, beating their chests, drowning out the chants of the Prakashamargis.

'Idolator!' the Pratham screamed pointing at Akrita. 'The very scum of the earth. Heathens who pray to lifeless stone statues. So many have we crushed, have we not?' The crowd flared up in wild jubilation.

'Their women,' the Pratham said, pointing at the female slaves. 'They walk beside their men, sometimes ahead, clad as they please, displaying their impurity and sinful form to the world. Look at the piety of our women, true followers of

Vallabha, who cover themselves from head to toe and thank Vallabha for the opportunity to serve their men.'

'Shame! Shame!' the cries were mocking. The loudest jeers came from the Shantimargi women.

'This wretch will teach us truth and wisdom!' exclaimed the Pratham.

Derisive laughter and applause greeted these words. Even the soldiers started to enjoy what was happening on the dais, many joining in the applause.

Akrita laughed back. He threw his mirth at the crowd, stunning them into silence with his audacity before this horde of believers.

'Listen sinners and deniers of god!' His voice was loud in the silence.

'To get a human life is a rare thing. Your soul has lived through millions of lives before it got the chance to be human. You neither live, only once nor die only once. It has taken many reincarnations for each of us humans to get here. Do not waste this chance! Do not forget its value!

'As a human, Paramatma has given you the power to choose between good and bad. Never should you think of yourselves as weak, as fallen, as sinners. To do so is a denial of Paramatma's blessing. To do so is the actual sin. If you didn't know this before, then learn now, do not be misled. Learn from the rishis and the Vedas and reach the Paramatma. Do not heed these creeds and throw away a diamond for a handful of dust.

'Self-denigration and meekness are not behaviours worthy of a human. These can be moral only for those who exist as slaves—not for those who live freely. Stand proud, stand tall and proudly claim that a spark of the divine rests in you.

'That spark is your soul, your Atma. It and the Paramatma are the same—the Atma a drop, the Paramatma an ocean. To merge the drop with the ocean is your life's purpose.

'That divine spark exists in everything, animate and inanimate. It lies dormant in stone, rock, metal and mineral. It is awake in plants and trees, in beings smaller than the eye can see. It walks in animals, big and small, of the earth, water and sky. And in humans, it thinks!

'From the field of feelings, experiences and good and bad thoughts, the rice of principle is harvested by the scythe of reason. This rice threshed with healthy debate gives birth to morality. Morality cooked with good sense gives philosophy, the food of the soul. The base of all this is intelligence. The supreme intelligence is Paramatma. This is what the Vedas teach us. Prajnanam Brahma!'

The Pratham moved forward to stop Akrita from speaking.

'The Paramatma is formless,' said Akrita. The Pratham paused, confused whether Akrita was refuting him or agreeing with him.

'That much the two creeds grasp. But that's where it stops. To really see the formless is extremely hard, even for a rishi,' Akrita continued. 'It isn't possible for the likes of you, who carp about our murthis all the time. A murthi is necessary for an ordinary devotee starting his spiritual journey. A picture is worth a thousand words, and a murthi a hundred million.'

'Enough,' said the Pratham. 'This is blasphemy!'

'There!' Rama suddenly screamed, and Suketu and his soldiers whirled. 'Continue,' he ordered Akrita. 'Do not stop this man until we've caught the assassin,' he screamed at the soldiers as he ran towards groups of people entering and exiting the tent. A dozen soldiers of each creed ran to catch up with him. The crowd turned towards them, distracted.

'Listen!' Akrita's voice was loud again. He waited till Rama and the soldiers had reached the mouth of the tent and the crowd had turned back to the dais.

'The spark of divinity in me creates the murthis of the Supreme Divinity. The divine in me sees God, godliness, feels bhakti and love, and performs worship. You, who consider yourselves sinners, see only clay, metal, stone and wood. At best, you may begrudgingly see some beauty. You do not see how the murthi aids in contemplation and helps turn the gaze inward. A murthi urges one through different forms to recognise the divinity within oneself. And in gratitude, we celebrate festivities, to spread joy and reverence in family and community.

'As one progresses, one discards form and finds the formless. No murthi, no scripture is needed then. The great rishis say it is then that you realise that what you were worshiping was your self. Ayam Atma Brahman. The self is Brahman.

'You are only an actor playing a part in the story of your life. Your soul watches. When the actor dies, a chapter ends and so it goes on. When you finally realise that you aren't an actor but the author of the story, the story ends, and you gain moksha.

'Paramatma can take any form it desires—male or female. But you malign the feminine, call it lesser and impure. A religion or spiritual philosophy without a sacred feminine, a goddess, is halfway to atheism. Akin to the dead, mirthless world of the Janamargis. You do not see that a man and a woman complement each other, rather you subjugate women, despise them as traps of temptation and cradles of sin.

'What a curse it is to have to love one's mother despite

her inferiority—a woman who is your father's slave. To love your wife knowing her to be lesser and to beget your children from an impure vessel. Yet, this is what the Prakashamargis and Shantimargis teach. It is the most depraved teaching I've ever heard.

'You who destroy our temples, decry our murthis as superstition and blind belief, do not realise that these physical murthis have saved us from the blind and mean superstitions that afflict all of you. True idolatry is saying—that only the name you give god is true and only your way of worship is right. The violence and grief this blind belief has caused is the gravest sin, a sin no god will forgive. You are the true blind idolators!'

Rama rushed back into the tent, the soldiers close on his heels. 'I saw him. If he's not outside, he must be still here. Fan out and find him before he strikes.'

The Pratham and the Pitah watched, unsure of whether to stop Akrita or to wait for the soldiers to finish this search. Akrita didn't wait.

'You look for a god to wash your sins, to ease your screaming conscience. Such a deity will only be a master to be fearful of. Never a friend, a companion, a parent or even a child to the devotee. A god renders justice, upholds dharma and does not wipe away your crimes because you confess. Or force, bribe, or scare others to accept your creed.

'All this talk of sin will breed two monsters from who you will never be able to escape. They will perch on your shoulders and gnaw away at your mind and soul. The monsters of guilt and repentance. You will wallow in one and make a great show of the second. On these two demons will rest your piety.

'You glimpse the truth, I accept that much. But your

teachings are but candles before the glorious sun that are the Vedas and Upanishads. They reveal the eternal truth, the Sanatana. They uphold dharma. Hence, it is called the Sanatana Dharma. Yet, you see not even the light of your own candles but gaze with fear at the shadows they cast. The shadows of sin. You struggle in vain to bury the shadows when you should seek to expand the light. As a result, you will always create an "other" to blame. You will always paint the "other" as a false villain and yourself as a false victim. The "other" will always be someone who doesn't follow your creed. You will signal virtue while throwing the blame of your vice on the "other" and calling them sinful.

'To claim that the blood of Alipta will cleanse you of sin, is not the teaching of a saint. It is the raving of a madman. Drop the delusion, pierce the veil of avidya. Bask in the brilliant sunshine of the Vedas.

'The Janamargis though, don't even have a candle. Their ideology is stillborn. They transform humans into blood-sucking leeches, living off the efforts of others. This path is fated to collapse, try as they might to delay it. It will give you a dreary, miserable life with no spiritual upliftment at all. Their leaders are worms who live in the dark because sunlight would burn their very existence away.

'The only way the three creeds can survive is through brutal violence and lies, to justify, deny or cover up the misery they cause. The more they spread, the more Valleys of the Dead will emerge. A philosophy that can spread only through violence is not a philosophy at all. It is politics and a play for power.

'Listen followers of Janamarga, Prakashamarga and Shantimarga—the creeds of no god, of a dead god and of a false god. Listen also, those of you with poor intellect, who think these creeds too can lead you to moksha, know that the Vedas deny them sanctity. When the concept of the divine itself is so wrong, no heaven can be won. You will only regress a thousand lives in your spiritual progress.

'And Sanatanis who accept only one form of God and deride all other forms, those who say that only one—Vishnu or Shiva—are superior, what can I say to such fools? The sun shines bright, but the cataracts in your eyes let in only a glimmer. To worship your beloved form, your ishta-devata is one thing, to deny others theirs is prejudice. That's no better than being a part of these cults. You create division where none should exist. Fie on you!

'And Arjuna, who spawns a cult of his own, who ossifies caste through paternity, is less of a samrat and more of a scoundrel. Him and these three cults, seek to imbue the Paramatma with their own likes and dislikes, whims and fancies. They seek to capture your mind, heart and body, but forget about your soul. But the atma knows the truth, and surely your conscience pricks your mind with strange, uncomfortable questions. Heed them! Do not allow ideology to come between you and the divine.

'Cast aside adharma, return to dharma, your one and only true home.'

Akrita paused a moment and proclaimed loud and clear, 'Sanatana Dharma Sarvottama!'

Silence reigned for a nimisha and then pandemonium broke out in the tent. The followers of the creeds screamed in anger. The captives roared with approval. The faithful pelted Akrita with anything that came to hand. He stood unflinching.

The Vadin's face was mottled with rage. He turned to confer with a clean-shaven old man clad in white, who in turn beckoned the Pitah to him. Rama watched the scene unfold. He had found the Parampitamaha. The three kings of Tripura were all on the dais and now known to him. Soldiers moved to quieten the captives, whipping them at will. The Pratham urged everyone to calm down as the Parampitamaha stood, raising his hands, asking for quiet. The crowd gradually settled down.

'Blasphemy!' he cried. 'Profane words have been spoken here. There is only one punishment.'

'Death! Death! Death!' the crowd screamed.

The Pratham roared. 'I will spit on their murthis, break them and trample upon them. I call upon the faithful to kill heathens wherever they find them.'

'Death! Death! Death!' the chant reverberated through the tent. Torches were lit, spewing copious fumes of black, blue and white. They hung in the air like a shroud.

Finally, the Vadin spoke in a thin, raspy voice. 'Men like these are the oppressors. They will never change. The only solution is to wipe them off the face of the earth.'

'Death! Death! Death!' the crowd repeated.

'Yes, death. But before that, the greatest pain his body can endure and we have people who will make sure he endures for a long time,' said the Parampitamaha. The crowd cheered. 'He will beg for the Redeemer's mercy, beg to be made a true follower, but we will not grant him that relief. When the Redeemer comes again as he once did when he rose from the dead, this man will roast before him for eternity.'

The crowd roared in approval, their frenzy at a fever pitch. The Parampitamaha quietened them again. Before he could say anything more, Akrita said, 'The Redeemer? Why, there he stands!' He pointed at Rama, and the crowd hushed into complete silence.

'You die now, Shiva,' murmured Suketu to Rama.

'The man who brought a dead leper—me—back to life. He accepted me as his shishya, won the blessings of Mahadeva and slew the asuras. My guru, the Redeemer.'

'I found him,' Rama said to Suketu.

'Where?' Suketu's eyes darted around. Rama strode towards the dais, with Suketu following. Signals were being passed around furiously; all the soldiers drew out their weapons. Rama leapt onto the dais.

'The man who killed all those soldiers last night is here,' he spoke loud and clear, his right hand outstretched. 'Hear me, sinners. His name is Renukaputra Ramabhadra.'

The Parashu tore through the sides of the tent and settled in Rama's hands.

'Parashurama!' Akrita announced.

'You!' Suketu screamed.

'Me,' Rama replied. He fixed his raptor-like gaze on the crowd, 'You asked for death. You shall have it. I have seen enough. There will be no compromise with adharma.'

Suketu leapt for Rama with his sword drawn. Rama beheaded him mid-leap. He turned and cleaved the Vadin in two, from where the neck met the shoulder, down to his loins. Blood burst out of the great rent, arteries spewing blood as the heart continued to beat. The two halves of the body fell away from each other, but even before they could hit the ground, Rama had whirled with the stroke of the axe. He used the momentum to crash the axe across the Pratham's neck, beheading him. The head arced across and above the captives and landed in the crowd. Everyone froze in shock for a nimisha. The Parampitamaha stood still in a pool of his own urine. The guards recovered and attacked. Akrita moved out of the way as Rama waded into the soldiers.

The assault was brutal and lasted a few nimishas. The corpses of the soldiers littered the dais. The hordes of followers and the faithful screamed and scattered in all directions, pushing and tearing at each other and the remaining soldiers. They tore open the sides of the tent made of cloth and ran for their lives.

'Send riders to the army encampments,' someone screamed. Rama turned to the voice; it was Upananda. His scream had jolted the Parampitamaha out of his immobility. He backed away. Rama caught the movement out of the corner of his eye. He turned towards the man, his axe coming up overhead.

'Mercy!' the Parampitamaha wailed as he went down on his knees. 'Ahimsa paramo dharma! Your own scripture says this. I beg for mercy.'

'The very scripture you deny? Every time you abuse the tolerance of ahimsa and mock it as a weakness, himsa whets its blade sharper. When the blade cuts, wretches beg for mercy in the name of ahimsa. I've walked the Valley of the Dead. A man who sanctioned that deserves no mercy. Die on your knees like the knave you are.' Rama shoved his axe into the man's skull.

Akrita threw the weapons of the dead soldiers to the captives, some of whom rushed to help him. The soldiers closed ranks according to their creed as more of them rushed in from outside. Rama attacked the Shantimarga soldiers, tearing through them, showing no mercy.

'Get the captives out, all the way to the jungle. Kill any soldier who stands in the way,' said Rama as he faced the remaining two formations. The captives led by Akrita streamed out of the tent, but the soldiers didn't move. They had seen what had happened just nimishas before. They knew they faced certain death. Upananda screamed at them to attack. The soldiers held formation, praying, waiting for reinforcements to arrive. But Rama didn't wait and hacked through them.

The mass of captives rushed towards the gate. The vendors and fortune-tellers had all scattered in the dusk when the faithful had rushed out. Fires had bloomed, and some tents were ablaze. The rampaging mob cut any soldier they came across or simply trampled on them in their headlong rush. Stands of produce and wares were knocked over, tents torn apart and carts upturned. They neared the gate but suddenly stopped, the front line falling as the people in the line behind crashed into them. They slowly regained their foothold and stared nervously. Heavily armed soldiers of all creeds stood at the gate, weapons ready, and they easily outnumbered the captives. Rama was back at the tent, and they knew they were no match for the soldiers.

'Look!' said Akrita, pointing towards the thicket. A torch shone through the rapidly growing dark. Suddenly, hundreds of torches could be seen shining all along the treeline of the jungle around the congregation.

Out of the jungle, the Malaya kshatriyas charged, men and women both, armed with swords and lances, screaming 'Courage is destiny!'

19

Rahasya

It was a day later. Dusk had turned to night as Rama stood with Akrita, Anantha and Bhargavi beside the flowering rudrapushpa shrub that marked the entrance of the sacred Naga grove and Bhadrakali shrine. The torches held by Anantha and the priestess threw little light and a lot of shadows.

'The captives camp with our soldiers half a yojana away, Swami. They will find new homes in our strongholds if they so desire. Else they can return to their homes once we have cleansed Tripura of its scourge. We have exterminated all the soldiers of the three cults at the fair. The kingdoms will fall soon.'

'It's good that you arrived in the nick of time,' said Akrita.

'The priestess insisted on a full-fledged attack. The warriors had all gathered to honour the quintet before their mission, and were already accompanying them part of the way. So, when I told the priestess all that had happened, she sent all of us to the congregation.'

Bhargavi smiled. 'I followed the Uddhatr's orders. I didn't send the quintet just as he had ordered. I sent the entire army.'

Rama smiled.

'We waited to see what we could do. When we saw the Adbhuta, the Parashu fly towards the enclosure, we knew something was up. Then the captives came rushing out, and we knew that this was the moment to act. In any case, there wasn't much to do since he single-handedly finished most of them,' said Bhargavi.

'So, who do you propose as the new king of Tripura?' Akrita asked.

'Someone from the old dynasty. Someone rooted in dharma. We will not rule here; this is not our final destination. We will settle where Swami says we should,' said Anantha.

'There will be time for that later, Anantha. For now, I need answers. Destroying the creeds is one part of why I arrived here. Meeting the Malaya kshatriyas—another. This shrine, I'm convinced, holds some answers. I must find them,' said Rama.

'But now? At night? Even we, Naga worshippers, never set foot inside the sacred grove after dusk,' said Bhargavi. She looked at the night sky. 'It is pournami today. The full moon is in Ashlesha—the watery constellation of the Nagas. I have done special pujas at dawn on such days. It is a time when the spiritual powers of the Nagas are at the zenith. The moon will soon cross into the fiery constellation of Magha.

'It is a time of gandantha—transition between water and fire—a time of karmic knots, of secrets that have a profound impact on our lives. It is a dangerous time to irk the Nagas. Wait till tomorrow morning. Why hurry? You've come back from an intense battle, take some rest.'

'It is some sense of unease that urges me to make haste. I've felt it for a couple of days now and feel it inside me as we speak.

It feels like Arjuna is aware of me. He feels like a malevolent, invisible eye in the sky. Something of great consequence is afoot; my instincts are screaming at me to go. I'm afraid I must enter the grove tonight, to find what I can.'

'As the Uddhatr wishes, may Bhadrakali keep you safe,' said Bhargavi as she and Anantha took their leave. Akrita borrowed Anantha's torch and followed Rama into the grove.

Eerie silence met them as they trod the narrow trail into the grove. The soft, moist ground ate up the sound of their footsteps. Rama walked slowly, trying to discern the twisting trail in the heavy darkness. The foliage closed overhead creating a living tomb, blocking out the light of the moon. The torch fought a losing battle against shadow and night.

'Acharya, wait,' Akrita whispered. They paused, and Akrita turned to shine the weak light on the path they had walked on. The trail died out a couple of paces behind them. It had disappeared into a wall of shrubs and undergrowth that hadn't existed when they had passed the spot a nimisha ago. 'The grove closes behind us. There is no way out.'

'Something meant only for our eyes and ears will happen here tonight. Let's move ahead on the only path we have,' said Rama. They walked in silence for a long time.

'The path is not as I remember it, Acharya. And it is a lot longer. It twists and turns a lot too,' Akrita whispered.

Soon, the first figurines of the Nagas appeared, lining both sides of the path. The number of figurines increased as they walked ahead. Whisper soft rustles followed them and a little while later they could also hear them coming from both sides of the path. Inarticulate, sibilant sounds rose around them. There was dead silence except for these rustles and sounds. Akrita shivered.

'I'm scared to look back, Acharya.'

'Keep your eyes ahead and don't stop,' said Rama.

The path twisted and turned for an eternity, for far longer than they had remembered. The sizes of the figurines kept increasing, many as tall as Rama, some far taller. Slithering sounds in the surrounding dark grew louder. It sounded as if a tremendous weight was being moved upon the soft earth, roots and fallen leaves. They turned one more twist in the trail, and the light of the lone lamp in front of the shrines shone before them. It blazed furiously, lighting up the deep purples, greens, reds and yellows of the Nagamandala that was drawn on the flat, hard granite surface of the shrine floor. It was intricate, with outlines of a snake drawn in white, weaving in and out of the brilliant colours, twisting and turning a hundred times, forming the sacred geometry of the mandala. Rama stood before it, examining it with care. Akrita stood close behind him. Realisation dawned on Rama. The twisting path they had just travelled on for what seemed like an eternity, exactly matched the outline of the serpent in the mandala.

Suddenly, some figures emerged from the darkness. Hundreds of them, of all sizes and colours, their scales glittering in the furious light of the lamp. Sibilant hisses filled the air, their bodies curling as they raised their heads and fanned their hoods out. The Nagas had come to their grove.

Some had three heads, some five and some seven. They gathered around the mandala, a few with heads as tall as Rama. They swayed gently as they waited, watching the two mortals with eyes that made Akrita's blood run cold. Rama stood still, unsure of what he was supposed to do. He prayed.

'*Bhagawati rakshaam dehi,*

Rakshaam bhagawati dehi.'

He sat down in padmasana and closed his eyes. He heard Akrita sit down behind him and whisper prayers for protection. Rama entered dhyana. He called out in his trance to the god who had given him the banalinga, sent him messages in his dreams. Guru Dattatreya.

Mahadeva had blessed him with a weapon; Devi with protection and aid. He beseeched the guru for answers, to help him understand. Rama sat in dhyana for a long time, till suddenly, he felt the Parashu vibrate in his lap. He opened his eyes into a blue mist and stared straight into the eyes of an iridescent cobra. The width of his twelve hoods was the same as the breadth of the mandala. Rama gazed wide-eyed without blinking, mesmerised with the naga's eyes. They were kaleidoscopic. The colours and patterns danced and transformed hypnotically. The cobra drew closer to Rama, the forked tongues flicking through the air around Rama's face, and slowly withdrew. The retinas of the eyes on each head contracted in a blink, and Rama woke from his stupor.

'Great Ahi, I bow to you,' said Rama.

'Rama.'

Rama stared at the cobra in surprise. It was the voice he had heard in the woods. A nimisha later, he understood. The guru had come to the sacred grove of the Nagas in the form of the Great Ahi, and the Nagas were here to honour his presence. Akrita prostrated himself before the guru.

Rama bowed to the Nagas.

'I am honoured to be in your presence. I pay humble homage to you all. Guru Dattatreya, blessed am I that you would speak with me.'

'Why are you here, Rama?' the guru asked.

Rama considered the question. The obvious answer was that he was here seeking answers, but the guru had asked first. He was not asking the obvious and 'here' could mean anything—the grove or Tripura or this earth itself. Rama answered with care.

'To learn some lessons, Gurudeva.'

'What have you learnt?'

'That there should be no compromise with adharma. If you permit it, soon you will tolerate it, partake in it and then celebrate it. Eventually, you will hate anyone who stands for dharma. A kingdom that disregards its ancestors and their sacrifices will soon disdain the descendants. The three creeds are symptoms of people forgetting or diluting dharma. They disregard pramana, the evidence before their eyes, and blindly follow lofty proclamations. On this path lies the loss of morality and heritage.'

Rama stopped, but the guru kept mum. Rama thought for a moment and then continued.

'If one desires to be peaceful, one must have the ability to punish, to inflict powerful violence. Else one is not peaceful, merely harmless. On this path lies defeat and slavery.'

Rama glanced at Akrita standing now with head bowed, close behind him.

'I also learnt that a guru can learn as much from a good shishya as the other way round. On this path lies true knowledge and humility.'

'Excellent!' the guru said. Rama bowed once more and pressed his palms together.

'A good shishya to have. What is your name now, child?' asked the guru turning to Akrita.

'Akritavrana,' Akrita whispered.

'A good name to have.'

'Do you know my old one, Bhagavan?' asked Akrita.

'Your past doesn't matter, Akritavrana. Your future started on the day you died. Look ahead.'

'Why send him, Gurudeva? The "voice in the woods" as Akrita described it, could have spoken to me directly,' Rama asked.

'A disease was cured, a life renewed, a good shishya gained. You tread where no mortal has gone before. It is good to have company. Perhaps one day he will tell the story of your journey to the world,' said the guru.

Rama didn't have to look back to know Akrita was beaming with joy.

'I seek answers, Gurudeva. Pray grant me the benefit of your wisdom.'

'But, do you know the right questions, Rama?'

Rama glanced into those kaleidoscopic eyes. There was nothing he could read in them. He gathered his thoughts; the opportunity was too precious to be squandered.

'What does it mean, to upraise the land and settle us down?'

'Good question, but not the right one. Also not my answer to give. You are the only one who can answer that.'

'How do I defeat Arjuna?'

'Better question, still not the right one. Maybe ask, *can you defeat Arjuna?*'

Rama didn't know. Would the Parashu and the divyastras be enough against the most powerful man in the three worlds? Arjuna hadn't lost a single battle yet. The devas and asuras feared him. He was head and shoulders above all of them in strength. For a mortal to have such extraordinary powers had to be a blessing. Rama knew that this strength came from Arjuna's spiritual prowess. And the guru was Arjuna's preceptor. Rama understood the question he had to ask. The right question.

'What is the secret of Arjuna's strength, Gurudeva?' Rama asked.

'Excellent question, Rama. Secrets, answers, stories and whispers—entire lives can be lived in the pursuit of those. Tell me, Rama, is it wise to seek a secret, and is it honest to reveal one?'

'Is it wise to conceal a secret that enables tyranny and brings misery to the world? Is it virtuous to deny knowledge to one who seeks to end this tyranny?'

'Well argued, Rama. Will you defeat Arjuna and spare his life or kill him?'

The question flummoxed Rama for a moment. He hadn't thought this over. He had accepted his father's judgement on Arjuna. Arjuna was the cause of untold misery, but did that warrant his killing? He had beheaded his mother on his father's orders; he had gambled on the chance that all was not what it seemed. What was at stake here? Could he defeat the man, render him powerless and walk away? Or would the killings only stop with Arjuna's death? Rama realised the guru had asked him to pronounce judgment. He was to be both the judge and the executioner. He thought for a long while. The guru and the Nagas waited for his answer.

The Nagas! That's another reason they were here, to await his judgement on Arjuna. Arjuna had ousted them from Mahishmati. They were the first victims of Arjuna's conquest. Their worshippers were wandering the forests, their homeland, Ahichchatra, sacked by Arjuna. Rama understood now why he had felt the urge to seek answers in this grove, and why Gurudeva had appeared as a great Ahi. He had arrived here from Indrapuri to help the Malaya kshatriyas. To defeat the three creeds and to gain knowledge of 'his people'. It was clear that Gurudeva had forsaken his disciple; he disapproved of Arjuna's actions.

Rama proclaimed judgement. 'Arjuna deserves to die.'

'Why does Arjuna deserve to die?'

Rama framed his answer with caution.

'There are three things a king must have—a sword, a jewel, and a mirror. The sword of valour and mighty armies, to defend and expand his kingdom. The jewel of wealthy citizens and a deep treasury, for the welfare of all citizens and for use in calamities. And the mirror of self-awareness. Arjuna has the first two, though he misuses them, but his mirror reflects untruth; it shows only what he wants to see. He deludes himself that what he does is dharma, but he does not see the pain of the world. Even if the mirror showed him the truth, the cataracts of ego and vanity cloud his sight. His mirror turns the sword on his subjects and he uses the jewel to hoard wealth. Arjuna is the alchemist who has turned gold into clay. He deserves to die for the woe he has caused the world.'

The Nagas stopped swaying, going as still as their stone figurines. Gurudeva was silent for a long while.

'I accept your judgement. I will reveal the rahasya.'

A susurration erupted among the Nagas. It seemed as if they were repeating his name. Parashurama ...

Parashurama ...

Parashurama ...

'Stories can change with the teller, but secrets can change the listener, Rama. Nothing can make one as lonely as a secret. Listen hard, my child, and listen well.

'Among all the boons Arjuna asked of me, there is one that is known to him and me alone. The rahasya behind his prodigious strength and vitality—his invincibility—is the divine power of the Sudarshana Chakra. He is the very embodiment of it. No mortal, deva, or asura can defeat him.'

Rama went slack-jawed with utter astonishment. He heard Akrita gasp behind him. This was not what he had expected. So many boons have been asked of the gods by so many mortals—asuras even. Every one of those boons had a loophole, a chink in the armour that enabled the downfall of the receiver should he abuse his power. Sometimes, it took a while to figure out what that chink was, but in the end it was found. But what could he do here? Arjuna's very being was imbued with the boon's power. Arjuna was the weapon itself, the very embodiment of it.

Despair clutched at Rama's heart. He had come all this way, striven so hard, won Mahadeva's Parashu—all this to be finally told that it was all in vain. His mind clutched at straws. Could Gurudeva make him the embodiment of the Parashu as well? Was that the answer; was it possible even? What was more powerful—the Chakra or the Parashu? Fool! he berated himself. Vishnu is Shiva and Shiva is Vishnu. Both are forms of the same Parabrahma. Rama failed to find an answer. He hung his head in hopelessness. He could sense the awe and disquiet of the Nagas. They had gone silent.

'Can I defeat Arjuna?' he whispered hoarsely.

'You will find death,' Gurudeva replied. Rama's shoulders drooped. Words failed him.

'Gurudeva, is there no way out? Surely you can save him, my Acharya?' Akrita wailed. Stony silence met Akrita's pleas. Rama looked around. The Nagas had all disappeared. Dead, stifling silence hung upon the grove and the shrine.

'Today is truly the day for answers and the revealing of rahasyas, Rama'. The iridescent heads of the cobra tilted up and gazed at the heavens.

'The past is a serpent of water, long flown. The present is a serpent of fire, blazing bright. Time is made of karmic knots and how to unravel them remains to be seen.

'A warning. A rahasya. A puzzle.

'The warning. If you battle Arjuna, you'll find death. No mortal can defeat him.

'The rahasya. It stops being a rahasya only through self-realisation. The rahasya realised in time, by oneself, becomes a boon.

'The puzzle. One who looks outside, dreams, but the one who looks inside, awakens. Awaken the Ahi in you. It is awakened in you already, just become aware of it and understand.

'Remember the beginning, Rama.'

The great iridescent Ahi head and the brilliant blue mist disappeared. Rama sat with his head sunk in his hands. A long while later, he rose unsteadily. Akrita rushed to help him. He leaned heavily on Akrita's shoulder, unable to stand straight on his own. He averted his eyes to keep Akrita from seeing the deep despair in them. His eyes fell on the Nagamandala. It was different now, the old intricate one was no longer there.

In its place was a simple circular figure of a snake swallowing its tail.

20

Golden Horn

Rama sat leaning against the tree in the darkness, stopping at last after a relentless trudge of four days, with no stop for food or rest. Akrita was curled up in a deep sleep of exhaustion, a little to the side. Rama hadn't spoken a word since he'd reeled out of the grove. He hadn't waited to bid farewell to Anantha or Bhargavi. He had wandered the forest with his mind and heart clasped in the icy embrace of despair. At long last, he had found enough sense to get his bearings by looking at the stars and had set out to find the Narmada. He found the river by walking towards the south-west and had followed its course westward, back home. Akrita had tried to make conversation, but Rama's stony silence rebuked every attempt, breaking his resolve within a day. He had followed Rama, after that, untiring and uncomplaining.

Rama felt sorry for him and castigated himself. He should have at least thought of the boy. He glanced at Akrita with a glow of pride. His shishya had learnt so much while he had been away. It was an exemplary speech he had delivered on the dais. So wise for one so young, and he had surrendered to the wishes of his guru and followed him without any complaint.

Suddenly, he felt some strange power uncoil and spring within him, taking him by surprise. Rama reached out with his mind to examine it, and it died away. He glanced at Akrita again, replaying the same thoughts again and again, waiting for that surge of power to reappear. Nothing changed within him. Rama sighed. Why did he sense this now? Rama thought hard. Perhaps it had been aroused earlier. When fury had flooded through him and the power of the Parashu had been at play; when he hadn't been paying attention. Something had risen in him during the battle with the asuras in Indrapuri too. No, it was before that, but when? Rama turned the thought over in his mind for a long time and gave up at long last. At least the despair had somehow lessened. He grew aware of his weariness and lack of sleep. He was a mortal after all, and no mortal could defeat Arjuna. Try, and one would end up as every mortal eventually did. Dead.

Death! Death! Death!

The cries of the frenzied mob in the tent echoed in his mind. Death was the end anyway, so why not meet it with honour and die fighting?

Life is a dream,
All must awake.
Death is the awakening.

The words of the Aghori song came to his mind. He had accepted his father's judgement of Arjuna, and he had made it his mission to kill him. It seemed impossible now, a mission doomed for failure. But his death could, perchance, give someone else a chance to succeed.

'So be it then,' Rama said into the darkness. Better that

than these horrible days of agonising despair. What had started with his mother's death would end with his. Rama resolved to die.

The tight knot of tension in his mind loosened, as he found relief in reaching a decision, never mind the fatalism of it. Rama's body relaxed, he breathed deeper, grew calmer and drifted into sleep.

He awoke as dawn was breaking. Akrita was already up, arranging jamuns and other assorted fruits on leaves for their morning meal.

'You will find a way, Acharya, I know you will.'

Rama smiled, rose and stretched. He walked to the cliff that overhung the valley. Below, the river was a gleaming serpent snaking its way through the green of the hills and the valley. The air was a brilliant saffron colour. Rama breathed in deep, wishing he could collect the saffron sunlight in his hands and drink it. A vague sense of unease was still within him, like a premonition that wouldn't reveal its secret. But he felt much better. What had to be done, had to be done. He would worry about the next step once he had reached his father's ashram.

'Let's go home, Akrita,' Rama said.

———

'Pranaam Samrat. Welcome to my humble ashram,' said Jamadagni.

Arjuna joined his hands together in namaste but didn't utter a word. He stared at the saptarishi without expression. He tried to probe Jamadagni's mind, but came up against an impenetrable barrier. Jamadagni guarded his thoughts; Arjuna wouldn't be able to read them.

Jamadagni gestured to his shishyas and the ashram renunciates, who stood gawking at the samrat and his royal retinue. They reluctantly dispersed from the elongated hut with open walls, which served as the pathashala.

'Do take your seats,' Jamadagni invited. Low wooden seats had been laid out for Arjuna, Suchandra and Brihadbala. The fourth seat for Chandragupta remained empty. The minister had insisted on walking around the ashram.

'My sons, Vasu and Vishwavasu.' Jamadagni introduced the two men who had laid out the seats. Arjuna seated himself in sukhasana as the two greeted the samrat. Arjuna probed their minds. They were filled with wonder at the sight of the samrat and awe-struck at the finery of the attires of their guests. Arjuna dismissed them from his consideration.

'It has been ages since the Haihayas and the Bhargavas sat together, Samrat. Your visit to this ashram gives us immense pleasure. We open our hearts to all of you in welcome. Accept our humble hospitality, be at ease as if you are in your own homes. And speak your minds without hesitation,' said Jamadagni.

The corner of Arjuna's mouth lifted in a slow, sardonic smile.

'What brings the Chakravarti Samrat to the deep woods, so far from Mahishmati?'

'A hunt. A sport I love,' said Arjuna 'I do not chase deer or other game, Rishi, that is not hunting. It's a predator I seek. To hunt it in its own habitat, to stalk it as it stalks its prey, to deny it a kill, that is sport for me. To look it in the eye and throw down a challenge. To hear its roar, to foil its attack, to dominate. To see the dumb surprise in its eyes when its very heart blood flows from its ripped chest. To do that is to hunt.'

'That is worthy of a Chakravarti, Samrat Arjuna. But what creature could stand against Sahasrabahu?'

'Some reports of such a one around these parts have reached my ears. I've come in search, and I will flush it out of its den. That's when I heard your ashram is here. An excellent opportunity to rekindle old ties and ask if you know of this creature.'

Jamadagni nodded. Both of them knew the implicit meaning of Arjuna's words. He wondered how Arjuna had found out. Jamdagni decided to probe further.

'How is your preceptor, Guru Dattatreya, blessed be his name?'

Clever one, this saptarishi, thought Arjuna. 'One can find the Avadhuta only if he wills it so. You know that as well as me. My prayers reach him,' he said.

'True, Samrat. A god who walks on earth, himself decides who can see him and where he can be found. And when. Wonder if he walks in shade or in a desert?'

Arjuna's face stiffened and his pupils widened for an infinitesimal fraction of a nimisha, but Jamadagni noticed it. It was enough to tell him two things. That the dream had been seeded in Arjuna's head too. Arjuna had seen Rama stand in the shade, while he himself wandered the desert. It also was clear that his guru had not responded to his prayers. His displeasure with and abandonment of Arjuna were evident in the dream, and the guru had not had a change of heart. Arjuna would have realised by now that Jamadagni also knew of the dream. Jamadagni watched Arjuna closely.

'My High Priest, Raikava, has divined, through the study

of the grahas and based on his deep occult knowledge, that strange spiritual energies have impacted this ashram. I find that remarkably interesting. Tell me about it, Rishi.'

'A hunt and a quest for spiritual knowledge. The samrat has eclectic tastes, but please, refresh yourselves first.'

Small clay tumblers of turmeric milk with almonds, cardamom and saffron were presented to the visitors. 'My third and fourth sons, Brihudyanu and Brutwakanva,' said Jamadagni. Arjuna appraised each of them and dismissed them from his thoughts in a nimisha.

'Excellent milk,' said Arjuna 'I await your answer.'

'This is an ashram, Samrat, devoted to spiritual upliftment and pursuit of truth. Parabrahma was pleased with our efforts and bestowed upon us blessings of certain aspects of the divine energy. That is all I can say. It is a matter for rigorous study and deep contemplation. Not a subject fit for casual conversation. And as you undoubtedly know, knowledge is imparted only to the deserving.'

A frisson of outrage ran through the visitors at Jamadagni's last words.

'So, which of these four sons of yours beheaded their mother?' asked Arjuna.

Jamadagni remained calm. Arjuna read disbelief and confusion in the minds of the sons. Disbelief that such weird stories had reached the samrat's ears and confusion that the high priest had divined it.

A series of thoughts ran through Arjuna's mind. What is happening here? The sons believed the beheading was a made-up story. But Chinnamasta, that was the name of the Mahavidya, who had manifested in their mother. Why did that happen? The ashram was a den of secrets.

'None of them,' said Renuka, as she entered the pathashala. She sat beside her husband and stared back at the visitors.

'It was the fifth son, then?' said Arjuna, his gaze fixed on the woman who hadn't even greeted him.

'Perhaps,' Renuka laughed. 'But he seems to have put it back where it belongs. It is always good to have one's head firmly on one's shoulders and not lose it in the clouds of fancy. Neither should one poke their head where it doesn't belong.'

Anger bloomed in Arjuna. A dangerous smile played on his face.

'You haven't introduced him to me yet.'

'His name is Ramabhadra, and he isn't here right now,' said Renuka.

'He seeks another guru? His father is not good enough for him? Or is he in some tapasya?'

Jamadagni smiled. 'Parents teach more with their actions than with words. The greatest teacher is, of course, one's self-realisation,' he said. 'Ramabhadra is in a tapasya of sorts. He aids Indra in his battle with the asuras. It has been about a year since he left with Indra.'

Arjuna thought for a moment. Didn't the saptarishi know that the battle was over? Was his son still in Devaloka? There were reports from spies about a man with an axe causing an upheaval in that nondescript kingdom Tripura. Was that him? Or was he hiding here and the parents lying?

'A warrior then, not a rishi?' he asked.

'His talent favours the knowledge and use of weapons. He is an exceptionally good exponent of the Dhanurveda and had learnt the science of weapons from me at a young age,' Jamadagni said with some pride. 'It's one's duty to give expression to one's talent within the bounds of dharma.'

'It is the writ of the samrat that brahmins will stick to their pujas, rituals and tapasyas. We have assigned each varna their tasks—no exceptions. It is the law of the land. It seems the Bhargavas disagree,' said Suchandra.

'It is better you ask the gods why they gave the talent of fighting to a brahmin instead of a kshatriya. You should punish them for disobeying the law of the land,' said Renuka.

'You mock my laws?' Arjuna's voice went up a notch. He probed Renuka's mind. She held it defiantly open, inviting him to read her thoughts. Daring him to. No, she did not know where her son was at the moment. She hadn't seen him for over a year. Arjuna then probed her mind about the beheading. All he saw was red, three streams of it. There was some divine essence about them. He didn't know what to make of it. He probed deeper. She thought of him as a spoilt brat, a petulant child, a cruel tyrant undeserving to be a samrat. She was contemptuous of him.

Arjuna stared at her, unwilling to attack a woman. But she would pay. She would see her son's body burn on the pyre. He would see her weep in sorrow.

'Would you prefer a shudra who is bad at his labour, languish in incompetence if he is good with rituals and mantras instead? When he can make a good priest? Would you make a vaisya bad with money, the head of the merchants' guild? Would you have a kshatriya bad at fighting, bear arms? Why is a new-born put in his parents' varna and profession by compulsion?' said Renuka.

'Such aberrations would naturally fall by the wayside. They will be rejected by their communities. Over time, such aberrations will be bred out. Only the ones fit for their station will survive,' said Arjuna.

'And thousands of good priests, good soldiers, traders, artisans and farmers and so on will be lost. Only because they were born in the wrong varna. Prakriti doesn't work that way, no matter what the laws of men proclaim.

'I am from a kshatriya clan, my husband from a brahmin clan. My sons all followed the path of brahmins, but which varna are they by birth and by the foolish law you impose?'

'Of course they became brahmins! Why would they settle for a lower rank?' Arjuna laughed.

'Ah! So that's it, then. Jealousy of brahmins. Despite Anasuya helping your mother, and your guru being one himself. I wonder why? Perhaps because enough of them still call out your wrongs, are willing to die for their dharma, and will not bend before you.

'You think brahmins are the highest? We get protection from the kshatriyas, coin from the vaisyas and food, skill and art from the shudras. We depend on all the other varnas to exist, and all we possess is our knowledge of the spiritual texts. Each varna has deep knowledge of the subjects they master. We have no wealth, no power, no skill. We have to follow the strictest rules, the harshest discipline. Everyone else lives with greater freedom and lesser rules. So why the jealousy?' continued Renuka.

'Your arrogance is insufferable. Brahmins think they know it all, claiming to have sprung from the head of Brahma,' said Suchandra.

'And since the kshatriyas sprang from the arms of Brahma, they are jealous of the brahmins—the head being above the arms! Do you have contempt then, for the shudras who sprang from the feet?' asked Jamadagni. 'It is the feet, Samrat, that carry the whole body around.'

'A blessing is given on the head, Samrat. For that, one has to do a namaskara. Take the weight off one's feet, lay the body on the ground, bend one's arms, press the palms together, and touch one's head to the feet of the person giving the blessing.'

'It is not the kshatriya, but the brahmin, who looks down on everyone else, Jamadagni,' said Arjuna.

'Then, such a one is not a brahmin. His knowledge isn't atmagyana, self-realisation. It is merely ahamkara, hubris. He is dharma-brasht. The varnas are bound together by duties and responsibilities towards each other. Not by assumed privileges. Beware of the ones that seek to sow enmity between the head and the feet. They are friends of neither, and seek to destroy culture, heritage and an entire way of living,' said Jamadagni.

'To separate the head from the body is to become, in essence, Rahu and Ketu. Greed, jealousy, lust for power, loss, isolation, decay and desperation are the fruits of this,' said Renuka. 'As I said before, my head is firmly on my shoulders. Think again Arjuna, of the broken dreams, unused talent and the sheer loss of human lives your laws lead to.'

'Such loss is temporary and for the greater good,' Brihadbala interrupted.

'You were right, Samrat,' said Jamadagni. 'One shouldn't forget one's station in life. One shouldn't play god.'

Arjuna struggled to keep his anger under control. He had been polite so far, far more than he usually was. The ashram, the saptarishi, and his patni held many secrets among them. That was the only reason for his continued patience. He thought about imprisoning and torturing them, but he didn't think they would break easily or reveal the truth.

Chandragupta would ask around the ashram. He would wait to see what information he brought. He swallowed his frustration at not finding Ramabhadra here and bided his time. An uneasy quiet snaked into the pathashala.

'Politics, war and what not! Unpleasant topics to discuss when one meets for the first time. Let's forget about all this; allow us to complete our athithi-satkara. Give us the privilege of serving the samrat lunch,' said Renuka, trying to placate frayed tempers.

'I eat with my fellow hunters. We eat what we kill. It is the tradition of a hunt. Have you forgotten all this, Renuka? You were a kshatriya princess after all.' Renuka startled, unused to anyone other than her husband calling her by name. Perhaps Arjuna could. He was many thousands of years older than her, despite his youthful appearance.

'We can manage to put up a meal for the four of you,' she said.

'Four of us? It is the Chakravarti Samrat who rides to the hunt! A small army of support staff camp half a yojana away. One lakh people, one lakh mouths. You can imagine how much we have to hunt each day,' said Brihadbala.

Jamadagni thought for a moment and said, 'I will arrange food for them too. Call your soldiers. They can all have their meals here.'

Brihadbala and Suchandra were taken aback. Arjuna looked on with sudden interest, his curiosity piqued.

'We wouldn't want the ashram residents to go hungry or to deplete their reserves. The ashram is no place for dignitaries, vassals and ministers, who are used to ... er ... the comforts of aristocratic life. Our camp is equipped for all that,' said Suchandra.

'No one will go hungry. Invite them here. We will give them a meal fit for the kings,' said Renuka.

Arjuna decided to stay. He had to see this with his own eyes. Perhaps there would be some humiliation for the couple, some joke at their expense.

'Send word with your charioteer. Bring them all here,' he instructed Brihadbala.

'Gather the residents to serve our guests,' said Jamadagni to his sons. 'I will see to the meal.' He rose, and with kamandalu in hand, walked away.

Chandragupta heard the excited chatter among the ashram residents—a feast for the entire hunting group! Nothing he had seen in the ashram could live up to that promise. They had neither the facilities nor the food, but the saptarishi would not give a false promise. Of this he was sure. Strange stories abounded among the residents about the happenings in the ashram. Each was more fantastical than the other. But they were all convinced that something tremendous had happened. Chandragupta believed that Raikava's divination was indeed true. But someone had cleverly confused the residents. He caught sight of Jamadagni walking towards the cowshed and decided to investigate. He slipped away, unnoticed in all the excitement.

Jamadagni walked to the very end of the goshala, nuzzling the heads of the cows and bulls he passed and playfully pulling the ears of the calves.

'Ma Surabhi,' he addressed the last cow. Chandragupta's breath caught as he watched, crouched near the entrance of the goshala. Did the saptarishi have Surabhi, the divine wish-fulfilling cow? Here, in this lowly goshala! He stared wide-eyed in disbelief. Surabhi shook her pendulous dewlap playfully.

Jamadagni slipped a small piece of watermelon rind in her mouth and stroked her hump. The small bells on her horns tinkled as she chewed. He squatted beside her forelegs and she put her head on his shoulder, as if hugging him close. He whispered something in her ear, her ear flicking as she listened and mooed. Jamadagni rose and chanted mantras, his lips moving without a sound, the fingers of his right hand forming a series of mudras as he chanted. Surabhi's body started glowing a brilliant white. Myriad yantras flashed and flickered on her flanks. Jamadagni sat by her udders, holding out his kamandalu. Surabhi's right horn turned golden and a drop of milk like liquid sunshine fell from her udder into the holy water inside the kamandalu. Jamadagni rose again, whispering his gratitude to her as her body returned to its normal appearance. He poured some water from the spout of the kamandalu into his cupped right hand, whispering mantras all the while, and threw the water in the air. Chandragupta hid behind a corner of the goshala as Jamadagni made his way to the kitchen hut. Then the minister ran back to the pathashala, excited to share this news with the samrat.

The environs of the ashram had changed in a blink. Chandragupta ran through immaculately landscaped gardens, lined with winding pathways and flowering shrubs. Fountains danced to birdsong, and the cool breeze was laden with the heady fragrance of thousands of blooms. The humble huts had become magnificent mansions reaching for the skies. He ran and stumbled and continued running, turning his head from side to side in amazement. It took him forever to cross the width of just one mansion, and there were so many of them. He reached the pathashala and stopped. It had transformed into a grand hall that stretched far into the distance. A thousand pillars of pure white marble stood clasped in embrace by flowering creepers, with diaphanous curtains hanging between them, filtering out the light of the noon sun. The floor was carpeted with exquisite rugs, and soft couches marked places for the guests to sit at ease and enjoy their repast. Low tables were laid out with plates and bowls of silver, and big platters of fruit stood on each alongside small casks of wine. He walked in, chest heaving with effort.

Renuka smiled at the utter surprise of the samrat and his companions. 'Sit, Minister. Regain your breath and refresh yourself with wine and fruit. I'll be back when the rest of your hunting party reaches here.'

Chandragupta waited until she was well out of earshot. 'I've found the golden horn, Samrat,' he gasped. 'It is Surabhi, the wish-fulfilling cow! The saptarishi has it here in this ashram.'

Excitement flooded through Arjuna's veins. An unforeseen treasure had fallen right into his lap. The prophecy was coming true. He would take the cow back to Mahishmati. Its loss would anger Ramabhadra, fill him with vengeance, and he would come there to meet his death. After that, the cow would grant him the magnificent temple he so desired and nullify the curse. He looked around at the wondrous vista before him. Such an extraordinary gift and the foolish brahmin didn't know what to do with it! A gift fit for the Chakravarti Samrat was languishing in the goshala of a hermit. All that big talk about dharma and ideals, and he was just being selfish, secreting away the best for himself and his family. He had been right. The brahmins always looked out for themselves first, the rest of the world and the gods even, came a distant second. He beckoned the minister closer. 'Tell me exactly what you saw.'

Arjuna bided his time. He ate very little while his entourage gorged on the delicacies. They praised the food as being divinely flavourful, demanding more. And the food came without pause. No wonder, given the provenance, thought Arjuna. He watched Jamadagni and Renuka all through the meal. Their athithi-satkara was flawless. He washed his hands and approached the saptarishi standing before his hut. The hut was the only thing that stood unchanged in the entire ashram. Such an eyesore among the gardens and mansions, thought Arjuna.

'How did you do it, Saptarishi?'

'Let it be, Samrat. I hope you enjoyed your meal. Let the source remain a secret.'

'A secret that stands tied in the goshala? How did you come by this extraordinary gift?'

Jamadagni hid his surprise well. 'It is not a gift, Samrat. It is a privilege and a responsibility. I tend to her like my mother. All I ask for is her milk, and that too, only for sacred rituals. And even then I take it only if she grants me permission.

'Today's meal is her blessing upon you all. Be grateful.'

'She doesn't belong in an ashram, and a samrat can care for her better than a rishi. Give her to me,' said Arjuna.

'She doesn't need to be taken care of. And her ownership is a privilege she gives as she pleases. It is not becoming of you to ask, Samrat, and not my right to give her to you. Ma Surabhi chose to live here. She is not something that can be granted or taken by force. She is a blessing that comes with spiritual power. Remember Vasishta and Vishwamitra.'

'Two foolish rishis fighting to possess Surabhi. And for

what? For more of their rituals and prayers? Such selfishness! You deny your samrat, Jamadagni. Think of the good she can do for this world. No one will need to go hungry anymore. No one will lack for anything. The divine cow gives whatever one wants.'

Jamadagni sighed. 'She is not just a cow, Samrat. She is Mata, mother. And no, she doesn't give whatever one wants, only what one deserves. Nobody gets more or less than their karma decrees and she stays only with those that are the deserving.'

'You call me undeserving? You insult your guest, Jamadagni.' Arjuna's voice was soft.

'Is that what you understand, Arjuna?' Jamadagni replied. Renuka slipped away from behind Arjuna. She had heard enough.

'I've had enough of this prattle. Let's stop this charade and talk without artifice. You know why I am here?' Arjuna said, with a hint of impatience in his voice.

'You search for my son. You came here to find him.'

'Yes. Ramabhadra is who I seek,' said Arjuna.

'But Samrat, Parashurama is who you will find,' said Jamadagni with conviction. Arjuna glowered at Jamadagni.

'Seize the cow,' Arjuna ordered Chandragupta. The minister mustered up a clutch of soldiers and ran towards the goshala. Jamadagni remained stoic.

Renuka finished her prayers as Chandragupta and the soldiers arrived. 'Go, Mother. It is not safe here,' she said and bowed to Surabhi, who disappeared in a flash. The ashram reverted to its original form. Renuka smiled in relief at the astonished faces before her.

The moment the gardens and mansions disappeared,

Arjuna realised he had lost the golden horn. He roared and transformed into Sahasrabahu. The roar rang loud across the ashram and the blood drained from Renuka's face. 'Hold her!' Chandragupta cried. A blow landed on Renuka's head, her hands were twisted behind her back, and a hand was clamped tight over her mouth. She struggled in desperation, half conscious, kicking at the soldiers, her eyes pinned on her hut in the distance. Sahasrabahu suddenly towered above the hut, gripping Jamadagni by the torso in his gigantic fist. Renuka froze, blood turning to ice in her veins.

Arjuna lifted Jamadagni to the level of his ochre eyes. The saptarishi didn't struggle, nor cry out. He gazed at Sahasrabahu with calm eyes and a gentle smile. Arjuna studied him in surprise. A saptarishi had enormous power, and this one had the knowledge of divine weapons, yet he did nothing. He probed Jamadgni's mind, who held it open for Arjuna. There was no fear, no outrage, no anger even. Deep in his heart, Arjuna felt ashamed. As Jamadagni's smile widened, Sahasrabahu flung him to the ground and trampled on him. Renuka swooned and collapsed; the soldiers let her limp body drop to the ground. Arjuna swatted away Jamadagni's sons as they rushed to help their father. The ashram's residents broke from their frozen fright and fled.

Arjuna looked down at the saptarishi. Blood spurted from Jamadagni's mouth as his body lay crushed and immobile. His eyes found Arjuna's, and he smiled again through his bloody teeth.

21

Yuddha

Manorama ran to Arjuna as he walked into his private chambers. Her breath was shallow, and her eyes were wide with fright. She ran her hands over his shoulders and arms and clasped his hands in her small dainty ones. 'You are all right. Devi be praised!'

Arjuna held her close. 'What happened? Why are you so worried?'

'A vision in my prayer. It was so real, so terrible. It is an omen, a nimitta, I'm sure. Something significant has happened. Tell me all that happened at the ashram, leave no detail out.' Arjuna sat her down on the couch and told her. Manorama remained silent.

'What was the vision?' Arjuna asked.

'I saw the silhouette of a person with a horde of crows perched on his head. I don't know if it was a man or a woman. It was pitch dark and the silhouette was a shade lighter. Then the head and the crows disappeared, and smoke started billowing out of the neck. And then I saw a severed head staring at its own reflection in a mirror. It sent shivers down my spine. It is an omen of impending death.'

'When did you have this vision?'

'During my evening prayers, four days back.'

'That was the day of my visit to the ashram,' Arjuna mused 'It is a nimitta of the prophecy coming true. The Bhargavas have lost the divine cow, the golden horn. Ramabhadra will swear vengeance for his father's death and come here, to me, to meet his own death.'

'The prophecy can cut both ways, my love. You desired to own Surabhi, but she is lost to you too. You have wreaked vengeance on the ashram. The implication of death can be for you too. What a prophecy means and what we want it to mean are two different things.'

Arjuna smiled. 'Quite the philosopher you are. You worry too much ...'

Manorama clutched at his arm as he rose. 'One thing worries me to no end. Why did the saptarishi offer no resistance?'

Arjuna stopped, remembering his moment of shame.

'Was he afraid? Was he stunned into immobility by the sight of Sahasrabahu?'

'No. He was calm. It took me by surprise. I've never seen anything like that before.'

'An ashram with a saptarishi; a patni who carries an aspect of Mahavidya. A son who is an amsha and a brahmakshatriya. And nothing happens? Leave aside attack, the saptarishi doesn't even defend himself?

'I worry for you like never before, my love. We should sit for a special puja together, to win Devi's protection for you. We must observe all the rules and rituals and put aside everything else till it is over.'

'You have already performed your own puja, Manorama.

Why one more? And my army has gathered outside the city, along with the armies of my vassals. It's been a long time since they last gathered like this. I must inspect them and attend to their needs. That's why I made my way back early with Suchandra, Brihadbala and Chandragupta, leaving the rest to strike camp and return. I cannot push this aside because you worry about a dream. Come, see the might of the largest army on prithvi. I promise you, your worries will disappear, and it will fill you with pride.'

Manorama stood. 'Arjuna, have my instincts ever led you wrong? Have I ever been this worried about any adversary of yours? Guru Dattatreya doesn't respond. Rishi Apava destroys our plans for the temple and curses us. The saptarishi does something completely unexpected and the golden horn disappears! There are forces at play here that we cannot even fathom. Let the army wait. It is my firm belief, a conviction of my heart that we have to do this if we are to kill this nuisance called Parashurama.'

Arjuna smiled when Manorama said 'we'. Her instincts had stood him in good stead before. 'So it shall be,' he said, trying to ease her trepidation. 'The army will wait, the queen's desire comes first.'

———

Rama walked on the path that ran alongside the brook. He was past the settlement and nearing his own ashram. Dawn was yet to break, and he was eager to get home and surprise his parents. Anticipation and happiness swelled in him, fighting back the uneasiness that had grown over the last few days. There was so much to tell them, and his brothers would each want him to sit with them and narrate his adventures over and over again. He wanted to discuss Guru Dattatreya's words with his parents. Rama turned over his words in his mind, again and again, as he walked, like an itch he couldn't help but scratch. He thought he understood what 'awaken the Ahi in you' meant, but he didn't know how to do it. Father would know, he thought. After all, there was little he didn't. Absorbed in his thoughts, he almost crashed into Dakini in the dark.

'Rama,' she exclaimed in surprise.

'Dakini, I'm so glad to see you. It's been ages ...,' Rama's voice petered out. He noticed her dishevelled appearance and distraught face. 'What's wrong?'

'Oh Rama!' Dakini burst into tears and buried her face in his chest.

'Don't worry, I'm here now,' he consoled her, hiding both his surprise and the sudden worry that had sprung up in his heart. She mumbled something against his chest, and he couldn't make out what she said. He glanced at Akrita, who shook his head. He hadn't understood either. Rama lifted her head.

'Your father ...,' said Dakini. Suddenly, the worry turned into panic and ripped through his body.

'Arjuna ...,' said Dakini, and in a flash, Rama was gone, running as fast as he could. He burst into the perimeter of the ashram, gasping for breath but not stopping. The ashram was still—no sign of disciples preparing for their morning prayers; no sign of any activity at all. He ran up to his parents' hut. He saw his brothers first, sitting hunched together at the entrance, tired, bruised, sorrowful and half asleep. Rama skidded to a halt in front of them.

On the raised platform beside the hut's doorway, lay Jamadagni's body, wrapped from neck to feet in a dhoti. His mother sat as still as a statue beside him.

Rama's mind reeled at the sight; he couldn't breathe in enough air into his lungs. He found himself kneeling by his father, not even aware that he had moved. Jamadagni had a smile on his face, calm and kind, despite the blood-stained teeth and dried blood on his beard and neck. Rama clutched at the dhoti beneath his father's chin. He paused, tears welling up in his eyes. He threw off the dhoti in a single motion and his eyes went wide with shock. It started as a sob; he forgot to breathe, his muscles clenching and refusing to let go. Tears flowed unchecked. He turned his eyes away and let out a loud and desolate wail into the darkness. The lone lamp on the platform flickered frantically.

Rama doubled over in grief. It hit him like a blow to his midriff. He crawled away from his father's body into the small open area. Jamadagni's body had been smashed beyond belief. The chest had collapsed, the ribs were broken and a couple of them stuck out from the sides of his torso; the insides had been turned to mush. The image burned in his mind, refusing to go away as he shook his head from side to side. He felt arms around him, and he clutched at them in desperation. Someone was calling his name.

It was a long time before he recognised his brother, Vasu's voice. His brothers were all around him, holding him close— afraid they would lose him too.

'Ma,' Rama said, his throat dry and painful.

'She hasn't moved ever since she recovered from her swoon and dragged father to the platform and laid him there. She won't let anyone touch father either. Arjuna's soldiers had pinned her hands and gagged her.' Rage erupted inside Rama, and the Parashu responded. Rama let the rage loose, immersing himself in it.

'Kill! Kill! Kill!' his mind screamed.

'Father didn't fight, Rama. We don't know why. He smiled as Sahasrabahu lifted him by the throat.'

Some incredible force awakened inside Rama. It shot up from the base of his spine. He didn't know what it was nor did he care to know why he was experiencing it right now, in spite of the fury of the Parashu. The Parashu was rattling, beating a frenzied metallic rhythm against the floor beside Jamadagni, where Rama had left it. Rama walked past his brothers and a grief-stricken Akrita, to his mother and gently squeezed her shoulder.

Renuka turned red, and the axe went still. Her whole body emanated a red glow from within. Her skin was the same colour as it had been on that incredible day of her beheading. She opened her eyes and Rama saw a timeless look in her eyes, as if there was some invisible power behind them.

'Once before. Now again. And again, soon,' she said in a voice that made his blood run cold. Her tongue shot out and extended past her chin. Rama heard soft laughter emanating from her mouth, but it seemed to come from some place far away. He stepped back a couple of paces in shock. Renuka's hands moved as if in a trance.

'He lives,' she whispered. Her hands hovered over Jamadagni's body and in a blink, it disappeared behind a thick red mist that covered him from head to toe. Ripples ran across the surface of it, down the length of his body and back again to his head. Rama retreated further, joining his brothers and Akrita as Renuka and the air around her pulsed with a warm red glow.

There was a dull thud, and the mist furrowed all of a sudden into Jamadagni's body. Renuka collapsed where she had been sitting. They rushed towards her. Rama and Vishwa were laying her down beside Jamadagni when Brihudyanu whispered in awe. 'Mahadeva be praised! He breathes! Father's alive!'

Rama stared at his father. His father's body had been completely restored, and he seemed to be in deep slumber. He watched the rise and fall of Jamadagni's abdomen as he breathed, willing it to go on, praying that it didn't stop. 'Ma Chinnamasta be praised!' he repeated over and over in his mind.

They all waited beside the two sleeping bodies, their spirits soaring and eyes darting between the rise and fall of Jamadagni's chest and Renuka's slumber. Dawn had broken, but nobody wanted to go inform the residents. The lamp stayed lit; Brutwakanva poured oil into it from time to time. No one wanted to turn it down, no one dared to.

Rama's thoughts wandered from one memory to another. He looked at the spot where he had beheaded his mother, where Ma Chinnamasta had stood headless. He remembered the last portion of the deer-antler dust. The extra portion that had been reserved for Akrita, who hadn't needed it. It was still in his father's hut. He rushed inside and found it lying in the corner of the lone shelf, still wrapped in a knotted cloth. Rama brought it out of the hut, and sat by Jamadagni's head, lifting and cradling it in his lap. He prised open his father's mouth with care and placed a pinch of the dust below the tongue. Then he waited, keeping his rage on a slow boil. The time would come to let it loose, he promised himself. Arjuna had made it personal now and no prophecy, no warning, was going to hold him back. He would have his vengeance.

Akrita watched him for a while and walked away around the hut. Rama's brothers gathered around him.

'Rama, why didn't father put up a fight? He is a saptarishi, an expert in Dhanurveda and the science of weapons and even the divyastras. He taught you so much of it, yet he didn't use his knowledge when the time came,' said Vasu.

Rama couldn't explain it. His father's teachings had helped him grasp the mantras of the divyastras and the techniques of each so quickly. He had trained all his sons in the Vedas and the shastras, but Dhanurveda was reserved for Rama alone. He knew his father could've been a formidable warrior himself had he chosen so.

'Tell me everything that happened. Leave out no detail.'

Vasu narrated the events of the day Arjuna had visited the ashram and falling quiet once he had finished, reliving the day in his mind.

'There's been a great change in father since you left. His irascible nature has disappeared, and a gentle calm has descended on him. We haven't heard him raise his voice or even show impatience,' said Brutwakanva.

Rama only half heard them. He remembered Ma Chinnamasta's words, and it filled him with dread. She appeared only when there was death. First at Ma's beheading, then now at Jamadagni's death, and she'd said she would come again soon. He was sure the third death would be his. Rama shut away his thoughts, not wanting to fall again into the morass of despair he'd so recently clawed himself out of.

'Even Ma has changed. She's managed to heal even the

patients who were at the very door of death. She's cured the most impossible of health problems. She doesn't even need the patients to tell her the problem anymore. She says she knows what it is just by looking at their aura. Now, she has brought father back to life. Where did she get this power from? Are those fantastical stories true?'

Rama kept mum, not wanting to explain things right now. That would have to wait. They sat there, huddled together with Rama cradling Jamadagni's head.

Renuka revived a muhurta past noon.

'Rama,' she mumbled. Rama reached out and held her hand in his. 'Deer antler,' said Renuka.

'I've already placed a pinch beneath his tongue,' said Rama.

'Not his time to go. Not yet,' Renuka paused and ran her tongue over her dry lips. Vasu dribbled water into her mouth from a small clay pot and she drank until it was empty.

'I will be fine,' she said as she sat up against the wall. She looked at Rama, saw the rage simmering in his eyes and spoke with cold, hard determination. 'It is time to bring Arjuna to heel, Rama. The wretch defiled this ashram with his presence. He dared to lay hands on your father. On a saptarishi. The fool coveted Surabhi and vented his rage on your father when he couldn't have her.'

'He came for Surabhi?' Rama asked.

'No. He came for you. To hunt you down.'

'I call upon Jamadagni's son, the Brahmakshatriya with Mahavishnu's Amsha and Mahadeva's Parashu, to render justice. Hunt that putrid beast down!' She clasped Rama's hand in both of hers and stared into his eyes, boring into his soul with the implacable fury she was feeling.

'Give me my vengeance.'

Rage exploded in Rama, the Parashu goading him to grasp it, to cut, to quench its thirst for blood.

'I accept,' said Rama.

Renuka smiled. 'Go.'

Rama held her hand to his heart. Renuka drifted back to sleep.

Rama touched the feet of his sleeping parents and hugged his brothers. He didn't know if he would ever come back. His brothers surrounded him with their arms, giving him tight hugs and saying goodbye to him with a hundred prayers and benedictions. Akrita reappeared from somewhere with a cloth bag hanging across his shoulders. If Rama was going to meet his death, his shishya would be there with him. He stood before Rama in silent supplication, imploring him not to leave him behind. Rama nodded his assent; he didn't have the heart to say no.

Rama bid his goodbyes and walked away with Akrita. He did not turn back even once.

He had walked for a muhurta at least, when he remembered. It was time to use his divine boons. He stood quiet for a nimisha and went deep into himself. He formed the image of the ratha in his mind and called it to come forth.

It stood before them, the magnificent war chariot. The charioteer was the same. Rama climbed aboard with the wonderstruck Akrita behind him.

'Mahodhara at your service, Swami. What is your command?' said the charioteer.

'To Mahishmati. To wage war,' said Rama. Mahodhara smiled, and the ratha started without the slightest jerk. Soon, he found the trail of the enormous hunting party and set course for Mahishmati. The jungle whizzed past in a blur.

It was still the wee hours of the night when the trees started to thin out and Rama got the sense that they were nearing the city. The smell of the environs had changed, the roads were wider and levelled, and they were passing carts and convoys with increasing frequency. He could only assume they were carts because the ratha sped past so fast that there was no time to clearly register their surroundings. He knew for certain that they were travelling at an incredible speed.

The ratha slowed; the two white steeds changing their relentless sprint for a slow amble. Up ahead on the path were a couple of torches being carried by foot soldiers and a dozen horsemen beyond them. Further ahead, Rama saw an array of lights strung out away from him, in a haphazard line tracing the path before him. Far in the distance, lit by a multitude of huge torches, was a gigantic archway with open gates and a drawbridge before it.

'Mahishmati,' said Mahodhara.

By now, two of the horsemen had turned and approached the ratha. The incongruity of two youthful brahmins in a war chariot had aroused their curiosity. One of them stopped right in front of the ratha and the other went round it, turning and reining in abreast of Rama.

'Name and business?' he asked perfunctorily.

'Parashurama, from Jamadagni's ashram,' said Rama. His name meant nothing to the soldier, but he was suddenly interested when he heard Jamadagni's name.

'The saptarishi killed by the samrat?'

'He lives,' said Rama, suspicion growing in his mind. 'Are these the troops that accompanied Arjuna on his hunting trip?'

'Address him as samrat, you country idiot,' retorted the horseman.

'Are you the hunting party?' Rama asked again.

'Uppity fellow, this one,' said the horseman in front of the ratha. 'Yes, we are the hunting party.' Rama hefted the Parashu onto his right shoulder.

'A brahmin with an axe and a war chariot. Looks like this fool wants revenge. Where is your army?' the horseman continued, mocking Rama. 'And from where did you steal the weapon and the ratha?'

'Ingrates who accept athithi-satkara and leave the host to die! Never mind, I don't really blame you; it is that wretch Arjuna I want.' Rama spat out the words. 'Get out of my way. This is the only chance you get to live.'

The horseman laughed and drew his sword. The other horseman did the same. One of the foot soldiers blew his bugle and the troops ahead turned, drawing their weapons. Rama turned to the horseman beside him and cut his sword at the hilt. He reached out and grabbed the soldier by his armour, pulling him closer. He hit him on the head with the base of the axe handle, knocking him senseless. Rama eased him off his horse onto the ground.

Rama leapt off the chariot as the two foot soldiers dropped their torches and drew out their swords. He hacked them both in a blink as the first horseman sat immobile in surprise.

'Sainikas! To me!' he screamed. He dug his spurs into the horse, and it rose, kicking at Rama's head with its forelegs. Rama sidestepped and cut through the underbelly of the horse, going through the saddle, lopping off the soldier at the waist. The upper body held still for a moment, then fell sideways as the horse crashed forward. Rama waded into the mass of charging soldiers.

Rama slapped the soldier awake. The man took a moment to come to his senses and struggled as Rama hefted him onto the ratha. He froze when he saw the blood splattered on Rama's face and torso. He slowly turned to face the road. It was strewn with dead bodies, mangled horses and smashed chariots as far as he could see in the light of the burning supply carts. He looked back at Rama's raptor-like gaze and stood transfixed in utter fright. He was the only man left alive of the hunting party.

Rama hurled the man at the group of soldiers bunched together defensively at the gateway of Mahishmati's fort.

'Tell Arjuna that Parashurama has come for his head!' shouted Rama.

The ratha turned and sped away into the night.

Dawn broke and as Rama waited, he surveyed the surroundings. Acres of land had been cleared and levelled around the fort as far as he could see. The drawbridge spanned a massive moat that wound around the fort walls. The gateway he faced opened to the east, and it was all forest behind him; perhaps the farmland lay to the other side of the fort. Mahishmati lay north of the Narmada so the river was to his left, edged with thick jungles and marshes. The drawbridge stayed down. No one had ventured out of the gateway, except for a troop of guards sent to replace the guards he had cut down last night. Nobody ventured towards the gateway either. The devastation of the hunting party would turn even the foolhardiest of wayfarers away. The destruction was now fully visible in the growing daylight, and word would have spread by now inside the city. Arjuna would know, even if the guard had not been able to deliver the message.

A posse of troops finally emerged from the far corner of

the fort in the south-east. Cavalry, hardly a hundred soldiers. They spotted the lone ratha waiting in the open field, and spurred their horses to a gallop. Rama invoked his bow. It appeared in his hand, as tall as himself and gleaming in the light. Two quivers appeared in the notches cut into the inner walls of the chariot at hip height. Rama twanged the bow string, and the sound carried across the field like a furious thunderclap.

Rama picked up an arrow, touched it to his forehead, saluting the bow and the arrows in the quivers. He nocked it to the bowstring and selected his target. He paused for a moment, brow creased in concentration. Rama remembered his father's training. In his mind, he called the target to him. That was how he had explained his unerring aim to Jamadagni. To see nothing but the target and focus so intensely on it that it loomed large in his sight, as if he had called it towards him. The distance vaporised in his mind; the cavalryman seemed only a yard ahead of him. Rama adjusted for the crosswind and stretched the bow, its base wedged against his toe, and let loose the arrow. A couple of nimishas later, the cavalryman fell off his saddle in the distance; the arrow lodged in his forehead as his horse continued to gallop ahead.

Rama's hands were a blur as he picked, nocked and shot arrows with blinding speed. No horseman survived the onslaught. They had not even come close to shooting their own arrows. Rama rested his bow and wondered why the soldiers had emerged from the side of the fort rather than from inside it. He instructed Mahodhara to go around the fort.

The walls of the fort were massive, stretching high as he rode closer to them. And long enough to hide the encampments from where the cavalry had emerged. The camps stretched upto the horizon; various pennants flying in different sections. Rama's amazement at the size of the camps and the number of soldiers grew as the ratha sped between the fort and the camps.

'Some sort of show of strength or of fealty by the vassals,' said Mahodhara.

Rama twanged his bow string again, the sound ricocheting off the fort.

'That should wake them up,' said Mahodhara.

The ratha sped round the fort. Rama shot down the soldiers who stood ahead to counter the ratha and those who gave pursuit. Soon, he was back at the east gate, from where they had started. The fort had three more gates, as huge as this one, each in a cardinal direction. The camps were all around the fort except in this field, which contained a mind-boggling number of soldiers.

'How many soldiers are there in all those camps?' asked Rama.

'Several akshauhinis, Swami. One akshauhini is 21,870 rathas, the same number of elephants; 65,610 cavalry and 1,09,350 infantry. The numbers are beyond overwhelming. You are but one warrior in a ratha. What is your plan?'

'Kill them here when they come. Kill them at the camp if they don't,' said Rama.

'Here they come,' said Akrita.

Soldiers poured out of the north-east side of the fort now, drumbeats keeping time as the infantry marched in formation. Cavalry and rathas coursed through the space between the formations of the foot soldiers.

'Cavalry and rathas first. The archers are still too far. They will take up formation as the horses charge,' said Mahodhara.

'Let's go meet them,' said Rama. He shot arrows one after the other as the ratha sped forward, his arrows having a much longer range than those of ordinary archers. He whispered mantras as he shot, and his arrows multiplied as they flew out of his bow. The charging cavalry and rathas saw a wall of death speeding their way. They shot their arrows in panic, but they hardly made a dent in the wall. Rama's arrows crashed into men, horses and chariots, tearing through flesh, wood and metal. Dozens of arrows pierced each of them, their charge ending just a few hundred metres from where it had started. Not a single man or horse survived. Rama shot a slew of arrows straight ahead, which thudded into the carcasses and broken rathas, pushing them out of his way. Rama's ratha crossed the dead bodies and paused.

The archers were now in position, nocking and shooting their shafts frantically, the foot soldiers preparing to charge. He noted their positions and started shooting again, countering their arrows with hundreds of his own. He stopped after a few nimishas. Not a single arrow had come close to him, not one archer remained standing. Rama picked up the Parashu and stepped out of the ratha.

'Go back and retrieve as many arrows and quivers as you can,' he instructed Akrita and Mahodhara. He swirled the axe around him as he walked towards the army.

The army stood stunned for a nimisha. The man had destroyed their cavalry, rathas and archers; now his ratha was turning back and he was coming towards them alone! They charged. Rama flung the Parashu from his hip as he ran. It spun as it cut through the soldiers, ripping limb and torso. Soldiers fell in mid-stride. Their compatriots beside them stumbled over their bodies, soldiers behind trying to sidestep the dead and evade the stumbling. They turned this way and that, to face the unknown attack, their eyes darting for the enemy in their midst as the axe flew at hip height, below their line of sight. Confusion broke through the ranks of soldiers as the axe returned to Rama, cutting another swathe of death on its return path. Rama ran, dodging javelins and spears, slashing at the men who drew close. He leapt into the gap cut by the Parashu, landing among the corpses, hewing at the soldiers closest to him.

He would be fighting five soldiers at the same time, and in a nimisha he would have disappeared, hacking into another set of troops several paces ahead, so fast was he moving. It was only by the time he started fighting the third set of soldiers did the dead bodies of the first set collapse to the ground. The soldiers tried to encircle him, but all they saw ahead was a blur of blood and gore and flying limbs. And then they were on the ground, breathing their last, unable to understand when death had come, disbelieving their fate.

Rama stopped when there were only a little over hundred soldiers left standing. They took one look at the carnage and ran for their lives. All except one. He stared at the Parashu, shivering in fright, an arm's length away from Rama. The gore and the gristle and fragments of bone was sliding off the blades and handle of the Parashu, but the blood was not. The soldier watched as a finger slid off the blade, falling to the ground, only a sliver of blood connecting it to the axe. The axe sucked the blood back into itself. The blood on the blades disappeared and they gleamed wickedly metallic again.

Rama moved the axe to his right. The soldier's eyes followed. He moved it to the left, and the soldier looked left. He simply could not take his eyes off the Parashu. Rama thrust it abruptly towards him, and the soldier jolted backwards. He swung reflexively at the axe and stared as the sword broke upon contact with it. He looked around for help. His fellow soldiers lay dead or had fled the massacre. His eyes settled on Rama, filled with horror. Rama walked past him.

'Go home,' he said.

The torches in the tent burnt furiously, matching General Brihadbala's mood. The vassal kings sat before him, some sombre, some angry.

'More than one akshauhini dead? How can one man kill so many?' Brihadbala spoke through clenched teeth. No one had an answer. He stared at each one in turn.

'Give me the details,' he said.

Silence again, nobody spoke up.

'Chandragupta!'

The minister gulped and mumbled, 'General ...'

Brihadbala stared daggers at him.

'Kings Mangala of Matsya and Kharapallana of the Shakas. Milinda of the Yavanas, Bhimapala of the Kambhojas and Parvataka of the Pahlavas are all dead. Their armies slaughtered to the last man.'

'But that is more than five akshauhinis.' said Brihadbala in astonishment. 'One man killed so many in less than a day?'

Chandragupta bowed his head.

'There's more, isn't there?' said Brihadbala.

Chandragupta spoke so low that the general had to strain his ears to hear him. 'The armies of the Dakshinatyas and the Pulindas have been annihilated. We don't know the fate of their kings. Good chance they are dead. Search parties are on the battlefield but with so many bodies ...'

Brihadbala groaned. 'You should have informed me earlier.'

'I had strict instructions from the High Priest Raikava and the queen herself. The puja was not to be disturbed. The dead kings were confident of being able to deal with Parashurama, either by themselves or together. Prince Jayadhwaja, King Suchandra, yourself and General Devadutta were all attending the puja. I didn't dare interrupt until ... I could think of no other way.'

'Where is Parashurama now?'

'He's in the jungles, somewhere between the east and south gates. His ratha hasn't left any tracks for us to know precisely. We had sent assassins in the night, since no one dared challenge him after the Pulindas fell.' It was Mahaveera, his second in command, who answered.

A long silence followed. 'But?' said Brihadbala.

'All were slaughtered. Their heads were displayed next to the drawbridge, mounted on spears driven into the ground. At the east gate,' said Mahaveera.

'How many?'

'Twenty-one.'

Brihadbala exhaled in frustration.

'He commands divyastras,' said Chandragupta.

'Isn't that obvious, you fool?' Brihadbala screamed, giving vent to his anger. 'It is the samrat he has challenged. No ordinary man can dare to do that. We have to stop him before the samrat rises from the puja.'

He looked at the kings, assembled from across the world. He did not even know some of them. None of them ventured an opinion. They were scared to voice a strategy that might fail, anxious about who would be picked to lead the next attack and secretly glad that they were at Mahishmati, the samrat's home territory. Here the final call would have to be the general's.

'All of you—get your best warriors together. Anyone who has knowledge of the divyastras or a special ability useful in warfare ... Here's what we will do ...' Brihadbala started when a soldier burst through into the tent.

'Senapati,' he panted, forgetting to salute. 'The camp of the Simhalas is on fire. Their king is dead and the soldiers are dying as we speak. Parashurama is in there.'

Brihadbala and the rest rushed out of the tent, calling for horses and reinforcements.

———

Rama awoke from his brief sleep, instantly alert. He estimated that he had slept only for a muhurta, vital and enough, given the circumstances. The faint smell of burning wood gave him pause. The Simhala and other camps would have controlled the fires by now, but their soldiers would be tense and nervous, anticipating surprise attacks and irritated by the lack of sleep. The fire-fighting and the feeling of high alert would sap their energy. But despite the slaughter and devastation he had wreaked, Arjuna's army was still humongous. Rama was reluctant to unleash the full power of the Parashu on ordinary soldiers. Besides, the rune hadn't yet glowed in the pattern, the way it had when he fought the asuras.

Mahodhara emerged from the woods, quickly making his way to Rama in the dark. It had been his watch, and he had news.

'Arjuna's army is burning down the woods in their search for you. Their Maharathis are using divyastras,' he said.

Rama grinned. They sought to smoke him out. But he wouldn't let them set the stage or the pace now that they had decided to pay him back in his own coin. He had not used his more powerful divyastras, reluctant to deploy them on ordinary soldiers or warriors did not have the prowess to fight or counter them. Even the agneyastras he had used to set the camps on fire had been limited in their potency. Warriors with the knowledge of divine astras were in the fight now, perhaps even Arjuna amongst them.

Rama quickly said his prayers and woke Akrita up to discuss his plans.

The army waited around the fort, facing the jungle, watching it burn. They knew Parashurama was in there, and they were ready and determined to put an end to the lone wolf who had visited death upon them. The fires raged, flames reaching the treetops, the thick smoke billowing upto the stars. The torches carried by the army looked like static fireflies suspended in the air from the burning jungle to the moat. A great torrent of water fell on the fires in an arc on the jungles from the east to the south gates, beating the fire down. The smoke, steam and heat were caught in the sudden wind that raced towards the soldiers. Bugles sounded and battle cries rent the air as huge phalanxes of the army disappeared behind the smog. The torrent continued to pour until it had extinguished the fire. The winds continued to snake through the ranks of soldiers who weren't able to see their compatriots even a dozen paces away.

'Varunastra! Vayavyastra! Counter measures!' someone screamed. Divyastras to dispel the smoke and repel the wind were deployed but were not powerful enough to counteract them for more than a few nimishas. And then the rain of arrows started.

The rain hammered down on the soldiers from the night sky, punching through their shields, canopies and helmets. Soldiers fell where they stood, scores of arrows piercing each one of them. Some arrows were as long as pikes, impaling the men and driving them deep into the ground.

'Into the forest. Find him!' Brihadbala shouted. Trumpets blared, signalling the manoeuvre. Soldiers ran forward, in an arc from the east to the south, pouring into the jungle where the fires had died down, their eyes streaming with water as the smoke stung their eyes and smothered their lungs. Rama raced his chariot towards them, ramming through columns of soldiers, the hooves of his horses trampling them and the heavy wheels of the ratha breaking bones and squelching flesh as it rode over the fallen.

Rama mentally chanted mantras as he shot through. Wind roared ahead of his ratha as he breached the front lines of the army, blowing men, horses and rathas out of the way. The blast of wind cleared the smoke for a few nimishas, and the soldiers were able to see an incredible sight as the ratha raced past them.

One man in a ratha moving so fast with his outstretched bow that it seemed like there were eight of him, each shooting an unending stream of arrows creating a circle of death. The arrows shot at him were met by his own arrows. The man extinguished and countered their divyastras even before they could deliver fully to their potential.

Rama cleared a path to the left with the Vayavyastra, the wind hurling the carcasses and broken chariots into the army.

The ratha turned and Rama scythed through the army, tracing a circular path down the middle, around the fort.

Dawn broke. The sun climbed higher in the sky as the battle raged on. The ratha stopped and the soldiers all around fell, more rushed in and fell themselves. Rama would again clear a path, and the ratha would move again. The Maharathis pursued him when he moved, encircled him when he stopped and attacked him from the front to prevent him from moving ahead. They challenged Rama with their own might and with the use of divine astras, singly and together. Every challenge ended in death.

Brihadbala, Mahaveera, the kings and their Maharathis surrounded Rama, shooting arrows at will, multiplying their own shafts with mantras of their own. None of them breached Rama's defence. They pursued his ratha and circled around it when it stopped, attacking, taunting, waiting for him to make a mistake, for him to tire, to sneak in one arrow through that would injure or kill him. Rama saw the foot soldiers suddenly fall back and make way for a battalion of war elephants. The general and his allies attempted to tie him down so the war elephants could trample over him.

'Nagastra! From the Nishada King!' Mahodhara warned, but Rama had already countered the attack. Hundreds of snakes flew towards him but were plucked mid-air by swarms of eagles and hawks from Rama's Garudastra.

'Not good enough!' Rama screamed at the king in rage. He invoked and let loose the Nagapashastra. In a blink, the Nishada King, his wheelmen, Maharathis, his charioteer, horses and ratha were covered with writhing snakes. They swarmed and slithered all over them, biting and spitting venom into their eyes. A gigantic python burrowed out of the earth and wound round the king's ratha and horses, constricting and crushing them in its coils, before dragging them back into its hole.

Rama shot his Garudastra again—this time to its full potency. It filled the air with the piercing cries and shrieks of eagles. They were massive, the shadow of their wingspans covering several metres of ground. The beat of their wings cleared the smoke, snuffed out the fires and toppled the men. They swooped down on the elephants and carried them up and away and dropping them on the rest of the army from above. The Vajrastra came next. Hundreds of bolts of lightning rippled through the air, white fiery streaks burning brighter than the noon sun. Chariots caught fire and exploded, horses were burnt to a crisp and men were reduced to ash.

'That's how it's done!' Mahodhara hollered at the army. 'Swami, the Kings of Magadha, Mithila and Vidharba are in the realm of Yama by your good hand.'

The soldiers and Maharathis kept coming, replacing the ones who were dead or retreating with injury or exhaustion. Brihadbala had the numbers to throw at him, to sacrifice in his quest to defeat Rama, and he would attack till Rama tired. And Rama was tiring. This was the fourth time he had gone round the massive fort, fighting every inch of the way.

The open ground was littered with carcasses of men, horses and elephants. Shattered rathas, broken blades, blasted armour and hewn limbs lay on the ground. Fires had broken out, spewing thick, pungent smoke into the air. Millions of arrows lay embedded on the corpses, some of them looking like human pin cushions. The fading sunlight filtered weakly through the haze of dust and smoke. Massive craters pockmarked the ground where Rama had blasted away entire battalions of troops. The craters were filled with corpses, some had become pools of blood, with gore and gristle floating atop the coagulating blood. The corpses stank to the heavens. The miasma of rotting corpses, blood and sweat, leather and iron, caught in the throats and lungs of soldiers, causing them to gasp and retch. And the scavengers had come to feast. Hundreds of vultures circled the sky and tenfold more covered the slain. They pecked and tore at the bodies. Hyenas roved through the dead. Crows, ravens and rodents swarmed over them, fighting each other for a morsel of flesh.

Pisachas and Vetalas, immune to mortal weapons, waited beside the soldiers who were still alive. They savoured the pain, fear and panic in the air and stared with their blood-red, unblinking eyes. They stood absolutely still, driving the soldiers mad with their eerie presence. They were biding their time for the soldier nearest to them to fall, so they could possess new bodies, drink the blood from their wounds as the soldiers breathed their last, and infest their innards with their spores. And the generals, Maharathis and their armies just could not stop the man who had done all this. His rampage of death continued long into the night.

Rama sensed his horses were tiring. It was close to midnight, and they had run almost continuously since he had invoked the chariot. He changed his strategy.

The Vayavyastra blasted a path towards the south gate, and Mahodhara turned the horses on that path. Rama blasted the gates into smithereens, and the adjoining walls cracked and crashed to the ground. He cleared a path through the debris and rode into the city, the army pouring in behind him. Rama caught a fleeing guard by the crook of his bow, and pulled him into the chariot as it raced ahead, twisting and turning corners. The guard wailed for mercy.

'The treasury, armoury, the food stores, the palaces of vassals, ministers and dignitaries. Direct me to them and you will live,' said Rama. The guard nodded in fright and desperation.

'Arjuna desecrated the sanctity of my father's ashram. I will lay his city to waste, and then we can find the samrat,' said Rama to Mahodhara.

'The horses need rest, Swami,' he replied.

'The treasury first, then rest. Let's ruin for Arjuna what he treasures most—his tributes.'

Rama killed the guards at the treasury, levelled it with the Vajrastra and burnt it to the ground with the Agneyastra.

'Where are the gardens?' Rama asked. The guard pointed, and Mahodhara rode through the deserted streets to the garden.

'Grass and water. Unhitch the horses. Let them rest awhile,' said Rama. He waited patiently for the army to catch up. Thousands of them came, signalmen having passed on the news of his location with short blasts of their bugles. They were wary and nervous, looking at the ratha and the untied horses in disbelief and anticipation. They took up their formations and advanced in tandem, wondering what the trap was. Rama waited until he thought they were close enough. Then he mentally invoked and let loose the Twashtrastra on the army.

'Don't let anyone harm my horses, ratha and charioteer,' he roared. As he said this, the soldiers turned upon each other, fighting, vying to kill. Rama waited to see if any Maharathi had the counter to this divyastra. No one seemed to know what to do or they were too busy fending off their own soldiers. Each soldier imagined himself the protector of the ratha and the other, his enemy. An enemy he would kill at any cost. Rama grabbed the guard by the neck.

'Where is Arjuna's palace?'

'A yojana that way,' the guard replied, his voice quavering.

'Let's go,' Rama pushed him ahead.

'B-but Swami, the samrat isn't there. He's been at the Devi shrine for the past three days.'

'Where is that?'

'Here, in the garden. Beyond that fountain.'

Rama ran towards the fountain, shoving the guard ahead, himself keeping away from the furious brawl that had erupted among the soldiers.

Four guards stood outside the temple, alert and ready. The sound of the brawl could be heard faintly here. They drew their weapons as Rama approached. He disposed them off quickly, smashing the base of the Parashu's handle into the temple of one guard, striking the side of the neck of another with the hard edge of his palm. The third had the wind knocked out of him with a kick to the groin, and the last was hit on the back of the head with the flat of the blade. They would all remain incapacitated for some time. The guard he had brought along stood still, unwilling to enter the temple, imploring Rama with his eyes. Rama let him be. 'Stay,' he ordered.

He entered the temple through the stone archway. Ahead of him was a spacious mantapa, and beyond that a simple garbhagriha with a murthi of the Devi. Torches were mounted on the high walls of the temple, on the four pillars of the mantapa, and on either side of the doorway of the garbha griha. A big lamp with four wicks burned at the feet of the Devi. A yagnakund blazed in the centre of the mantapa. A priest and his assistant sat on one side, chanting mantras softly. Opposite them sat five men and a woman.

Rama looked at the handsome, prodigiously well-built man. It was the man he had seen in his dream. Arjuna.

Arjuna turned, sensing a new presence. He saw the axe first, and in the next instant he found Rama's eyes. The young man in the dream. Parashurama.

Karthavirya Arjuna and Parashurama locked eyes with each other. Neither uttered a word. The priest turned to check what had distracted the samrat. His chant petered out when he saw the man inside the archway. The others turned. All eyes were on Rama now. He walked forward.

The men behind Arjuna scrambled to their feet. Arjuna motioned for them to sit back down, his eyes still fixed on Rama who climbed the five steps of the mantapa and came to a stop a few feet away from the yagnakund.

The two men continued to stare at each other. The tension in the air rendered everyone else at a loss for words. They waited with bated breath. Arjuna probed Rama's mind, and was almost startled out of his sukhasana posture at what he saw there.

Thoughts flew at a furious pace in his enemy's head. Rama had the mantapa and the people in it drawn like a painting in his head. He remembered every single detail of that picture. The colours of their clothes, the distances at which they were seated with respect to each other, the expressions on their faces, the vessels and items being used in the yagna, even the number of bricks used to build the yagnakund. He was assessing the time each would take to reach for a weapon, how fast they could stand up, which arm they preferred, and how much strength each had. Suchandra moved quietly to the left as he sat. Arjuna saw Rama reassess and note his new position immediately. He spent the longest time assessing Arjuna's prodigious physique, noting the breadth of his palm, and the length of his fingers, and the reach of his arms. He wondered how he transformed into Sahasrabahu and why Arjuna didn't topple with the weight of a thousand arms. He correctly deduced that Arjuna would have to grow to an enormous height and girth to manage all his arms, and wondered if that was possible in the confines of the mantapa. Again, he arrived at the right conclusion. Arjuna would just smash through the mantapa. Only one thought now, what did Sahasrabahu look like? Arjuna watched him worry it over. He couldn't devise a strategy unless he knew what Sahasrabahu and his arms were capable of. Rama thought a bit more about it and then just dismissed it. He remembered the last words of the mantra as he was walking towards the mantapa and wondered why the samrat was here when there was a battle raging outside. He also understood the sankalpa of the yagna. He deduced everything correctly; it was for the safety and long life of the samrat. But he didn't know this ritual, and what or who was being invoked was a mystery to him.

Rama dismissed this thread of thought too and considered what he knew about Arjuna. Jamadagni's image appeared in his mind, talking about Arjuna. The words flashed across his mind. *Arjuna has the ability to read the thoughts of others.* In an instant, all the thoughts and pictures disappeared from Rama's mind to be replaced by an image of the Parashu.

Arjuna probed deeper. No, this was not an image. The Parashu was a living thing *inside his head! Something sentient!*

Arjuna's mind went numb with shock. How was this possible?

He probed for a few nimishas more and then, gave up. He glowered at Rama.

The priest finally found his voice.

'Who are you?' he asked hoarsely, his eyes darting from the man to the menacing axe. Rama smiled, his raptor-like gaze still fixed on Arjuna.

'Parashurama,' he replied. A frisson of nervous excitement ran through everyone except Rama and Arjuna.

'Who is he?' Rama asked, pointing at Arjuna with his axe. Arjuna smiled.

'Kill this wretch,' the lady cried, but Arjuna waved for the men to remain seated even before they could move. He motioned to the priest to answer.

'Chakravarti Samrat Karthavirya Arjuna,' said a haughty voice. It was the lady who had answered.

Rama looked at her. She stared back at him with anger, but there was deep fear dancing in her eyes. Rama pointed to her and looked at the priest. The priest hastily glanced at Arjuna and replied into the awkward silence, 'Queen Manorama.'

Rama looked at the four men glaring at him. The priest answered again. 'Crown Prince Jayadhwaja, King Suchandra and his son Prince Pushkaraksha, General Devadutta. I'm High Priest Raikava and this is my assistant.'

Next, he asked more confidently, 'What is your business here?'

Rama dropped the Parashu on the smooth stone floor with a clang, startling everyone except Arjuna. He pressed his palms together and gestured towards the murthi.

'The temple is closed to the public till the samrat and queen finish their puja at dawn. Leave now and come back later,' said Raikava 'How did the guards allow you in?'

'They're dead,' said Arjuna.

'They're unconscious,' said Parashurama, at the same time.

'You can finish your puja. I will not kill in a temple,' said Rama. Arjuna laughed derisively.

Rama looked at the murthi of the Devi. It was elaborately decorated with flowers and jewellery. Three hands of the murthi held the pasha, ankusha and kamala, and the fourth was in surya mudra. 'Devi Adi Parashakti,' Rama whispered under his breath as he looked at the powerful and serene face of the goddess in the light of the torches and the lamp.

He lay down on the mantapa floor in shastanga pranama and went into dhyana.

'Devi Ma, your devotee beseeches you. Show me a way to defeat Arjuna,' he prayed in his mind. He paused and from deep within him, the words emanated, 'I offer my own head as sacrifice.'

The unknown power roared through Rama's being. He didn't examine or try to understand it. Rama kept his mind blank. He rose and opened his eyes. Only the whites of his eyes were visible now. Raikava gasped and Arjuna stared. The four flames of the lamp at the Devi's feet gathered and blazed tall, dancing in the shape of a serpent.

Arjuna probed again. But, he only saw the brilliance of the golden Parashu in Rama's mind.

Rama's vision filled with the serpentine flame, the third eye of the goddess on her forehead and the full bloomed lotus adorning the crown of her head. He closed his eyes and bowed to the Devi again. When he opened his eyes, his pupils stared at Arjuna and then he looked at the fire in the yagnakund.

'I guess Arjuna won't get up until the yagna is done. He didn't respect the sanctity of my father's ashram. Good that he respects the sanctity of this ritual. I will too. Finish the yagna. I will kill him on the battlefield.'

Manorama laughed, throwing her utter lack of respect for him into her demeanour and her words. 'The samrat will tear you apart, fool.'

Rama turned and walked away without a word.

Arjuna stared at Rama's retreating back. Anger growing at the audacity of the man. His eyes fell on the Parashu still lying where Rama had left it. He glared at it. It suddenly stood upright, startling Arjuna and whipped away, out of the temple, into Rama's hand. Rama laughed.

22

Mrithyu

Rama made his way out of the garden in his ratha. Arjuna's soldiers filled every inch of every street as far as he could see. They were in a pitched battle against each other. The trained and armed mob had formed groups. They were cutting down anyone who belonged to a different group and were turning on each other when they couldn't find anyone else. General Brihadbala's chariot was overrun with a murderous swarm of his own soldiers, hacking and stabbing him, killing his charioteer and disembowelling his horses. The mob attacked everyone but Rama. Maharathis fought their own troops and used their divyastras to dispel them, but no one had a counter to the Twashtrastra. The humongous army had turned on itself. They would do Rama's job for him. The ratha sped towards the gates, the mob parting to make way.

Raikava was starting the puja again when Arjuna asked him, 'What is the meaning of the omen? The serpent of flame we all saw?'

Raikava pursed his lips in thought and replied, 'I do not know, Samrat. I can meditate on it after the puja if you wish, but it is vital we finish the puja before dawn. There are only a few muhurtas left.' Arjuna gestured for the puja to continue.

Three muhurtas later, Mahaveera stumbled into the temple, bleeding profusely from half a dozen wounds. He dropped his sword and battered shield and clambered up the mantapa steps.

'Samrat,' he rasped, blood bubbling at the corner of his mouth. 'Parashurama has turned the soldiers against each other. They have slaughtered General Brihadbala and dozens of other officers and are now destroying the city. They have turned against unarmed citizens, even women and children. It is some divyastra. Nobody out there knows how to counter it.'

'Twastr,' said Arjuna.

'I have the counter, Samrat. Allow me to leave, else there will be no army and no city left,' said Suchandra. He paused. 'Bhimapala and Mangala know the counter too. Where are they?' he asked Mahaveera.

'Dead. In the last two days, Parashurama has killed at least ten akshauhinis. We lost count after that.' Everyone gasped in astonishment except Arjuna. He glanced at the sky. Couple of muhurtas more to dawn.

Manorama held his arm. 'What damage has been done, cannot be undone. It makes no sense for you to leave the puja now, so close to the end. It will give you your greatest victory, my love. I promise. Let Suchandra handle this problem.'

Arjuna sighed and nodded. 'Take Devadutta with you. Jayadhwaja, get this man a vaidya and return.'

Suchandra bowed to the samrat and the queen, prayed to the goddess and left with Devadutta and Pushkaraksha.

'If he kills Parashurama, this puja would no longer be of any use,' Arjuna said to Manorama.

'If Suchandra kills him, the victory will still be yours. A challenger who died at the hands of a mere vassal of the samrat. If Suchandra dies, you will ride out after the puja and victory will be yours, I promise. Both ways you win. I don't care how many lives Parashurama takes, be it Suchandra's or Brihadbala's or any other king's. But he will not take yours. We will rule for a thousand years more and fashion the world as we see fit,' said Manorama. Her eyes gleamed with passion and ambition. Arjuna smiled.

'Continue,' he ordered Raikava.

The ratha rolled into the small clearing in a different part of the jungle. Mahodhara had found it on his rounds during the watch. It wouldn't be wise to rest at the same place again. Akrita peeped out from behind a tree and came running to meet them.

'The samrat?' he said, hoping to hear the news of his death.

'I met him. He sits in a puja till dawn breaks and will fight only after. We have some time,' said Rama.

'You met the samrat?' Akrita said in astonishment. 'What did he say?'

'Nothing. We didn't say a word to each other.'

He alighted from the ratha and sat down against the nearest tree. Akrita mulled over Rama's words for a while and then busied himself in building a small fire to cook their meal. Mahodhara drew a knife from his waistband and slipped into the woods to go round the camp and to check for spies or assassins.

The blood rush and battle rage ebbed away from Rama

and weariness set in. He slumped in exhaustion, stretching his legs out. The silence and darkness wrapped around him like a comforting blanket. He sat awhile and then gathered himself in padmasana and began his pranayama, easing his breath in through one nostril and out through the other. He then lay flat on the grass and relaxed his muscles, breathing in, holding his breath and exhaling, just as he had practised since childhood. His muscles relaxed further, and his body went completely still. His mind, however, was furiously at work, turning Guru Dattatreya's words over, trying to make sense of them and of the omen at the temple. He grew more desperate for an answer, and the more he searched, the more anxious he grew. Rama finally gave up and relaxed his mind, letting the thoughts come and go as he paid attention to his breath. He eased into yoganidra, the state of complete relaxation.

He awoke a muhurta later and found Akrita and Mahodhara beside him, waiting for him to wake up. They had extinguished the fire. The three of them ate silently in the darkness, thinking ahead to the dawn and of Arjuna's arrival on the battlefield.

They were resting after the meal when a few explosions rocked the forest. Lightning arced down in the darkness, burning some trees to ash and causing others to explode. Someone was trying to flush them out of the forest; someone was calling them to battle.

'It's not dawn yet. Has Arjuna forsaken the puja?' Mahodhara asked.

'Let's find out,' said Rama.

Rama's ratha emerged from the forest. The explosions went on, randomly going off in different parts of the forest. The fires on the battlefield did not reveal the identity of the warrior who sought to fight him. There was a distant glow in the horizon in the direction of the fort. Mahodhara coaxed the horses forward. Akrita crouched in the shelter of the metal cladding that ran around the three sides of the ratha. He lifted his head to peep over Mahodhara's shoulder.

Rama invoked and shot the Suryastra. Blazing light filled the sky, shining through the haze that still hung over the battlefield. He saw a mammoth army awaiting him in front of the fort. Soldiers were still pouring out of the destroyed east gate. The distant glow was the city of Mahishmati burning within the fort. Someone had, indeed, countered his astra, but not before a good amount of damage had been done.

'Unbelievable! Still more soldiers,' said Rama.

'I estimate you've slain more than half of the army gathered here, Swami,' said Mahodhara.

Rama noted the variety of pennants and standards in the army, led by three chariots in the front. He peered at the maharathis in the chariots.

'Suchandra, with Pushkaraksha and Devadutta,' said Rama.

'And the Haihaya horde,' said Mahodhara. 'The Vitihotras, Sharyatas, Bhojas, Avantyas and Tundikeras. Elite soldiers, the very core of Arjuna's military.'

The light of the Suryastra was abruptly cut off when Suchandra countered it with the Parjanyastra. Masses of dark clouds appeared, thunder boomed, lightning flashed and rain pelted down in the darkness. Clarions sounded across the field and the ground shook as the army charged ahead.

'You have a conch, Swami. Amrutajit. It's in the recess behind the quiver notches.'

Rama found and blew it; its sound deep and resonant,

as his ratha raced forward. He handed the conch to Akrita and started shooting his arrows, chanting mantras mentally. Thousands of arrows flew from his bow. He shot the Aindrastra to shower shafts from the sky and the Vayavyastra to blow the army off their feet. They countered all of his arrows and divyastras. The lightning flashed again, and Rama saw the army still charging ahead, much closer now. He shot again and again, nocking two and three arrows at once, moving blazingly fast. His astra exploded in the wall of men racing towards him and in the next moment, Suchandra was there, countering him, buying time for the men to regroup.

Pushkaraksha and Devadutta swept around him and attacked his flanks. Rama counterattacked, not allowing any arrow to sneak through, but he could not break through their defences either. Rama's ratha turned, looking for an opening to break through. Suchandra and his compatriots fought furiously, keeping him on the defensive. The ratha turned a complete circle and Rama realised the tremendous disadvantage of his position. The army had encircled him, and it was protected by three warriors of high calibre and with the knowledge of divyastras. The three rathas orbited around him like planets revolve around the sun, seeking a chance to converge upon him.

Suchandra attacked, and his two partners sought to tighten the circle. Rama fended them off, cutting off their bows, using the momentary gap of time before they lifted new bows, to inflict as much damage as he could. He drove Suchandra wide with his arrows, all the while defending his ratha, horses and Mahodhara from harm.

He moved faster than he ever had, his left hand holding the heavy bow rock steady while his right hand was a blur.

The wall of arrows flowing out from him in all directions was relentless and deadly. Arrows pierced the defences of the three warriors, killing scores of soldiers behind them. He shattered their rathas and killed more as they jumped into new chariots. The three Maharathis protected each other, preventing Rama from harming or killing any of them. They rained boulders at him from the sky, he smashed them. Arrows rained down on him, he blew them away. He countered every divyastra they unleashed on him.

———

Dawn broke and Raikava signalled the end of the puja, thanking the Gods for their blessings and for the safe conclusion of the ceremony. Manorama applied the victory blessing, the vijaya tilaka, on Arjuna's forehead.

'My life force is now yoked to yours, my love. It is the protection of the love of the queen for her samrat. You cannot be killed before my life is taken from me,' said Manorama.

'That was not necessary, my love, but I honour your wish. You humble me with your love,' said Arjuna gently.

'I will stay here and continue my prayers until that wretch dies,' said Manorama.

'Eat first. You've stayed hungry for four days.' Arjuna fed her a little of the prasada from the puja.

'Long live the Samrat!' said Manorama.

'Long live my Queen!' Arjuna replied.

A soldier entered the temple and whispered in Jayadhwaja's ears. The prince listened and dismissed the soldier. He approached his parents.

'The Haihaya army and Suchandra have surrounded the wretch. It is only a matter of time now.'

Arjuna looked at the horizon. The smoke from the burning city billowed and hung in the air like an insult to his power. Parashurama had burned his city while he sat in puja in deference to Manorama's wishes. His aura of invincibility had been damaged forever. One man had done this—a formidable and worthy adversary. Arjuna wondered if Suchandra could bring him Parashurama's head.

Arjuna bade Jayadhwaja remain and attend to his mother. He walked out of the temple to see with his own eyes the destruction Parashurama had wrought on his beloved city. The four guards still lay crumpled on the ground. Further ahead, as far as he could see, the garden was littered with thousands of slain soldiers. Anger bloomed inside Arjuna. He saw a lone soldier standing to the side of the temple entrance and walked up to him. Utter terror danced in the soldier's eyes.

'P-p-pranaam S-s-samrat,' he said, quaking in his boots. Drool dripped from a corner of his mouth. Arjuna waited.

'Parashurama ordered me to stay here when he came to the temple,' the soldier mewled. He saw the rage in Arjuna's eyes, and a small moan escaped his lips. Arjuna looked long and hard at him and turned away with a mighty effort.

'Go home,' said Arjuna.

———

Rama fought on. Many muhurtas had passed since dawn had broken, but the battlefield stayed under the darkness of dust and smoke. He concentrated his attack on Pushkaraksha and Devadutta. Rama knew by the stretch of their bows and the power of their arrows that they were weaker than Suchandra.

He targeted them relentlessly, injuring them dozens of times. His arrows sneaked past their defences and destroyed their bows, rathas and even the army flanking them. But Suchandra was always there to save them, to counterattack, to give them time to recoup. Rama grew desperate. Two days of continuous warfare with hardly any respite had put him at a disadvantage against these fresh warriors. He had to end this impasse.

Rama invoked and shot the Narayanastra.

'Drop your weapons!' Suchandra screamed. His charioteer blew short blasts on his conch. The cue was taken up by the signalmen, who began blowing their bugles and clarions for downing arms.

The astra hurtled through the air, its power radiating outwards. It pulverised anyone holding a weapon in the blink of an eye. Great swathes of the army fell, reduced to piles of pounded flesh, iron and leather. Blood burst into the air and turned into a fine red mist. The survivors watched in horror, frozen at the incredible power of the astra, splattered by the gore and blood of their unfortunate compatriots.

The power of the astra roared through the army and dissipated. Rama hurried to shoot his arrows at Suchandra before he could pick up his weapons. Suchandra stood defiant, smiling insolently, daring Rama to do his worst. Rama shot his shafts in a blur, hundreds of arrows racing like the wind towards Suchandra who swatted them away with his trishula. Rama stood stunned. That was impossible ... unless the trishula was divine, a blessing upon Suchandra.

He watched in horror as Suchandra threw it at him. He knew that ordinary arrows would have no effect on it and he knew of no divyastra, which could counter the trishula. In desperate panic, he dropped his bow and called the Parashu to hand. He flung it at the trishula.

The two weapons collided, and it seemed that the world would end. A piercing, grating sound made them all drop to the ground. The ground heaved and shock waves emanated from the two weapons, the waves threatening to unravel the very fibre of his being. The sound was a merciless throb in Rama's head. The ferocity of the waves increased, and the ground shook as if gigantic hammers were battering their way out. Rama recalled his Parashu to end this insanity. He collapsed to the floor of the ratha, waiting for the trishula to impale him and end his life. It never came. Suchandra, too, had recalled his weapon too and fallen in a swoon inside his chariot.

Rathas careened around the field, the horses maddened by the sound and the shock waves, the charioteers slumped in their seats. Not a single soldier had managed to remain on his feet, and the horses and elephants trampled over them in their mad rush. Rama fought to ignore the pain in his ears, the angry throb in his head and the wayward course of his ratha. He controlled his breath with great difficulty and calmed himself, closed his eyes and let his mind go blank. Rama invoked the yagnakund in his mind and fed the pain into the agni, dismissing its hold over him. He cleaved his mind. His pupils turned upwards beneath his eyelids.

Rama invoked the battlefield in his mind. He saw Suchandra collapsed in his hurtling ratha. He probed the essence of his spiritual power and the strength behind the trishula bestowed upon him. Complete pitch black surrounded the yagnakund, blanking it out. Eerie laughter echoed through his mind, making his hair stand and a shiver run down his spine. Some power, mind numbingly potent and infinitely dangerous had descended upon him. A brilliant, long, blood red tongue appeared in the dark. A garland of laughing skulls emerged beneath it. A shining scimitar rose high above the tongue.

Bhagawati rakshaam dehi!
Rakshaam bhagawati dehi!
Rama chanted.

Bhagawati vijayam dehi!
Vijayam bhagawati dehi!
Bhagawati bhiksham dehi!
Bhiksham bhagawati dehi!

'Ma Bhadrakali, judge my intent, judge my dharma. Grant me victory,' he prayed.

Rama held his palms together and turned them upwards. He asked the Devi for alms. Turmeric glowed in his left palm, fire in his right. Rama understood. The dust from the shrine of the Malaya Kshatriyas was to be his shield, and the fire his sword.

On the battlefield, Rama withdrew the small piece of cloth he had in his waistband at the temple in Tripura and stood. He threw the yellow dust in the air and it settled all over him, leaching through his dhoti, covering him from neck to toe in yellow.

The pitch black disappeared from around the yagnakund. Rama's ratha came to a stop as Mahodhara recovered and controlled the horses. He saw Akrita curled up on the floor of the ratha, his head clutched between his hands. Suchandra also reined in his steeds, his charioteer still slumped in his seat. He picked up his bow and saw Rama stare back at him, unarmed. He shot an arrow straight at Rama's chest. Rama caught it in mid-air and broke the shaft in half. Suchandra nocked another arrow. The surprise on his face turned to panic as he struggled in vain to remember his mantras.

'You have misused Ma Bhadrakali's blessings. She has withdrawn her boons. Time to pay for your crimes,' shouted Rama.

Suchandra dropped his bow and grasped the trishula. He flung it at Rama. It hit Rama on the chest and landed uselessly at his feet. Rama took up his bow, nocked an arrow, and shot the Agneyastra at incredible speed. He burned Suchandra to a crisp. The trishula disappeared.

Rama put away his bow. The Parashu flew upto his hand as he jumped off the ratha and sprinted. He leapt into Pushkaraksha's ratha and hacked him into two, from the top of his skull to his loins. Rama flung his axe. It decapitated Devadutta and returned back to his hand. Bugles sounded. The army had recovered. They had seen the three Maharathis being slain, and now saw Rama without his bow. They charged. Rama roared, battle lust raging through him. Not the time for the bow and arrow, time for the Parashu. To kill, to cut flesh and spill blood. To give the 'drinker of blood' a river to swallow. He picked up a battle-axe from Pushkaraksha's ratha. Parashu in his right hand and the battle-axe in his left, he invoked the image of the Parashu in his dhyana. The rune on the Parashu glowed. Spokes radiated out from the bindu to the circle, and started turning like a wheel. A small movement, each nimisha. Rama understood.

Mahakaal's weapon. The rune was the wheel of time. In his mind, he slowed down the spin of the wheel. The charge of the army towards him also slowed down. They looked as if they were moving not through air but thick sludge. Rama leapt off from the ratha, whirling the Parashu and the axe. He danced through the soldiers, cutting them down while they looked like they were standing still.

One muhurta later, he stopped. Nothing more, man, horse or elephant remained to be cut. He returned to his ratha. Akrita and Mahodhara looked into his eyes and froze.

He invoked the Vayavyastra and released it to do his bidding. The wind whirled through the field, gathering and piling up the thousands upon thousands of corpses. When the wind died down, he invoked the astra again. A column of wind swept towards Mahishmati. Rama blew the blast of Amrutajit into it.

The conch's blast roared like a thunderclap through Mahishmati and Arjuna's palace, which was yojanas away from the field. It froze everyone to a numbing stillness, making their hair stand on end, petrified to even draw a breath. Manorama's eyes flew open, her mind and mouth forgot the words of her incessant prayer. A ruthless silence clamped down as the blast rolled away. The silence lay thick, pungent and oily on the skins of soldiers, citizens, priests and royalty alike threatening to smother life, shatter bones and pulp the innards of every living thing.

'ARJUNAAAH!'

Rama screamed into the silence, the power of the invoked wind ripping through it. Men reeled and toppled, women swooned, the children stood mute, unable to cry in their utter terror. The scream was everywhere at once, and inside everyone's head, turning their minds into mush with the brawn and rage imbued in it. It cascaded through the streets, flooding the gardens and markets and temples and mansions. It echoed in the high-ceilinged court and palace of the monarch of the world.

Arjuna stared stonily at nothing; his face as hard as granite. His fists clenched involuntarily as virulent rage blossomed in his heart. He knew what it meant. Arjuna got up to prepare for battle.

———

Arjuna rode through his desolate city. There wasn't a single man or woman alive on the streets, except for the remnants of his army that marched behind him. Corpses were everywhere, covered with crows, ravens and rats. Citizens who had walked proudly as the residents of the capital of the world, now huddled in their homes in fear. The sounds of the horses' hooves, the wheels of the ratha, and the boots of the army echoed in the quiet of a city holding its breath and in the dim light of its broken magnificence. Arjuna's ratha wound through streets that had been cleared of dead bodies. They were piled up like macabre head-high walls. Vultures perched atop them, not pecking or tearing at the flesh but watching the procession with beady eyes, like sentinels of death.

Arjuna rode out of the destroyed gates of his fort and gazed at the devastation Parashurama had wreaked. Death had reaped an extraordinary harvest in the last three days. The dead were piled up in countless pyramids as far as the eye could see. Corpses of twenty akshauhinis. The remaining akshauhini marched behind him. The haze hovered, thick, dark and menacing like some creature from Naraka. The stench, already bad in the city, was a hundred-fold worse here.

His breath clenched as if a snake had wound itself around his lungs and squeezed. Fires pockmarked the battlefield like virulent blisters, some glowing red hot with bitter malice and others blazing with a vengeful fury, roaring with the hunger to devour more.

Arjuna gazed at the unbecoming of his empire, of his invincibility and his legacy. All brought about by the single most powerful threat he had ever faced. Parashurama's death would be the start of a new era. Arjuna would reign for thousands of years more and become the greatest samrat of this Chaturyuga. Arjuna saw the lone ratha in the distance, only a charioteer and a slightly built, young brahmin boy in it. He scanned the battleground for Parashurama.

He saw him, standing atop the largest pyramid of corpses, twirling his axe, framed by the blaze behind him.

Rama watched the huge ratha emerge from the gates. It was built long and high and needed scores of horses and tens of wheels to move it. Soldiers assembled behind it, but the army didn't matter anymore. Arjuna's reputation had been destroyed. His death would be the final unbecoming. After that, the world would heave a sigh of relief; it would heal and become a better place.

'Can you kill him?' a small voice in his head asked. 'I have to,' Rama spoke to himself. 'I will find a way.'

Arjuna's ratha moved forward, leaving the army behind. Rama smiled. It would be a man-to-man duel. Arjuna would want to defeat him without transforming into Sahasrabahu, to show the world that Parashurama had not been worthy of his full power. The samrat was bare-chested; he wore no armour, not even a war helmet. The man's vanity and ego were enormous. Rama leapt off the pile of corpses and climbed into his ratha. He took up his bow as Akrita crouched low and Mahodhara sped forward. Rama twanged his bow string.

The arrows came thick and fast. Rama countered them in the nick of time. Thousands of bolts flew from each bow as Rama's ratha circled Arjuna's. Rama couldn't help but admire the sheer power and grace of Arjuna's skill with his bow. He made it look so effortless. Rama forgot his tiredness and lost himself in the joy of battling with the most powerful man in the world.

Arjuna poured all his prowess and ability into his attack. He probed for Rama's weaknesses and found none. His attacks were all repulsed, his ploys understood and parried. Parashurama was an incredible warrior, his movements dizzyingly fast, his focus sharp and unerring. He felt a grudging admiration for his enemy. This was the definitive battle of his life, and it would be remembered for centuries.

And then the divyastras came into play.

The fires of the battleground blazed with extraordinary fury and immense columns of fire flowed, converging on Rama's ratha. Rama rushed to counter it with the Varunastra and Vayavyastra. The wind spun outwards from Rama and gathering the water of the Varunastra, exploded outwards and upwards. Wind and water raced past Arjuna, killing the fires and filling the air with steam. The piles of corpses lifted to the sky and crashed downwards at Rama. Mahodhara pushed his horses to a full gallop, turning the ratha this way and that, buying time for Rama to counter. Rama blew as many of the piles as he could into smithereens, while the rest landed where the ratha was nimishas ago with a loud sickening squelch.

Rama cleaved his mind. He couldn't see Arjuna invoke his divyastras in time—only his speed was helping him counter them in the nick of time. Arjuna's mantra siddhi was intensely powerful. Rama invoked the battleground in his dhyana and gazed at Arjuna. All he saw before him was a brilliant revolving disc. He tried to draw the chakra into the yagnakund fire. It wouldn't budge at all, but he could sense the next divyastra being invoked. He had won himself precious fractions of nimishas to counter Arjuna.

Arjuna shot the Nagastra and Rama countered with his own. Two giant serpents fought on the field, their hoods as high as mountains, swaying far above the rathas. They twisted and wound around each other, spewing venomous fumes, biting and spitting at each other. Arjuna let loose the Garudastra, but Rama blew the gigantic eagle away with a blast of wind from his Vayavyastra. Arjuna stared in disbelief.

Rama's reaction to his divyastras had been immediate, much faster than earlier, as if the man was reading his mind. He shot his arrows in a fury, invoking his divine weapons, multiplying his arrows. Rama staved off all of them. He counterattacked, paying back Arjuna in his own coin. He couldn't breach Arjuna's impregnable defence. The weapons of the slain warriors lifted from the ground and hurtled towards Rama. He deflected them towards Arjuna who blew them away into dust. They fought on, both seeking an opening, a lapse, a delay of a fraction of a nimisha to gain the upper hand. Both were unable to break the deadlock.

Arjuna roared in anger and frustration. In a blink, Sahasrabahu stood in the chariot. Rama stared in awe as he saw the gigantic form for the first time. He understood the purpose of the huge ratha. It was to bear Sahasrabahu's weight and his weapons. Five hundred arms took up bows, five hundred arms nocked arrows in them and shot them at Rama, each arrow multiplying to thousands as it flew out. Rama countered with thousands of his own and the Vayavyastra. Arjuna stared in disbelief. On and on they fought, caught up in frenzy and battle lust.

In his dhyana, Rama saw Arjuna invoke the Brahmastra. He was stunned by Arjuna's action. The weapon could destroy the very weave of reality if deployed with its full potency, and Arjuna had done so. The only counter was a Brahmastra of his own. He invoked it and let it loose.

The five elements seemed to pause for a nimisha before they began to pound. Rama's very being throbbed and an ear-splitting, mind-numbing shriek roared through his mind. The tremendous potency each had imbued in their astras clashed against each other and the energy spewed out, uncontrolled. Rama glanced at Arjuna, the immense heat turning his sight watery. His mind reeled when he saw Sahasrabahu roar with maniacal laughter. Arjuna didn't care, he would destroy the universe if that's what it took to win.

In his dhyana, Rama saw the brilliant point of energy that had been generated by the opposing Brahmastras. It pulsed virulently—the force of the energy and the intensity of light growing with each pulse. The battleground disappeared in his dhyana and a still, pregnant darkness replaced it. The darkness of emptiness, of the absence of any form of matter. The universe seemed to hold its breath. The point of energy grew to the size of an egg, gathering power, concentrating it on itself. Don't let the egg crack open, Rama's mind screamed. He fought his panic. The energy of the egg was stupendous, and once released, it would destroy all creation. Revoking his astra would be of no use now. The energy had grown enormously. Arjuna's astra would alone destroy the world and every living being in it. He emptied his mind, not thinking but giving in entirely to instinct. Rama imagined the Parashu over the yagnakund, and it appeared, its power surging through him. He replaced the Parashu with the golden egg of energy. Rama paid homage to it and to Brahma, the creator of the astra and the universe itself. He sought Brahma's permission and surrendered to him again. The unknown power surged through him again. Cracks appeared on the surface of the egg; it would explode any nimisha now! He saw the stream of Arjuna's yogic power flow into the egg like a river in spate, and his own power cascading against it. He invoked the Parashu again and cut off Arjuna's stream of power. It wasn't enough. The incredible potency of the twin Brahmastras colliding now had a life of its own.

Rama's mind raced. He didn't know what to do. Even if the energy had been just a point and not a brilliant egg on the verge of explosion, he wouldn't have known what to do.

A word blazed across his consciousness.

Bindu! The rune on the Parashu!

Rama focussed on the rune. He willed the circle around the bindu to glow. The Parashu responded. Then, he imagined the circle as a sphere containing the egg. A golden orb materialised around the egg. The egg exploded.

The energy crashed against the golden sphere. A long, keening boom erupted from the Parashu as it thrummed in frenzy, struggling to contain the power of two Brahmastras.

Rama willed the sphere to contract. The sphere didn't budge.

And, then ...

... ever so slowly, it grew smaller and smaller. Rama contracted it as much as he could.

Arjuna sensed a subtle shift in the stupendous power coursing around them on the battlefield. Alarms clanged in his mind. He probed into Rama's mind and almost dropped his bow in astonishment. He could see two minds in Rama's head. Or was it one mind divided in two? He didn't know. But he could suddenly see two Ramas—one on the battlefield and the other in dhyana before a yagnakund, controlling the Brahmastras.

How? Arjuna's mind screamed. How could any mortal do that? Could even the devas do that? Unbidden, something from Pulastya's thoughts from the past raced to the front of his mind. Rama was a Brahmakshatriya!

And that Parashu, it wasn't merely a weapon, he had guessed right earlier, it was ... it was ... a part of Parashurama's mind.

Arjuna watched, fascinated, despite himself.

Rama fused his Brahmastra with Arjuna's and chanted the mantra for its revocation. He withdrew them both in the nick of time. The egg blinked out of existence. The Parashu went still. The golden orb dissipated. The battleground slammed back into his dhyana.

Arjuna stood stupefied in his ratha. Parashurama had revoked both the Brahmastras. No mortal had ever done such a thing before. Even the devas wouldn't know how to. It was beyond his own powers, even.

Rama leant back against the flagpole of his ratha, panting from exhaustion at the enormous mental and spiritual effort he had expended. It began to rain gently, and the rays of the setting sun broke through the smog, bathing everything in an orange-red glow.

'Enough!' Arjuna roared. 'Enough of these playthings.

Let's settle this man to man. Fight me and die like your cowardly father!'

Blind fury exploded in Rama, the wrath of the Parashu surged through him. Sahasrabahu leapt. Rama dropped his bow and hurled himself out of the chariot, the Parashu flying back into his hand. They met in mid-air. Rama chopped off Arjuna's fists and arms as he swerved to avoid the punches and the grasping hands coming his way. Arjuna laughed as he landed. The chopped arms and fists regenerated. He charged again.

Rama moved as fast as he could, in the grip of rage, instinct and the power of the Parashu.

Kill! Kill! Kill! His mind urged.

He hacked through the forest of arms, weaving through them, slashing at the knees and calves of the gargantuan form. Arms regrew again, wounds healed and disappeared without a scar. Arjuna attacked again. Rama moved in a blur, dodging the blows, whirling the Parashu continuously around him. He invoked the Vayavyastra as he leapt. The wind thrust him upwards and onto Arjuna's bent back. Rama roared as he plunged the Parashu into the prodigious mass of flesh on Arjuna's back from where the arms had sprouted. Arjuna screamed in pain. Rama hacked, tearing off huge chunks of flesh, blood and gore splashing on the yellow of his skin. He cut the arms that twisted to grasp him and drove the axe deeper into the flesh with every stroke.

'Why wasn't the Parashu cutting through?' Rama thought in desperation.

Arjuna threw himself backwards to crush Rama between the ground and his tremendous weight. Rama jumped out of the way as Arjuna crashed to the earth. In a nimisha, Arjuna was up again, laughing, his thousand arms mocking Rama's effort.

Lightning crashed as Rama leapt away in the nick of time. He cut through the next strike, caught the third with the Parashu and hurled it back at Sahasrabahu. Sahasrabahu bellowed. If Arjuna didn't need anything material to invoke the Divyastras, neither did Rama. He called the lightning down on Sahasrabahu. He was too large to avoid the strikes. They hit him with a ferocious force. His arms flailed as Rama sliced them away, littering the ground with them. Arjuna let the lightning burn through his body, watching Rama all the while. His body healed in a couple of nimishas as his hands continued to flail at Rama, trying to smash his fists into him. Rama was wonderstruck at the amount of battering Sahasrabahu's body was capable of enduring, even as he continued to hack away at Sahasrabahu's torso. He moved in a blur but one of the hundreds of fists hit him with tremendous force. It flung him several feet away. Rama struggled to get to his feet as the battlefield heaved and swayed in his vision. His body throbbed with agony. He thanked the gods that it was only a glancing blow, else his body would have been broken by now. He managed to stand up on his third attempt, gasping for breath.

Fight! Fight! Fight! His mind screamed.

The lightning died away as Rama used the Vayavyastra to blow Sahasrabahu back. He crashed into his humungous ratha, smashing it into a misshapen heap. It bought Rama some precious time to regain his breath and steady himself.

Sahasrabahu laughed. He grew even larger. He lifted the squashed ratha, dead horses and all, broke it across his thigh and hurled the pieces at Rama. Rama leapt away, escaping the two halves of the ratha by a whisker. Sahasrabahu roared and pummelled the ground with his fists. The ground cracked open. Dead elephants, horses, rathas and soldiers slid into the chasms that had opened, pulling Rama along. Rama hurled the Parashu at Sahasrabahu's neck as he held on to the edge of the gorge, scrambling for a foothold. He pressed himself against the walls of the gorge to avoid the falling debris. He waited for the flood of dead bodies and equipment to subside below him and then climbed out.

He saw Sahasrabahu twist and contort his arms to keep the Parashu from reaching his neck. He was straining and grunting with all the effort. It was taking all his superhuman strength to fight the Parashu, but the Parashu moved inexorably forward, inch by inch.

Now! Kill him! Rama's mind screamed.

Rama scrambled around for a weapon. He found a broadsword, invoked the wind and leapt high. The wind aided his flight. He landed on Arjuna's shoulder. He swung the sword with both his hands to behead Sahasrabahu. Sahasrabahu shrank in size, letting go of the Parashu. Rama fell to the ground with a thud next to Arjuna in his human form, his sword clattering away from him. The Parashu sped to the place where Sahasrabahu's neck had been a moment ago, and stood still for a nimisha, not finding its intended target. Arjuna kicked Rama in the midriff as the Parashu sped back to Rama. The kick knocked the wind out of Rama's lungs and turned his vision watery. He struggled onto his knees. Rama grasped the Parashu and swung blindly as Arjuna morphed into Sahasrabahu again. It sliced open Arjuna's belly, spewing out his innards. Arjuna screamed in agony.

Rama rose unsteadily, pushing the Parashu into the

ground with shaking hands to support his weight. He blinked to clear his vision, gasping big gulps of air. He watched as Arjuna continued to morph.

Arjuna tore out his own intestines and threw them at Rama. He bent over quivering in incredible pain. A few nimishas later, he stood tall, whole and strong again. All traces of pain had left his face. Arjuna laughed.

'I cannot be killed, fool!' Arjuna mocked, his ochre eyes as malevolent as ever. Rama stared at him, his pupils widening in disbelief.

Mahadeva! Was it impossible to kill this creature? Rama's mind cried in anguish. Where is that strange power when I need it? Was it of any use? Remember, remember! He berated himself. His mind raced as images from the past flashed through it. He could find no answer.

In desperation, Rama imagined the rune of the Parashu, the turning wheel. He slowed down the movement as much as he could, straining hard, using the last dregs of his energy. He stopped when he couldn't slow the movement anymore— only Mahakaal himself could stop or reverse the motion. He threw himself at Arjuna, the furious swings of whose arms had slowed down by now. He would get to Arjuna's neck and behead him this time. Rama cut away at the swinging arms, but one fist sneaked through and hit him. Even with the slow momentum, the impact was tremendous. He was flung yards away, his body and mind in a world of hurt, as if his bones had cracked and his muscles smashed to a pulp. He desperately drew air into his empty lungs, holding on to the image of the rune in his mind, trying to keep its spin slow. Arjuna's arms regenerated slowly. Rama hung on to dear life, willing himself to get up.

He pushed himself to his knees, the battleground wobbling in his sight. His body was still intact, but it throbbed with agony. The image of the rune slipped and blinked out. Arjuna's next punch crashed into him like a hundred thunderbolts. The world went dark as he lost consciousness.

Sahasrabahu's stupendous roar brought him back to his senses. The roar of victory. The army waiting at the fort erupted in joy. Manorama heard the roar and the bugles and dundhubis floating in faintly from the battleground. It was enough to bring her to her feet.

'Kill that insolent wretch. Tear his head off. Kill him without mercy,' she screamed into the dusk.

Arjuna drew close to where Rama lay. He stopped when he saw that the Parashu that had fallen from Rama's hands. He tried to pick it up. It did not budge. Arjuna threw all his strength and as many arms as he could into the effort. The Parashu stayed on the ground. Arjuna walked away. Rama tried to breathe deep, but he could not get enough air into his lungs. An enormous fist wrapped around his waist and lifted him up. Sahasrabahu's ochre eyes stared into his. Rama opened his mouth and blood coursed out like a river, staining his teeth, beard, neck and chest. His vision spun; all he could see were those malevolent ochre eyes with golden motes floating in them.

Events from his life flashed before his eyes again—the fragility of his mother's bent neck, Ma Chinnamasta, the banalinga, the battle with Mahadeva, Nandin and Indra, the sacred grove and Guru Dattatreya's words, his father's crushed body.

'Like father, like son,' said Arjuna as one of his hands tightened around Rama's throat.

Rama imagined his father being held in Sahasrabahu's fist, as he himself was now.

'Why had Father let Arjuna do that?' A thought flashed in his mind.

And Rama finally realised why.

He realised it all.

The power surged up his spine to his forehead. The Parashu beat against the ground in a frenzy. Arjuna glanced at the Parashu for a nimisha. Rama cleaved his mind again. The pupils turned upwards, and their whites stared back at Arjuna.

'Jamadagni lives,' Rama gasped. He smiled through his blood-stained teeth. It was a gentle and calm smile. Arjuna was puzzled for a nimisha, by the sight of Rama's eyes and the words he had spoken. He squeezed Rama's throat.

Rama smiled as he embraced Mrithyu.

23

Avatara

'Am I dead?' Rama asked himself.
'I should be.'
'Am I alive?'

Rama looked down at his body. It was smeared with turmeric, blood and the dust that the war had unleashed. He pinched himself and felt the sensation on his forearm. It was a body, but was it his? Is this me? He was strangely detached from it.

'I shouldn't be.'

Tree falls in the jungle,
No one to hear.
Mind it has fallen,
Matters not the sound.
Neti Neti.

The words were all around and inside him.

He looked around. Soft, impenetrable fog was all he could see. He could taste it, and feel its feathery touch on his skin and deep inside himself. Rama could smell its sweet,

sweet fragrance and hear gentle whispers, like the fog was chanting mantras he couldn't comprehend. He held up his hand, and the fog streamed through his fingers, like an ephemeral liquid.

'Am I dreaming?' He did not know the answer.

'Am I in dhyana?' He tried to form the yagnakund in his mind and failed. Rama tried to form the image of the Parashu but failed again. He remembered it but couldn't form an image of it. Curiously, he felt like he had transcended the state of dhyana and gone deeper and above it at the same time. He couldn't explain it to himself.

Un-ask the question,
Dive into yourself,
Find the universe.
Dive into the universe,
Lose yourself.
Neti Neti.

Rama stood in absolute peace, letting the serenity of the fog wash over him. The tiredness and battle rage were gone. He was completely relaxed.

'Where?'

Rama did not know where he was.

'When?'

Last he remembered, he had been smiling at Arjuna's puzzled face. He didn't know if that had happened a nimisha or aeons ago. He had no sense of time here. Or space, he realised. Rama sensed everything was happening at the same time, and only to him.

'Why?'

He had finally understood, that is why. Rama realised the implication of Guru Dattatreya's words. He now knew the rahasya. The energy of the Ahi, his kundalini shakti suffused his being and merged with the light of the amsha on his forehead. He understood the greatest lesson his father, his first guru, Saptarishi Jamadagni, had taught him.

'What?'

Self-realisation. The lesson that cannot be taught but must be realised by oneself. His gurus had opened the door; it was his responsibility to enter and understand what it meant. He had come this far. He realised there was still some more way to go.

'How?'

Rama did not know how. It had all begun with mother's beheading. His father's death at Sahasrabahu's hands had brought him to his end. It had brought him here. But was this the end? Rama thought hard.

Unbecoming, death, becoming ...

He had un-become. He had died on the battlefield. Now he had to become ...

Remember the beginning.

Guru Dattatreya's words came to him. Nandin had also reminded him of the same thing. The image of the Nagamandala flashed in his mind. A snake swallowing its tail. A full circle. Back to the start.

Rama understood.

The beginning ...

The fog disappeared, and Rama entered another world in a blink. He was in front of his father's hut, but not of the world he knew. It was surreal, bathed in shadow and in an eerie light that was everywhere, from a source he couldn't see.

Jamadagni knelt before him, facing away, his head bowed and eyes closed. It was the very spot where he had beheaded his mother. The Aghoris danced and sang in a tumult. Their dreadlocks flying and damarus whirling as they blew their bone trumpets. The macabre sound made his hair stand on end. The air was thick with their bhasma—the sacred ash—and the smoke of their incense pots. A great sea of them, men and women, swirled around Rama and Jamadagni. Their faces were hidden in shadow and their forms kept changing from mortal to bhoota to skeleton.

Mountain of ego,
Scorpion of lust,
Tread her path,
Turn them to dust.
Free the Atman,
Be the Brahman.
Burn the body,
Eat the mind.
Mahavidya awakens,
Mother comes.

The world turned red.

Renuka Chinnamasta stood before him, as big as Sahasrabahu. Her body was the red of the rudrapushpa. A belly chain of bones and a garland of skulls covered her nudity. A hissing green serpent for a yagnopaveeta. Dakini and Varnini appeared, naked and dancing in rapture, tossing about their loose tresses.

The Mahavidya stood waiting, her blood red tongue hanging out of her mouth, going past her chin. Her breathing echoed throughout the world. She breathed in and the world seemed to want to rush into her nostrils. She breathed out, and the world relaxed. Her giant eyes, primordial and timeless, stared at him unblinkingly. Waiting ...

The Aghoris suddenly went quiet and still. The silence was deafening.

The prophecy! Rama thought. The words that had had such a profound effect on Renuka's life. His life. The words that had sparked all this.

The beginning ...

Rama uttered the prophecy from Renuka's childhood.

Mounds of ash four,
Streams of blood three,
Head of one,
The price to be paid,
A test by fire invoked.
Fork in the path of dharma,
Rests on the edge of a blade.

Rama's Parashu appeared in Renuka Chinnamasta's right hand. She held it out to him. Her mouth did not move, neither did her tongue, but her powerful voice rang out in the space.

'Behead him. Vengeance is mine,' said Chinnamasta gesturing towards Jamadagni.

Rama stared back at the Mahavidya. This cannot be happening again. This was wrong, it made no sense. He remembered the Devi temple in Mahishmati.

'No,' said Rama. The world froze.

'The power of Chinnamasta manifested in my mother because of him. My mother saved his life with the same power after Arjuna killed him. There is no cause for vengeance. It is I who beheaded my mother. It was my decision alone.

'I offer my head as sacrifice,' added Rama.

The Mahavidya smiled. Rama saw a flash of Renuka's innocence in it.

'So be it,' she said.

In a blink, Rama was kneeling before her, looking up at her face. Jamadagni sat in padmasana to the side, the pupils of his eyes turned up, the whites staring at Rama.

———

Sahasrabahu squeezed Rama's throat as hard as he could. The skin was soft but refused to collapse under the enormous pressure. The neck wouldn't snap, neither would the spine. He turned Rama horizontal and dug his hands into the torso to rip it apart. His fingers couldn't penetrate through the skin. Arjuna went wild with fury and frustration. He threw the body on the ground, stomping on it with his feet and pummelling it with his fists. Rama's smile remained unchanged and his body remained undamaged. Sahasrabahu roared in disbelief. He picked up Rama's body to examine it again.

The Parashu rattled on the ground. Arjuna watched, puzzled. One of his hands extended towards the Parashu. He could pick it up with ease. He turned it over, scanning every inch of it, not understanding why he could pick it up now. Arjuna dropped Rama's body to the ground. He would cleave Rama with his own weapon. Rama's body landed on its knees, with his face upturned. The whites of Rama's eyes stared back at Sahasrabahu.

———

Clay pots appeared around Rama in six concentric circles. Sixteen in the outermost circle, twelve in the next inner one, then ten, eight, six and four.

'One pot for each week you were away from the ashram,' said Renuka's voice.

'Mounds of ash four,' Chinnamasta's voice boomed.

Rama invoked Agni into his eyes.

Sahasrabahu appeared suddenly, charging with fury at Rama.

'Vengeance is mine!' said Rama and burnt him to ash with the streaming Agni of his eyes.

Karthavirya Arjuna stood before him, magnificent and handsome. The monarch of the world. Rama burnt him down to another mound of ash.

Arjuna appeared again. Much younger than before. He sat in padmasana. Eyes closed, his face suffused with the joy of dhyana. He became the third mound of ash.

Rama gasped when he saw what came next. There were two apparitions before him. It was a choice. A queen, her face serene and filled with love for the infant gurgling in the safe embrace of her arms. Rama knew who it was immediately, though he had never seen her, only heard of her. Queen Padmini, holding baby Arjuna.

The second apparition was himself. Parashurama, filled with wrath at the queen and the baby. Ready to kill them.

Rama went numb with shock. He was drowning in a whirlpool, unable to find his way to the surface for air. His mind screamed at him that it wasn't real, that these were only illusions. But he couldn't believe that in his heart. This test was real in more ways than he could comprehend, he had no doubt about that. No! He couldn't kill a mother and an innocent baby, and he couldn't kill himself. Both were mahapaaps, grievous sins. He turned to the Mahavidya to beg for mercy.

There were no eyes behind her eyelids. The Mahavidya had invoked Varuna into her eyes. Oceans of water surged from her eye sockets, streaming down her face.

'Choose wrong and oblivion awaits,' Chinnamasta said calmly, ruthlessly.

Burn them both, a part of Rama's mind wailed. Only four mounds of ash, a second part reminded him. Two mahapaaps at once, another part mocked. Sacrifice yourself, a fourth part advised. Let someone else kill Arjuna and free the world from misery. The gods will surely heed the prayers of so many millions. Would you judge the actions of gods, fool? His mind cried. You were granted an amsha, blessed to become a brahmakshatriya, trusted to make your own decisions. And here you are wallowing in self-pity. Shame bloomed in Rama's heart.

Rama reeled in confusion. He didn't have much time. This test of dharma was excruciating, but he had to act fast. He glanced at Jamadagni. The saptarishi's face stared back at him with compassion. So very like the compassion on Renuka's face when he had beheaded her.

Rama calmed his frantic mind and focussed on what he knew. The apparitions he had seen. The first one had been of Sahasrabahu denoting Arjuna's extraordinary strength. Second was that of Samrat Arjuna, signifying his dominion and vitality. Third was that of young Arjuna in prayer. It showed his devotion, to a guru who had later discarded him for his adharma. He had burnt them all. Rama realised he was burning Arjuna's spiritual power. The fourth apparition of Arjuna's mother cradling him as a baby showed the power of her prayer and her love. The child had grown to plunge the world into misery, he already knew that. It would be wrong and an undeserved mercy to spare the child. Arjuna hadn't spared a thought for the thousands of mothers who had suffered because of his adharma.

Rama's own apparition was an embodiment not only of his righteous wrath but of all those mothers' curses. Compassion wouldn't be in sacrificing himself or refusing to make a decision. Compassion would be in honouring those mothers. He remembered Jamadagni's words when he had questioned him about the rishis cursing Arjuna.

Curses abound, but the protection is powerful.

He was looking at that protection. He burnt the Queen and baby into the fourth mound of ash. The apparition of himself blinked out of existence.

'You have chosen the fork in the path of dharma. The head of one is the price,' Chinnamasta's voice rang.

The raging water disappeared from her eyes and Rama knew he had chosen right.

Three streams of blood erupted from the mouths of Chinnamasta, Dakini and Varnini. The Aghoris launched into their mad euphoria. The blood bathed Rama and the Aghoris. The Agni vanished from his eyes as Rama stared up at Chinnamasta with the whites of his eyes. Chinnamasta raised the Parashu.

'Blade be true,' Rama whispered. The Parashu responded to his call. It turned golden.

Chinnamasta held the Parashu overhead.

Sahasrabahu, too, held the Parashu overhead on the battlefield.

Rama remembered the lesson he had realised by himself.

The lesson his father had hoped he would realise within his soul.

Rama surrendered.

It was not about the Parashu or the Sudarshana Chakra. It was something beyond that. The source behind them. The source that Jamadagni had surrendered to. Of which, the Mahavidya was only a portion.

He surrendered his five organs of perception. Gyanendriyas.

He surrendered his five organs of action. Karmendriyas.

The five functions of the life force. Panchaprana.

The five elements of his body. Panchabhoota.

As the twenty-first, he surrendered his mind.

The golden beam of light on his forehead blazed, shining on the Mahavidya's face.

Rama said the word for the first time.

'AMBA!'

Chinnamasta crashed the Parashu downward on his skull.

Sahasrabahu, too, crashed the Parashu downward on his skull.

The energy of the Ahi in him, the kundalini shakti surged from the agya chakra on his forehead to the top of his head. The force exploded out from the inside of the skull.

Rama did not feel any pain. He felt the rapturous, euphoric joy of a lotus with thousands upon thousands of petals blooming.

JAGAD-AMBA!

Mother of the Universe. Of all Universes.

The Rahasya.

The Beginning. The Beginning of it all...

LALITHA.

The universe was her play.

Beyond wakening, sleep and dream.

Beyond life, mrithyu and rebirth.

Beyond unbecoming, death and becoming.

TRIPURASUNDARI.

Rama floated in the nothingness. He, saw a single, tiny point of light and wondered what it was. He, suddenly, found himself inside it. Immense universes drifted in that infinitesimal space, infinite dimensions to each. He saw worlds reflected like two mirrors facing each other, each same as the other but somehow different. Stars were born, blazed yellow, ballooned into glowing red and then black, collapsing upon themselves. Entire galaxies came into existence in his thoughts and simultaneously, he realised he was just an ant in one of them.

'JAGADAMBA!' He cried with joy.

And then, he was before a mirror. There was a lady a little away from him, standing before her own mirror. Queen Manorama. She stood transfixed by what she saw in her mirror, utter horror and disgust writ large on her ashen visage.

A voice as came from inside him, around him, from everywhere and nowhere. Rama yearned to merge with that sweet, gentle vak.

A voice as loud as a whisper, as quiet as thunder.

'Karma comes calling.'

Manorama disappeared into a mound of ash.

In the Devi temple, in Mahishmati, Manorama collapsed. Dead.

'Amba!' Jayadhwaja screamed, cradling her head in his lap as he tried in vain to revive her. He shouted frantically for help.

Rama saw nothing in his mirror. The feather light amsha of Mahavishnu and his soul fused together. His image appeared in the mirror, glowing golden from head to toe.

He had un-become, had died and had become ...
AVATARA.

The mirror disappeared, and Rama contracted into a single point of light. Pure energy, pure consciousness, adrift in the nothingness. Whether for a nimisha or for eons, he couldn't say. The point of light grew larger, elongating and moulding itself. He felt himself in some warm, invisible fluid, swirling around him, as if he was afloat in the Narmada. He grew aware of constellations gathered around him in a circle. No, not a circle. A pot. A kalasha. The flux of the fluid in the fixity of the stars. An indescribable feeling of ecstasy and utter peace coursed through him.

Sree Matre Namaha! His consciousness exulted in rapture.

He saw himself, a being of light, grown back into his original form, turning ever so slowly in a foetal position. The kalasha was a womb, and he was a child among the stars.

Jagadamba! His soul cried again.

'Chiranjeevi,' said the voice.

And Rama felt himself fall away. He was back in front of Chinnamasta. The entire world hushed, waiting. Rama saw the Parashu frozen in mid-air, a hair's breadth away from his forehead.

———

Sahasrabahu sat a little distance away from the kneeling Rama. The Parashu had stopped just before it could hit Rama's head. He couldn't move it after that, neither could he budge the immobile form of Rama. The army surrounded the two of them and Rama's ratha, waiting for their samrat's order.

Arjuna felt enormously old, tired and inexplicably

vulnerable. He looked towards the city. Something had happened there, he was sure of it, but he didn't know what. A small shiver ran up his spine.

He looked at Rama's divine ratha. The charioteer stared back at him, unperturbed. The young boy in the ratha, unmindful of the samrat, the army and the ocean of corpses, stared in a trance at Parashurama.

The Aghoris took up the chant in their frenzy.

Man awakens,
Avatara comes!
Man awakens,
Avatara comes!

Akrita climbed out of the chariot with the conch in his hand. He began to sing. Arjuna gasped as he realised the voice was that of his guru, Avadhuta Dattatreya.

Delve into the void,
Merge into the night.
Avatara awakens,
Behold his might.
Burn the body,
Eat the mind.
Purusha awakens,
Avatara comes.
Life is a dream,
All must awake,
Death is the awakening.
Behold the one,

Who dreamt in death,
Who awoke in life.
Parashu he wields,
Purusha awakens,
Avatara comes.
Power of the Parashu,
Power of the Chakra,
Neti Neti.
Beyond and beginning,
Rahasya one and true.
Jagadamba smiles,
Avatara comes.

Arjuna stood bolt upright. His secret, known only to him and his guru. Parashurama knew it!

———

The pots around Rama exploded with tremendous force. A square with four nested sides formed on the ground. He saw the yantra shining in the air above him. Six concentric circles of red lotus petals, a petal for each pot. It settled upon and around him; he was the focal point, the bindu. Rama reached up and gathered the Parashu.

The conch's blast tore through the air on the battlefield.

Parashurama stood, snatching the Parashu from where it hung frozen. The whites of his eyes stared at the stunned Arjuna.

In his trance, Rama invoked Arjuna in the yagnakund. He saw him clearly now. Rama sensed the power of the sudarshana chakra in every cell of Arjuna's body. He paid homage to that power, poured out his devotion to it and called it to him. The power responded, leeching away from Arjuna, moving towards Rama. He gathered it and it shone in his hand, a brilliant disc with a thousand prongs. The light on Rama's forehead drew the chakra into it, and it slowly disappeared in the light.

On the battlefield, Sahasrabahu charged at Parashurama in rage. Rama hacked his arms off, his movements faster than lightning. He cut the back of Sahasrabahu's legs and sent him crashing to his knees. Sahasrabahu willed his arms to regrow and for his wounds to heal. But the thousand arms were gone; only two were left now, and he continued to bleed. He was back to his original form, as Arjuna. He would never be Sahasrabahu again. Rama's left fist crashed into his jaw, rocking him, making his head yaw and pitch. Arjuna's powerful frame fought in vain for balance. He felt blood trickle down the corner of his mouth.

The army charged when they saw Arjuna on his knees. The rune of the Parashu flashed in Rama's mind. It was a chakra with thousands of prongs. Rama held up the Parashu. Arcs of golden lightning shot straight into the sky, blindingly bright in the darkness. Thousands of golden filaments emerged from the blades of the axe, impaling each of the rushing soldiers. The brilliance of the filaments framed the gold of the Parashu, like a golden disc on an axe. In a blink, the filaments turned blood red and withdrew into the Parashu again. Huge swathes of the army collapsed dead. A nimisha later, the survivors, a few thousand, turned tail and fled.

Arjuna looked at the carnage and back at Rama. His power was gone, he had lost, and he did not know how Rama had done all this. But he could still do one thing. Arjuna probed

Rama's mind ... and went slack-jawed with amazement. A joyous quiet, a deep calm suffused Rama's mind. A quietude that was more chilling than the white-hot rage he had seen there before.

In that deep, dark quiet of Rama's mind was the golden Parashu, framed by the brilliance of a thousand-pronged chakra. The young brahmin lad's words sprung into his consciousness.

Avatara!

Arjuna gasped. He could still fight, but he knew he was no match for this man. He had thrown all his strength, skill and yogic power into this battle, and it hadn't been enough. He had been beaten into submission.

'Vengeance is mine, Samrat,' said Rama.

'Karma comes calling,' Arjuna's voice was quiet.

'Yes,' Rama replied.

'One more rahasya, perhaps the guru didn't tell you. I could only be defeated by a yoddha greater than me. It took an avatara and a brahmakshatriya to do it. I'm proud of that.'

He closed his eyes, whispering his last prayers. He turned his face to the sky and looked into the dust and smog of the battle. Rama heard him murmur. 'This journey ends, another one begins. Another life, another realm perhaps. As the guru wills. I surrender to his judgement.'

His voice grew louder, more commanding.

'Parashurama! Chakravarti Samrat Karthavirya Arjuna gives you his final order.'

Rama waited.

'Give me the death I deserve. Fulfil your purpose.' Arjuna didn't bow his head. He looked up at Rama. Rama nodded.

'Long will you be remembered, Samrat!' said Rama.

He whispered, 'Om Namah Shivaya,' swung the Parashu and beheaded Arjuna. The cut was clean. Blood gushed out of the neck in three great spouts, bathing Rama red. The red of the rudrapushpa.

Arjuna's torso crashed forward, falling at Rama's feet. Rama picked up the head, whirled it, and flung it away with a deafening roar. The head disappeared into the darkness and haze.

He pressed his palms together and prayed for the souls of Arjuna, Manorama and all the soldiers who lay dead.

Om Shanti! Shanti! Shanti!

He climbed back into the ratha with an ecstatic Akrita and said to Mahodhara, 'Let's go home.'

Jayadhwaja sat cradling his mother's body when something landed inside the temple, bounced into the mantapa and stopped before him. Arjuna's head stared at him with dead eyes. Jayadhwaja screamed.

END OF PART I

Acknowledgements

Writing is a solitary endeavour, not a lonely one. Our perceptions, experiences, feelings, impressions, memories, and thoughts are all at play when the pen moves across the paper. The story is inevitably coloured by all these, and also by our own character. These are the unseen elements that help the reader 'see' the story, each in their own way. So, I think my first acknowledgement should be to the life I've been given and tried living. The good and bad of it, warts, beauty and all.

Notwithstanding all that, this book couldn't have happened without:

My family. Amma, Sudeep, Priya, Radhika, Sanvi and Eshaan. Acchan, hope this book reaches you in the good place you are in and you see your son's name on the cover. I've counted my blessings and here I name them.

My first readers—my mother, Priya, Sreelekshmi and Prathyush Ramakrishnan. Thank you for the feedback and, more importantly, asking for more. It helped me finish what appeared daunting when I started. Thanks also to Bharathi Venkat for her spot-on critical evaluation and insight.

My friends, Chandrashekhar Jayaraman and Tasneem Nakhoda, for being who they are. The warmest, nicest couple

I know. Santosh Janardhanan, who always seems to know someone somewhere, and is always willing to help. Garima Louckx for her timely advice. 'Resilience' is my motto. He-who-shall-not-be-named, no, not the bad wizard guy, a good guy in fact, who played a vital role in finding me a publisher.

Karthika V.K. for believing in this manuscript, and Sanghamitra Biswas for being the awesome editor she is. Pallavi Mohan for her keen eye in shaping the manuscript. Nithin Rao Kumblekar for the powerful cover design. I thank you all.

Sanchith Sanjeev and Vasuki Vasudev for the wonderful trailer. Vijay Kumar A.G. and Vineet V.M. of Pixelclay Design for the artwork, and Shashi Ukkinagatti of Magic Trunk Studio for the video animation. All young guys with incredible talent.

All the authors I've read, whose books I loved, hated, re-read or never read again. They planted the two magic words in my head, 'What if ...'

To my pitrus, my kuladevi and my ishta-devata. May I always be in your service. Bhagawan Parashurama, I'm just a nimitta. A paltry imagination attempting to capture your magnificence.

Finally, to my readers. Thank you for the indulgence. It will always be a privilege to write for you. This too is a blessing. I hope you will love reading Rama's journey as much as I loved writing it. Love it or hate it, I humbly request you to leave a review on platforms like Amazon and Goodreads. It will help me grow and improve as an author.

Onward then, into the story ... where lies mantra, prophecy and magic.

Ramabhadra and his epic saga await ...